# Easy Web Design

*Mary Millhollon with*
*Jeff Castrina and*
*Leslie Lothamer*

PUBLISHED BY
Microsoft Press
A Division of Microsoft Corporation
One Microsoft Way
Redmond, Washington 98052-6399

Library of Congress Control Number 2005936846

Printed and bound in the United States of America.

1 2 3 4 5 6 7 8 9    QWT    0 9 8 7 6 5

Distributed in Canada by H.B. Fenn and Company Ltd.

A CIP catalogue record for this book is available from the British Library.

Microsoft Press books are available through booksellers and distributors worldwide. For further information about international editions, contact your local Microsoft Corporation office or contact Microsoft Press International directly at fax (425) 936-7329. Visit our Web site at www.microsoft.com/learning/. Send comments to *mspinput@microsoft.com*.

**Acquisitions Editor:** Juliana Aldous
**Project Editor:** Kathleen Atkins
**Editorial and Production Services:** Steve Sagman, Studioserv

Body Part No. X11-74975

# Table of Contents

## Part 1: The Talk—Web Basics

In the six information-packed chapters of Part 1, you'll learn all about Web site creation and design, and you'll acquire the knowledge you need to move forward with confidence. In these early chapters, you'll enjoy a bountiful serving of theory, illustrations, tips, and pointers from professionals in the field along with a wealth of online resources and examples. By the time you've finished Part 1, you'll be ready to create the five Web sites described in Part 2.

# Part 2:  The Walk—Creating Web Sites

Part 2 presents five projects designed to help you acquire hands-on experience with the
Web site creation process. Each walkthrough includes the planning and building steps
required to create a Web site. In addition, you'll find pointers to online bonus steps that will
take your experience even further. The walkthroughs are arranged progressively, occurring in
the simplest to the most advanced Web development environments, thereby enabling you
to ease your way into using and understanding advanced features and tools.

## Chapter 11:  Going All Out with FrontPage          334

# Part 3:  The Rest—Going Live

After you post your Web site, you should count on showering it with some ongoing
attention. Sure you could slap up any old Web page, call it a Web site, and leave it
unattended, but your site would grow dusty and visitors would never return. For a truly
successful Web site, you need to tend to it on occasion—even if all you do is fluff it up a bit.
The purpose of Part 3 is to show you how to make a site go live and then stay alive.

## Chapter 12: Sending Web Pages into the Real World          362

## Chapter 13: Updating, Archiving, Moving On          384

*As always, we dedicate this book to our readers—who time and again prove to be some of the most interesting, eclectic, and friendliest people online.*

# Acknowledgments

As you might imagine, developing a comprehensive full-color book like this takes a village (of the digitally connected sort). First and foremost, please put your hands together for Jeff Castrina and Leslie Lothamer for infusing their creativity and talents throughout this book and its companion Web site.

Now let's give a rousing round of applause to the people who made this book possible in the first place: Claudette Moore at the Moore Literary Agency; Juliana Aldous, Program Manager at Microsoft Press; and Kathleen Atkins, Project Editor at Microsoft Press.

Next major props and an extended standing ovation to the people who really got in way past their elbows to ensure that this book is the wonderful book that it is: Steve Sagman, project manager (and clearly part magician); Jennifer Harris, editor extraordinaire; Audrey Marr, desktop publisher of all hours; Joel Panchot, graphic artist at Microsoft Press; Jim Kramer, book designer; and Tom Speeches, indexer.

Finally, last but never ever least, my most heartfelt thanks go to Robert and Matthew for their patience and understanding, and for just being themselves—two of the most exceptional boys in the world, who contribute laughter and joie de vivre to the universe every single day. Rage on nerds!

# Introduction

Welcome to Easy Web Design! If you have read either (or both) of our earlier Web development books, *Easy Web Page Creation* (1st edition; Microsoft Press, 2001) or *Faster Smarter Web Page Creation* (2nd edition; Microsoft Press, 2002), we want you to know that this edition provides information for both new and past readers alike. In this edition, we've updated the theory and information in Parts 1 and 3 to incorporate current technologies and trends. In Part 2, we went one step further and created all new projects. We focused on making the new walkthroughs span as many new technologies and processes as we could possibly squeeze between this book's covers.

In addition to the updated theory and new walkthroughs, we're continuing to support and grow www.creationguide.com as a dynamic companion to the book and ongoing resource for readers. We whole-heartedly believe in putting the Internet to work instead of including CD-ROMs with our Web books, and we continue to do so. Please visit us online anytime, regardless of whether you read *Easy Web Page Creation*, *Faster Smarter Web Page Creation*, or *Easy Web Design*.

## Where We're Coming From

With so many resources in today's world, you might be wondering why we wrote this book. In a way, this book found us—we certainly didn't get into Web development with this book in mind. The tale starts a few years ago, when we (Jeff and Mary) were coteaching a course on graphics and Web design. As the course progressed, a nagging suspicion solidified into crystal clarity—people from all walks of life want to build Web sites, but they don't have the foggiest idea where to begin. Since then, the Web has woven itself more and more into all of our lives, and we've found that an even greater number of people are interested in posting information online.

Because we tend to be helpful types, we initially searched high and low for a good resource to recommend to people when they asked us for direction. We checked out bookstores and online resources only to find reams of good information scattered all over the place. That was nice, but we were looking for basic information concisely compiled in an understandable manner in one book—a book we could just hand to people when they looked at us with questions in their eyes and said, "I want to build a Web site, but..." Ultimately, we never did find a true one-stop resource to turn to, so we wrote the first edition of this book.

We worked diligently to combine our knowledge and research into an organized and easily digestible book that blended a bit of theory with plenty of hands-on practice. We wrote a book for our students, friends, peers, neighbors, and associates who found computers interesting but didn't necessarily want to earn full-fledged geek status anytime soon. Since then, we've been revising and updating the text (and the companion Web site) to keep up with the ever-evolving Web. We're happy that our book serves as that one-stop book for Web site basics. And now, we have a resource to hand to people as we definitely say, "Here you go—this has all you need to know to get your Web site online."

## Why This Book Could Be for You

Easy Web Design focuses on the great number of people who want to create a Web presence. This book is for you if you have basic computing skills (such as the ability to use a mouse, open folders, run desktop programs, and so forth) and are actively contemplating building a Web site. This book is for you if you've already tasted the art of Web design but want an introduction to some of the newer technologies, such as XHTML, CSS, XML, and Microsoft Office 2003 Web creation tools. This book is for you if you want to review today's basic Web development concepts and technologies without trudging through today's tangled forest of technobabble.

As you'll soon see, Easy Web Design is written in an easygoing style and is packed with all the information necessary to enable you to create, post, and maintain Web sites. The text is divided into three parts, with each part (and each chapter within) building on information presented in prior sections and chapters—concept by concept. Part One, "The Talk—Web Basics," provides all the information you need (and then some) about text, graphics, page components, planning, site creation, and tools. Part Two, "The Walk—Creating Web Sites," provides step-by-step, practical hands-on experience by walking you through the process of creating five complete Web sites, using five different utilities—MSN Spaces, WordPad, Microsoft Office Publisher, Word, and FrontPage. Part Three, "The Rest—Going Live," shows you how to upload, archive, and maintain your Web site in addition to suggesting future directions you can take in your Web development effort.

## But Most of All...

We must admit that we do have an ulterior motive. You see, beyond this book, our sincere underlying goal is to educate and inform—we want to get you into the realm of realizing that you can build a Web site, and pretty easily, too. We specifically designed this book to give you a strong foundation in Web development—a foundation that will serve you well now, while you create an immediate presence, as well as in the future, when you work on more advanced Web development endeavors. We wrote this book so that you can experience firsthand the enjoyment of building, and the value of owning, your own Web site.

# the talk—
# web basics

# 1

The other day, we went hiking with some friends. But we didn't simply wake up, run out the door, and start climbing a mountain. Instead, the event sort of evolved:

"Hey, want to go on a hike this Friday?"

"Sure—sounds good. Where should we go?"

And without realizing it, the planning process had begun—we were talking about taking a hike. We were calling friends, checking online databases for nearby trails, selecting a time to meet, thinking about supplies—all this, and we hadn't taken a single step.

Web design follows a similar path. Before you build a Web site, you need to mull it over, talk about it, learn some Web site design principles, plan how to best create your site, and gather your supplies—basically, you need to allow yourself to comfortably slide into the natural progression that takes place whenever you embark on an undertaking. You need to plan. Fortunately, planning doesn't have to be synonymous with boring.

The goal of Part One is to be the "Where do you want to go for a hike, and who's going to drive?" portion of this book. Here's where you satisfy your instinctive planning urges and move beyond gut-level reactions. In this part, you'll learn about Web site creation and design, quell feelings of doubt (yes, you can create a Web site), and gain the knowledge to move forward with confidence.

# demystifying
## your (future)
## web site

Clarity—that's the goal. So let's start by pulling back the drapes, opening the shutters extra wide, and cranking open the window. See—same room, different perspective. Opening a few windows and doors to air out your preconceptions can eliminate a lot of the mystery surrounding Web site creation.

# Basic Hoopla

Obviously, you're familiar with that not-so-newfangled invention called the Internet. Further, we're willing to bet that if you're contemplating the idea of creating a Web presence, you know how to use a computer on some level. We're also assuming that you've surfed the Web at least a few times, you can use basic applications (such as word processing packages), and you can click a mouse with the best of 'em. Fortunately, your basic computing knowledge is all you need to be able to create a Web site—well, your basic computing knowledge along with this book, of course.

Your first undertaking on the road to becoming a Web site developer entails building on what you already know. For instance, in addition to moderate computing capabilities, you should have an inkling of how the Internet, the Web, Web pages, and Web sites relate to one another. Therefore, in the spirit of our goal of clarity and simplicity, we'll cut to the chase in this chapter and briefly describe the main elements of the world's largest network. After we get the fundamentals out of the way, we'll spend the remainder of this book talking about planning and building your Web site. If you're already comfortably familiar with the relationships between the Internet, the Web, Web pages, and Web sites, feel free to skim through this chapter and move on to Chapter 2—we'll be ready to chat about Web text as soon as you get there.

> **lingo** The *Internet* is the hardware that's connected together to create a massive worldwide network.

> **lingo** *Routers* are relay components between networks. For instance, you might link to a wireless router in a coffee shop or an Internet café to link to the Internet.

## The Internet—Just a Bunch of Hardware

To put it simply, the *Internet* is hardware—lots of hardware—connected together to create a massive worldwide network, as illustrated in Figure 1-1. The Internet's hardware encompasses all the components that a person can physically touch, including computers, *routers*, modems, cables, telephone lines, high-speed data circuits, other physical network pieces, and *radio frequency (RF) waves*. (OK—radio frequencies are a little hard to touch, but technically they are physical and measurable.)

For now, that's really all you need to know about the Internet—it's the hardware. No need to regale you with a long diatribe about how the U.S. government's Cold War paranoia spurred the development of a

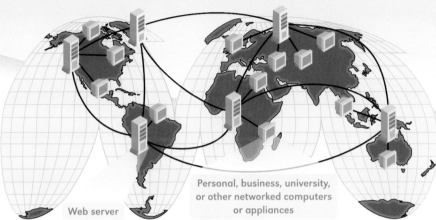

**Figure 1-1** *Hardware relationships on the Internet, the world's largest computer network*

Web server

Personal, business, university, or other networked computers or appliances

noncentralized computer network. If you're curious about the history of the Internet, you can find information online and at your local bookstore or library. (Also, see the resource section on this book's companion Web site, at www.creationguide.com/resources, for some history-of-the-Internet resources.)

Now that we've clearly identified that the Internet is the hardware, let's take the next logical step. Like all computer hardware (think of your desktop or laptop computer), the Internet needs software—otherwise, the Internet's hardware components would simply sit and gather dust on a worldwide basis. Enter the World Wide Web.

## The Web—Some Software for the Hardware

The *Web* is a little more esoteric than the Internet. That's because the Web consists of *software* (including programs and files) that enables information to travel around on the Internet's hardware. Way back in the 1990s, we used to tell a short story about insects and arachnids to help illustrate the relationship between the Internet and the Web. You can view the story online, if you want, at www.creationguide.com/webstory, but we think that the relationship between hardware and software is much easier for most people to grasp these days.

So let's put this together. The Internet is the hardware infrastructure used to transmit electronic information—an infrastructure made up of

> **note** In a *wireless* (WiFi) computer network, *radio frequency (RF) waves* carry data, voice, and video information, much like cell phones. The RF waves are invisible energy waves of the *electromagnetic spectrum*. The electromagnetic spectrum covers the range from AM radio through FM radio, TV, radar, WiFi, cell phones, infrared, visible light, ultraviolet light, x-rays, and gamma rays. Because radio frequencies can penetrate non-metallic walls and obstacles, visibility between computers on a wireless network isn't required.

**lingo**   The **Web** consists of software that enables information sharing on the Internet.

**lingo**   *Servers* are powerful, high-capacity, network-linked computers that store files and respond to users' requests to view and access the stored files.

**lingo**   A *protocol* is a set of rules that describe how data should be transmitted. For example, the Web uses Hypertext Transfer Protocol (HTTP) to transmit HTML and other Web-centric documents.

computers, routers, modems, cables, telephone lines, high-speed data circuits, RF waves, and information bases called *servers*. Unfortunately, not all computers and components attached to the Internet's infrastructure can support all computer file formats. Furthermore, including every available method (or *protocol*) for understanding the various document formats on all computers would be highly impractical. So the Internet community devised the World Wide Web—software that enables information sharing on the Internet regardless of the type of computer connected to the network.

In a nutshell, a computer scientist named Tim Berners-Lee conceived and began developing the Web in 1989 at the CERN laboratory in Switzerland for the high-energy physics community. (You can learn more about Tim by visiting *www.w3.org/People/Berners-Lee*.) The Web quickly attracted a great deal of attention and spread beyond the physics arena. As with the history of the Internet, you can find reams of information about the history of the Web online or in numerous computer books.

For our purposes, you need to know only that the Internet is the hardware and the Web is the software. Simple enough. We're ready to move to the next level—to the files that the Web software supports on the Internet hardware.

## Web Pages—A Few Files on the Internet

Now we come face-to-face with the heart of the matter—Web pages. Basically, when you strip away all the highfalutin technobabble, Web pages are files. To be specific, Web pages are usually Hypertext Markup Language (HTML) files. No need for your eyes to glaze over at the sight of *HTML*; in Part Two of this book, we'll clear up the mysteries of HTML and even XHTML. At this point, all you need to know is that Web pages are simply files that the Web software can interpret and display, just like the document (.doc) files that Microsoft Office Word uses and the workbook (.xls) files that Microsoft Office Excel creates.

Because Web pages are files, you don't have to stretch your imagination too far to realize that creating a Web page is simply the act of creating a specific type of file on your computer. Word documents, spreadsheets, databases, Web pages—they're all specific types of files. The bottom line is that Web pages are computer files, and you've worked with computer files numerous times.

Of course, this isn't to say that Web pages don't have a few idiosyncrasies that set them apart from other files. Namely, Web pages almost always incorporate multiple files and hyperlinks, and they are frequently corralled into groups called *Web sites*.

**lingo**  A *Web site* is a collection of related Web pages, usually including a *home page* and related *subpages*.

### The Multifile Nature of Web Pages

Granted, we just said that Web pages are simply files, and we stand by that. But we should clarify a bit regarding the kinds of files we're referring to. While you read the next few paragraphs, you might think we're providing a little too much information at this point—but we're really not. You should have at least an inkling (not necessarily a firm grasp, just yet) of Web page components and inter-actions before we progress too far along. (Enough of the disclaimer; on to the information.)

First, at the most basic level, every Web page is a *text document*. A text document is a file that contains words, letters, and numbers with-out any formatting. For instance, opening Notepad or WordPad in Microsoft Windows (click **Start**, point to **Programs** or **All Programs**, click **Accessories**, and then select **Notepad** or **WordPad**) and typing your name, a catchy phrase, miscellaneous letters, a few numbers, or

**lingo**  A *text document* is a file that contains words, letters, and numbers without any formatting.

# Web Pages and Browsers   To view Web pages, you use a *browser* (such as Microsoft Internet Explorer). In most cases, a browser application resides on the *local computer* (the computer that you're working on). You can delete, install, upgrade, and customize your browser just as you delete, install, upgrade, and custom-ize other software applications on your computer (including Microsoft Office pro-grams, such as Word and Microsoft Excel). One slight confusion occasionally crops up regarding where the Internet ends and your computer begins. The clarification is easy—when you view a Web page in your browser, the toolbars, menu bars, status bars, and so forth surrounding a Web page are part of the browser application, which resides on your computer; the content within the browser's main window comes from the Internet.

anything, really, creates a text document–not a Web page, mind you, just a text document. Figure 1-2 shows a simple example of a text document open in Notepad.

**Figure 1-2** *A simple text document in Notepad*

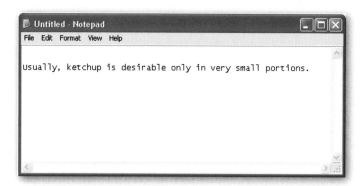

To upgrade your text document to a potential Web page, you simply add specific HTML commands, as shown in Figure 1-3.

**Figure 1-3** *A text document with fundamental HTML commands added*

After you add HTML commands, you save the text document with an .html or .htm extension in place of .txt or .doc. (Don't sweat the specifics at this point.) Then you can open the document in a browser application, such as Internet Explorer.

Figure 1-4 shows how the text document with the HTML commands shown in Figure 1-3 appears in a browser. (To see the page online, visit *www.creationguide.com/ketchup.*) Notice that only the body text, and not the HTML commands, appears in Figure 1-4. Just the body text shows, because HTML commands provide instructions to browsers regarding *how* to display information and the body text tells browsers *what* information should be displayed.

**Figure 1-4**   *A basic text document with HTML commands in a browser*

Don't worry if this HTML explanation seems a little vague at the moment. We'll walk you through the process of creating a Web site by using HTML in WordPad later in this book (in Chapter 8, "Demystifying Basic CSS and XHTML"). You'll see then that HTML is fairly straightforward if you take it one step at a time. (And for added inspiration, you'll find that you can create Web sites without knowing HTML at all in the other Part Two chapters.) At this point, you mainly need to recognize the following basic premise:

> *Web pages are text documents.*

You might've noticed that a paradox seems to be emerging here because we've adamantly stated that Web pages are text documents. But if Web pages are text documents, why does the Web overflow with graphics? Fortunately, you can use HTML text documents in conjunction with specific graphics file types on the Web. Namely, the Web supports graphics files with .gif, .jpg (or .jpeg), and .png extensions–but let's save the graphics file format discussion for Chapter 3.

Here's the scoop: To show a graphic on the Web, you can create an HTML (text) document that includes commands that tell a browser where to find a particular graphic and how to display it on the page (including position, size, and so forth). Thus, the multifile nature of Web pages is unveiled. Generally, when you look at a Web page online, you're looking at a few files–an HTML (text) file, some graphics files, and maybe a multimedia file or two.

**try this!**
You can see for yourself how HTML works. First ensure that Windows is configured to show file extensions:

1 Open Control Panel. (In Microsoft Windows XP, on the **Start** menu, click **Control Panel**; in earlier versions of Windows, click **Start**, point to **Settings**, and then click **Control Panel**.)

2 In Control Panel, double-click **Folder Options**, and then click the **View** tab.

3 Clear the **Hide Extensions For Known File Types** check box, and then click **OK**.

After you've configured Windows to display file extensions, type the HTML text shown in Figure 1-3 into a Notepad document. (To open Notepad, click **Start**, **Programs** or **All Programs**, **Accessories**, and then click **Notepad**.) Save the Notepad document to your desktop (so that you can easily delete it later) as a text (.txt) file by selecting **Text Document** in the **Save As Type** box in the **Save** dialog box. Close Notepad.

Next, display your desktop, right-click the text file that you just created, and click **Rename**. Replace the .txt extensions with an **.html** extension. When Windows displays a message box asking whether you're sure you want to change the file type (and warning you of potential "dangers"), click **Yes**—you're not wreaking any sort of havoc in this instance. Note that you can also save documents in Notepad as HTML documents by typing *filename***.html** in the **File Name** box in the **Save As** box. We show you how to manually rename a .txt file here because later you'll learn that knowing how to rename a .txt file as an .html file will come in handy.

Now you're ready to view the document in your browser. To do so, you can use any of the following methods:

● Double-click the HTML file that you just created.

● Open your browser, and drag the HTML file's icon into the browser window.

● Open your browser, and type the path to the HTML file in the browser's Address bar.

If your file doesn't look similar to the file shown in Figure 1-4, visit www.creationguide.com/ketchup, click **Source** on your browser's **View** menu to display the page's source code (for more information about source code, see the sidebar "A Little More HTML," later in this chapter), and compare the online source code with the document you created. Keep in mind that after you change a .txt file to an .html file, you'll need to open the document from within Notepad if you want to edit the file's text.

To illustrate the multifile concept, take a look at Chris's Music Instruction home page, shown in Figure 1-5.

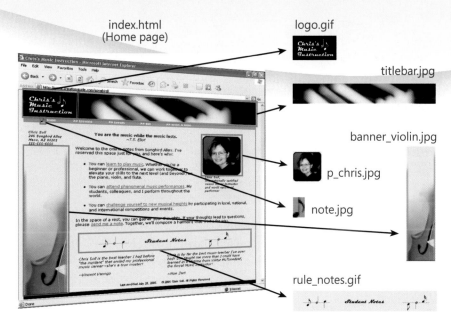

index.html
(Home page)

logo.gif

titlebar.jpg

banner_violin.jpg

p_chris.jpg

note.jpg

rule_notes.gif

**Figure 1-5** *An HTML text file and six graphics files combined to create the Music Instruction home page*

As you can see, the page consists of seven files—an HTML document (index.html) and six graphics files (.gif and .jpg files):

| | |
|---|---|
| **banner_violin.jpg** | **logo.gif** |
| **note.gif** | **p_chris.jpg** |
| **rule_notes.gif** | **titlebar.jpg** |

Figure 1-6 depicts a Windows Icons view of the files used to create the home page illustrated in Figure 1-5. (Notice that the Windows folder contains the same HTML file and graphics files.)

After reviewing Figures 1-5 and 1-6, you're ready for another "bottom line" blanket statement. Basically, you need to walk away from this discussion with the following information:

> *When you view a Web page in your Web browser, you're usually viewing a number of files working together to create a single page.*

**Figure 1-6**   *Icons view of the Music Instruction home page files*

Having safely tucked away the knowledge that a Web page consists of multiple files, you should now consciously consider that a Web page isn't a solo form of communiqué, like a flyer on your car windshield. Instead, a Web page almost always uses *hyperlinks* to link to other Web pages.

## Hyperlinks and Web Sites

**lingo**   *Hyperlinks* are clickable text or graphics that enable you to access additional Internet resources.

As we stated at the beginning of this chapter, we're assuming that if you want to create a Web site, you've surfed the Web. Thus, you've clicked numerous hyperlinks. As you know, hyperlinks are clickable text or graphics that enable you to access additional Internet resources and Web pages. More technically speaking, hyperlinks are elements included in HTML documents that point to other Web pages or Internet documents (similar to how some HTML commands point to graphics files). Figure 1-7 shows how a few hyperlinks on the Music Instruction home page point to other Web pages—specifically, the Lessons and Events pages. Clicking a hyperlink displays a linked page, which can be any page on the Internet (not just a Web page that you've created), located anywhere in the world. You can see this relationship in action by visiting Chris's Music Instruction site online at www.creationguide.com/songbird.

As a Web designer, using hyperlinks naturally progresses to using multiple Web pages. Generally speaking, you won't want to place all

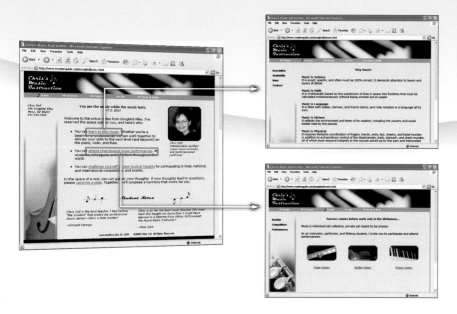

**Figure 1-7** *Examples of hyperlinks, which take viewers to other Web pages or Internet resources (see www.creationguide. com/songbird)*

your information on one big, long home page. Instead, you'll want to create a series of more concise Web pages that relate and link to one another. This collection of related Web pages forms your Web site.

## From Your Head to the Web (and Back Again)

At this point in the chapter, the components are laid on the table: the Internet, the Web, browsers, Web pages, hyperlinks, and Web sites. This roll call of components is a good start, but we face the small detail of how a text file and a few graphics files that you've created on your computer are turned into a Web page on the Internet. Before we wade too deeply into the muck and mire of Web page transmissions, let's debunk a surprisingly popular myth:

> *People who view your Web pages on the Internet have access to your desktop computer.*

The preceding statement is *not* true! Rest assured, "live" Web pages are not stored on personal computers. Instead, the Web page files are stored on servers. (Refer to Figure 1-1 to see an illustration of how servers fit into the Internet's infrastructure.)

## The Client/Server Nature of the Web

Servers are simply powerful computers—much more powerful than desktop and laptop computers—that store Internet files and run special software designed to respond to *client requests*. Of course, now we've introduced the term *client*. Let's stop this circuitous approach and briefly indulge in some geekspeak.

Basically, Web files are transmitted using what is known as the *client/ server model*. In the client/server model, one system (a server) connected to a network serves the request of another system (the client). For the purposes of Web design, a *client* is a fancy name for a browser

## A Little More HTML
The text and HTML commands used to create a Web page are collectively called the Web page's *source code*. Most browsers enable you to display a Web page's source code. For example, to display source code by using Internet Explorer, you click **Source** on the **View** menu, as shown here:

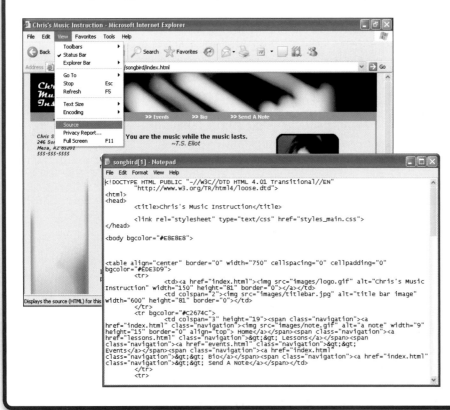

(such as Internet Explorer) running on a user's computer, and a *server* is the combination of a powerful computer that stores Web pages and the software that responds to requests to display Web pages stored on the powerful computer. Therefore, when you access a Web page, the following process takes place:

1 This part's familiar—you connect your computer to the Internet and open your browser. Then you type a Web address (URL) in the Address bar and press ENTER, or you click a hyperlink on your browser's start page.

2 The client (your browser) sends the typed URL or the URL associated with a hyperlink across phone lines, cables, or WiFi waves; through routers; and to your Internet service provider (ISP). Your ISP is the company that you pay to provide you with access to the Internet.

3 Your ISP then sends your URL request across the Internet via more cables, routers, and other high-speed data circuits to the computer (the server) maintaining the requested Web page.

4 The server sends the Web page information across the Internet to your ISP, and, finally, your ISP forwards the information to your computer.

> **lingo**  *URL*
> (pronounced "you-are-ell") stands for *Uniform Resource Locator*. A URL refers to an Internet address that tells your Web browser where to look on the Internet to find a specific Web page.

This process is illustrated in Figure 1-8

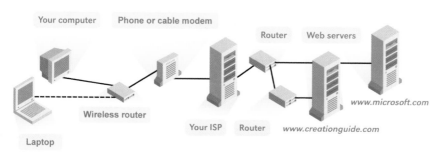

Your computer    Phone or cable modem

Router    Web servers

Wireless router

www.microsoft.com

Laptop

Your ISP    Router    www.creationguide.com

**Figure 1-8**  *The underlying concept of accessing Web pages on remote servers*

From a Web designer's perspective, after you create a Web site, you copy your Web site's files to a server that will be hosting your site—similar to how you can copy a file from your hard disk onto a CD or USB flash memory drive (except that you copy your Web site's files across Internet lines, as described in Chapter 12, "Sending Your Web Pages into the Real World"). Using File Transfer Protocol (FTP) tools,

My Network Places, or Web publishing wizards, the process of copying your Web site's files to a server can be as simple as dragging files from your local folder into a folder on the server that you're using to host your Web site. Then, when others view your published Web site, they access the server that stores copies of your files, not your computer.

That's a wrap on our fundamentals review. At this point, you're ready to forge ahead with the design and implementation of your Web site, as described in the upcoming pages. But before closing this chapter, we'd like to brief you on what's coming in the next few chapters.

## Progressing at a Steady Clip

As you might suspect, much of the work of creating a Web site involves that much maligned concept known as *planning*. You need to spend at least a little time thinking about content–including text and graphics–as well as devising your site's structure. Although Web design is a creative process, it's not a black art devoid of structure. Throughout the course of this book, we'll pass along a few basic tenets that will help make the process of creating your Web site easier. Our expertise comes not only from our own years (and years) of online experience but also from numerous professional allies and usability studies that many other designers, engineers, and information specialists have performed. From these sources, we have drawn some basic conclusions about text, graphics, colors, usability, and design on the Web that we have proven in practice. Therefore, the remaining chapters in Part One–Chapters 2 through 6–address the information you should know to make your Web site design endeavors successful, including issues surrounding text, graphics, colors, layout design, helpful tools, and Web site planning. Therefore, we highly recommend that you read (or at least scan) Part One before diving into Part Two.

Of course, we also know that you might be champing at the bit to create a Web presence *now*. We know the feeling. While we present some hands-on information and exercises in Part One, you simply might want to go ahead and skip to Chapter 7 to learn how you can dabble with some *free* server space. In Chapter 7, we introduce a project that lets you get online quickly for free–by setting up a *blog*. That way, you can set up a simple online presence within a couple

**lingo** *Blog* is an abbreviated term for *Web log*. A blog is a frequently updated (usually daily) Web site that presents personal information, opinions, and links. It's designed to reflect the personality of the author and present a mixture of personal updates and reflections about current events, the Web, or society in general.

hours, and you'll have your first Web site with your very own URL posted today. If you do jump ahead to Chapter 7, be sure to return to Chapters 2 through 6 to brush up on the basics of creating Web sites before you go any further. That way, you'll be fully prepared to create the more advanced Web sites presented in Chapters 8 through 11.

Finally, regardless of how you wind your way through this book and onto the Web, when all's said and done, remember to review Chapters 12 and 13. Chapter 12 describes how to go "live" (if you're using any Web publishing method other than a free hosting service), and Chapter 13 addresses updating and archiving your information as well as future advancements you might consider as your next step in Web design. Although updating and archiving might sound fairly dull, these processes are critical. After all, if you spend time and effort to create a Web site, you probably won't want it to shrivel and die from neglect within a few weeks.

All in all, by the time you complete this book, you'll have mastered the basics of creating Web sites in a number of ways. You'll no longer cringe when you see expressions like *XHTML* and *cascading style sheets*, and your skills will serve as a strong foundation that you can build on to create a wide variety of more advanced Web sites.

# check it!

- The Internet is hardware. The Web is software (including programs and documents).
- Browsers are applications that enable you to view Web sites.
- Most basic Web pages consist of multiple files—such as an HTML (text) file and graphics files.
- A Web site is a group of related Web pages.
- Hyperlinks provide access to other Web pages and Internet resources.
- The Internet uses the client/server model, in which a server responds to client requests for information.
- Internet users access Web pages that are stored on servers.
- If you can use a computer, you can create a Web site!

# A

# composing
## and shaping
## web text

# 2

Like a great meal, a successful Web site should look good as well as offer rich, satisfying content. A restaurant that serves artistically arranged yet cardboard-flavored dishes or, alternatively, uninspiring-looking piles of palate-pleasing delights rarely earns return visitors. Just as a gourmet restaurant must provide tasty and visually attractive fare if it wants to build a clientele, a well-designed Web site needs to incorporate quality content with good design to inspire users to visit time and again.

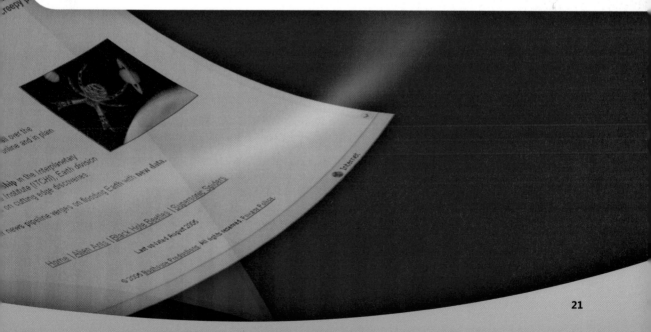

# Text Matters

When people contemplate building Web sites, they usually think of design first—that is, how the site will look rather than what it should say. And that's understandable as well as desirable, because thinking about design is always good. In fact, quite a bit of this book is devoted to Web design. But at the heart of every Web site is *content*. After all, most people build Web sites because they have a message they want to share—even if that message simply asserts, "Look what I've been up to lately!"

To be successful, your Web site must provide information that quickly captures viewers' attention; otherwise, viewers won't stay more than a couple of seconds and probably won't return. Therefore, start by thinking about your Web site's content before you design.

> **tip**  You might be happy to learn that the Web doesn't require you to be Hemingway to build a good site. Online audiences generally prefer relevant mediocre writing over irrelevant awesome writing. Fortunately, this chapter tells you how to create relevant *and* better-than-mediocre writing, with an emphasis on clarity and organization.

If you follow along with this text, you'll be well on your way to having your Web site's content fully spelled out and formulated by the end of this chapter. But even if you don't progress that far in creating content for a particular Web site, you'll be able to identify and create good Web text in general. Further, you'll know how you can maximize the use of text on your future Web pages. With this know-how, you'll be able to ease into blending content and design when you start to build your Web pages.

Now, back to the matter at hand—online text. Reasonably enough, you might be thinking that you're quite capable of using words so you don't really need to read about Web text. But rest assured, even if you're a full-time writer, you can benefit from the tips in this chapter. Although good online text has a lot in common with good printed text, it also varies from printed text in a number of key ways. You'll see as you progress through this chapter that creating effective online text involves mastering and blending the arts of clarity, marketing, visual appeal, technological limitations, and a little reader psychology.

# Readers' Approach to Online Pages: Scanning and Skimming

The first concept you need to address is that readers respond to Web pages differently from the way they respond to printed pages. In early studies, Web experts found that reading a block of text online took approximately 25 percent longer than reading the same text on a printed page. In other words, in the amount of time you spend reading 75 words online, you could read 100 words on a printed page. Experts now debate whether online reading speeds are on the rise due to improved monitors, use of color, or general increased familiarity of reading online text. Regardless of exact percentages, the majority of experts agree—people's reading speeds slow down significantly when they read online text (as compared to hard copy text), even though many people are getting better at reading online. One way people have adapted to the slowness of online text reading is that they frequently scan and skim Web text instead of reading every word on the screen.

Recent research studies by organizations such as the Nielsen Norman Group (www.nngroup.com) and Eyetrack III (www.poynterextra. org/eyetrack2004) have further reinforced the scan-and-skim theory in relation to reading online content. Therefore, you should be aware

---

**try this!**

In March 2000, Webreview.com conducted an informal poll in which readers ranked their general impression of the quality of writing found on the Internet. Of those responding, 55 percent ranked the quality of online writing as fair, 22 percent ranked it as poor, 21 percent ranked it as good, and only 1 percent ranked it as excellent. More than five years have passed since that poll, and we haven't found any comparable data being gathered online. Therefore, we've posted our own unofficial Web Writing poll, at www.creationguide.com/2cents. Feel free to take a moment and let us know how you feel about the overall quality of writing on the Web. As with all parts of the CreationGuide Web site, your privacy is respected and the poll is completely anonymous.

of the differences between *scanning* and *skimming* so you can design your Web site in a way that addresses both processes.

*Scanning* occurs when a visitor lands on your Web page and quickly looks over the page, mostly to see if the page is relevant or interesting. If a Web page doesn't grab the visitor quickly (within 7 to 10 seconds, according to most usability studies), the visitor will very likely move on to another page or another site altogether. Therefore, you should present your content to accommodate scanning research findings. According to usability studies conducted with left-to-right readers, visitors' eyes most often first fixate on the upper-left corner of a Web page, hover there for a moment, sweep across the page from left to center to right, and then finally move farther down the page. Figure 2-1 shows an image based on the Eyetrack III research that uses color to show the areas on Web pages that receive the most focus and attention from visitors. As you can see, the upper-left corner and center area are high-focus areas for most people.

**Figure 2-1**  *Key focus areas on a Web page*

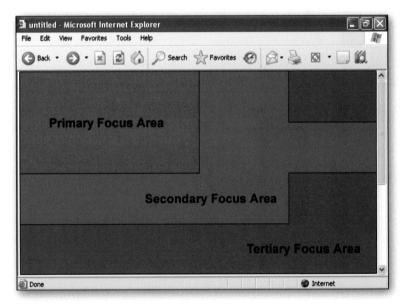

*Skimming* comes after scanning. After a visitor scans your page and determines that it's sufficiently relevant or interesting, the visitor skims the content to quickly identify the main ideas of the page. Skimming generally occurs three to four times faster than reading content word by word. When a visitor skims a Web page, the eyes look at headlines, hyperlinks, boldface or italic text, first and last sentences in paragraphs, bulleted lists, tables, captions, and sometimes images. Skimming helps visitors decide whether they want to dive deeper into your content. The best content developers help readers skim text by providing just the right visual emphasis on main ideas and points of interest.

Now that you know how visitors look at your Web content before they read it, you can keep the scanning and skimming ideas in mind while you develop your Web site. Increasing the scanning and skimming potential carries the triple benefit of aiding visitors' comprehension, increasing your Web site's credibility, and improving your site's chance of being ranked higher by search engines (because your Web site's main ideas are easier to identify). In other words, paying attention to content is worth it. In this chapter, we describe a variety of methods you can employ to improve your Web pages' scannability and skimmability (and yes, we did make up those words expressly for your benefit). We also drop scan and skim reminders throughout the planning chapters and walkthroughs later in this book.

To illustrate the scanning and skimming concepts, compare Figures 2-2 and 2-3. (You can view the Web pages shown in these figures online, at www.creationguide.com/cosmic/alienant-bad.html and www.creationguide.com/cosmic/alienant-good.html.) Figure 2-2 shows a Web page that doesn't adhere to good online-text practices, whereas Figure 2-3 follows the textual advice presented in this chapter. Notice how much faster you can identify the text's main points in Figure 2-3 than in Figure 2-2. The upcoming text explains why and provides pointers for you to use when creating your own online text. After you read this chapter, you should return to these images to see if you can identify all the ways in which Figure 2-3 has been improved over Figure 2-2.

**note** Please note that we use the words *link* and *hyperlink* interchangeably.

**Figure 2-2**  *An ineffective presentation of Web page text*

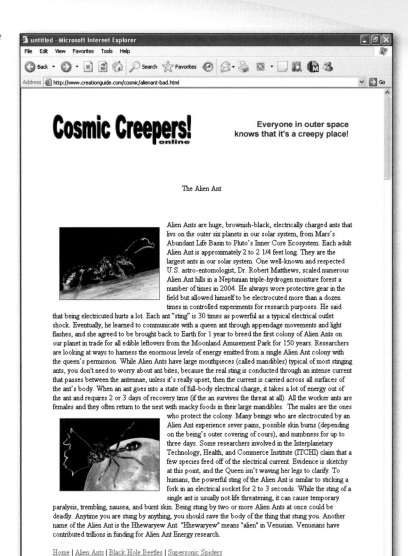

Alien Ants - Cosmic Creepers - Microsoft Internet Explorer

File   Edit   View   Favorites   Tools   Help

Back | Search | Favorites

Address http://www.creationguide.com/cosmic/alienant-good.html

# Cosmic Creepers!
online

**Everyone in outer space knows that it's a creepy place!**

Home | Alien Ants | Black Hole Beetles | Supersonic Spiders

## Alien Ants

### Habitat
Outer six planets in our solar system, from Mars's Abundant Life Basin to Pluto's Inner Core Ecosystem

### Threat
Electrical current, causes excruciating pain

### Quick Facts

- 2 to 2 1/4 feet long
- Largest known ant in our solar system
- Brownish-black exoskeleton protected by synaptic electrical web
- Large mouthpieces (called *mandibles*)
- Mandibles used to carry food to the colony
- Females gather and store food; males defend colony
- Intense electrical current runs between antennae for defense
- Electrical current spreads across exoskeleton in extreme situations
- Also called Hhewaryew Ants (*hhewaryew* means *alien* in Venusian)

### Alien Ant "Stings"
Alien Ants protect themselves with self-generated electrical currents. In battle and defense, they "sting" by zapping foes with a current generated between their antennae. A single zap can transmit up to 30 times more energy than a typical electric outlet.

An Alien Ant that faces a life-threatening attack can become fully electric across its exoskeleton. This full-body charge often proves effective, but it takes a toll on the ant's health. A healthy ant requires 2 to 3 days to fully recover from a full-body charge if it survives the attack.

A single Alien Ant's sting isn't deadly to most species, including humans. A sting usually causes severe pain and can produce any of the following effects:

- Numbness (up to 3 days)
- Trembling
- Temporary paralysis
- Nausea
- Skin burns

Multiple stings can result in severe burns, permanent paralysis, or possibly death.

### Recent Research
In 2004, renowned U.S. astro-entomologist Dr. Robert Matthews scaled numerous Alien Ant hills in a Neptunian triple-hydrogen moisture forest. During his studies, he allowed himself to be electrocuted more than a dozen times in controlled experiments. He fully recuperated from the paralyzing effects and made astounding progress in understanding Alien Ant culture.

Dr. Matthews successfully learned to communicate with a queen ant through appendage movements and light flashes. She recently agreed to live on Earth for 1 year to help set up the first Earth-based colony of Alien Ants. In trade, her Neptunian colony will receive all edible leftovers from the Moonland Amusement Park for 150 years.

The Earth-based colony allows researchers to study methods of harnessing the enormous levels of energy emitted from a single Alien Ant colony. Venusians have contributed trillions in funding for Alien Ant energy research and plan to send a team of researchers to participate in the Earth-based research project.

Home | Alien Ants | Black Hole Beetles | Supersonic Spiders

**Last updated August 2005**

Done | Internet

**Figure 2-3** *An effective presentation of Web page text*

Now that we've made a case for thinking about your text and recognizing how online readers scan and skim before reading, let's briefly look at the fundamental roles text plays on a Web site. Then we'll discuss the details and the how-tos involved in shaping and streamlining online text.

## Textual Elements of a Web Page

Most Web pages use a variety of textual components, as illustrated in Figure 2-4. These textual elements are described in the following subsections. In this section, we talk about the individual parts. Later, we talk about building them.

**Figure 2-4**   *The various textual elements of a Web page.*

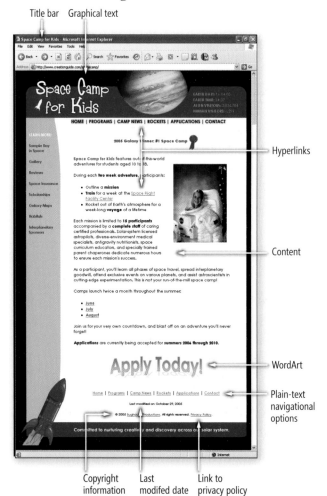

## Title Bar

Let's take it from the top—literally—by looking at the title bar. When you create a Web site, you create the text that appears in a browser window's title bar for each Web page. The key to title text is to make it concise, clear, and useful. Notice that when you open a Web page, the Web page's title text also appears in your Microsoft Windows taskbar. Taskbar text simplifies a user's job when switching among a number of open windows. Therefore, although you can insert clever or witty title text if you want to, you should generally lean toward useful and clear instead. Notice the lame vs. helpful title bar text shown earlier in Figures 2-2 and 2-3.

## Content

A Web site's *content* refers to its substance—the reason people are visiting your site. As described in the next few sections, Web site content should be clear, brief, easy to scan and skim, informative, timely, and grammatically correct (among other select qualities). Keep in mind that no matter how beautiful a Web site, the Internet's most engaging feature is text. After all, in addition to Web sites, a few hundred million people regularly rely on online text to send e-mail messages, chat using instant messaging (IM), communicate on Web logs (blogs), and post to discussion groups.

## Hyperlinks

Hyperlinks provide form and clarity to a Web site. They link the pages of your site to one another, they provide access to additional information on the Internet, and they aid in scanning and skimming by their very nature. They also keep your pages from becoming "dead ends" on the Web. In other words, hyperlinks help you to organize your information, and they enable visitors to access and process information quickly and easily. Textual hyperlinks are the "meat and potatoes" hyperlinks, because all browsers and visitors can access text links. Therefore, make sure your textual hyperlinks are clear, consistent, and appropriately placed, as we discuss later in this chapter and in Chapter 4, "Mastering Web Design Basics."

**tip** For added clarity (on taskbar buttons especially), skip leading articles (*the*, *a*, *an*) in a Web page's title bar text, and use important keywords in your title bar to aid search engines. Using snappy, descriptive, relevant titles helps your pages stand out within users' workspaces as well as stand out in search engine results that organize Web pages by titles or scan titles for keywords.

**tip** One way to obtain content for your Web site is to take advantage of Web content providers. A number of news bureaus, media centers, special interest groups, private contractors, and other information specialists provide Web content to Web sites on a regular basis, usually for a fee. To find a content provider, visit your favorite news provider or special interest site, or use a search engine (such as www.msn.com) to locate Web content providers or copywriters.

## Logos, Graphical Text, and WordArt

You can use *logos, graphical text*, and *WordArt* to add a professional look to your Web site. Figure 2-5 shows a few examples of logos, graphical text, and WordArt. As we explain in Chapter 3, "Creating and Using Art on the Web," you can use graphical text to add a consistent and unique look and feel to the group of related Web pages that make up your Web site. Having all the parts of your Web site appear interrelated clearly indicates to visitors that they are still within the realm of your Web site even as they click from page to page. Furthermore, logos, graphical text, and WordArt are frequently used to provide a unique and consistent graphical link to a site's home page. You might have discovered while surfing the Web that you can usually click a company's logo to return to the site's home page. (If you haven't discovered this practice, you should test it out during your next Web surfing session.) Whenever possible, link your logo to your home page throughout your Web site.

> **lingo** A logo is the graphic identity of a trademark or brand. Logo text is usually set in a special typeface, or *font*, and often arranged with a simple graphic in a specific way.

**Figure 2-5** *A few samples of logos, graphical text, and WordArt*

> **tip** Logos should almost always appear in the upper-left corner of your Web site—especially on your home page.

If you're viewing the "good" Alien Ants Web page (Figure 2-3) online at www.creationguide.com/cosmic/alienant-good.html, you can click the *Cosmic Creepers!* online WordArt logo in the upper-left corner of the page to display the fictitious site's home page, shown later in this chapter, in Figure 2-9.

> **lingo** *Graphical text* is a general term that refers to text used to create graphical elements on your Web pages, including stylized buttons, banners, logos, and so forth.

## Forms and Menu Items

Some Web sites use text for forms and menu items. Figure 2-6 shows a simple, clear, well-aligned form that visitors can use to sign up to receive an online newsletter. We imagine you've run across online menus and forms (especially if you've purchased a book from Amazon.com or viewed an online map in MSN Maps & Directions). Effective forms and menus are simple, logical, clear, and visually well-aligned—users must readily know what to select, which labels go with which box, how to enter text in a form's text boxes, and which action they should perform next. We show you how to add a form using FrontPage later in this book's walkthrough section. In the meantime, if you're interested in reading up on the role that text plays in creating forms and menus, thumb through some graphical user interface (GUI, pronounced "gooey") books, which you can find in bookstores and libraries. Be careful before you invest in a GUI book, though—many GUI books target programmers and software developers, and the text might present more information than you need.

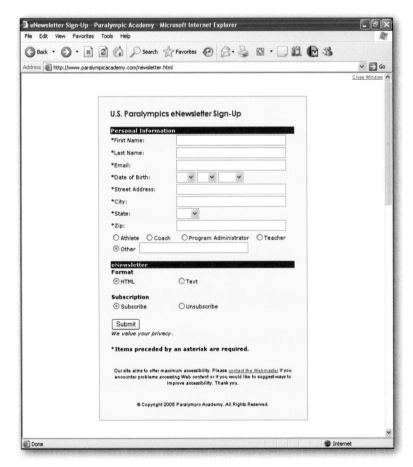

**Figure 2-6** *A well-designed online form*

**lingo** *WordArt* is a Microsoft Word feature that enables you to create stylized text-based graphics, such as custom headings and logos. For example, in Figures 2-2 and 2-3, we created the *Cosmic Creepers!* online logo element by using Word's WordArt feature and the Drawing toolbar, and in Figure 2-4, the *Apply Today!* graphical text is a WordArt element.

## Plain-Text Navigational Options

**note**   As an added bonus, adding text-based navigation links to the bottom of your Web pages means that users can move to other pages in your Web site without having to scroll to the top of the current page to access your main navigation links.

Many Web designers opt to format their menu bar and navigation elements (buttons) only as graphics. (In Figure 2-4, the buttons across the top essentially serve as the site's main navigation bar.) Using graphical navigation elements is fine, but we recommend that you display your navigation hyperlinks as plain text in conjunction with your graphical elements. If your Web site's design uses a graphical menu bar or buttons, you can avoid disrupting the layout of your Web pages by including textual hyperlinks along the bottom of your page (as shown in Figure 2-4). Offering an alternative to graphics-based links is useful because some viewers turn off their browser's graphics capabilities to expedite Web page downloads. Furthermore, textual hyperlinks aid screen-reader tools used by visitors with low vision or other vision impairments. Keep in mind that if you don't provide text-based navigation components, some users might not discover how to get to your site's ancillary pages. If that happens, you can bet your last pixel that visitors won't be hanging around your site for long.

## Date or Last-Modified Information

Generally, you should include a date element on your Web site. The date can be as nondescript as a small line of text located near the bottom of a Web page. If regularly updated content is one of your page's main selling points, however, you might want to make the date much more noticeable by placing it higher on your page and nearer the "prime" upper-left area. On the other hand, if you don't plan to update your site regularly, you might opt to omit publishing a last-modified date. Frankly, we don't recommend that you plan on *not* updating your site, but in some circumstances, you might be able to get away with a static page or two within your site. For instance, if you're presenting instructions for an antigravity coffee grinder you invented that won't be changing in the next 10 years, copyright the page of instructions and don't bother with a last-modified date. Conversely, on large sites (like the CreationGuide Web site), you can usually get away with adding a last-modified date to just the home page. A date on the home page inherently implies that you've paid attention to your site and have made recent updates as required.

## Copyright Information

You own the copyright to all original text and graphics you create. Therefore, to protect your property, you should add a copyright notice to your Web pages. By law, you're protected regardless of whether you include a copyright statement, but the statement shows readers that you value your copyright and that your information is up-to-date. Keep in mind that if you use freeware (such as copyright-free graphics that you've downloaded from another Web site) on your Web page, the freeware is free for anyone else to use as well; you cannot copyright freeware.

> **tip** To create the copyright symbol © in Microsoft Word, press CTRL+ALT+C, or if AutoCorrect is turned on (the default setting), type **(c)** and Word automatically changes the text to ©.

When you add copyright text, the information can be as simple as © 2006 *Your Name or Company Name*. And for added emphasis, you could add *All Rights Reserved*. Furthermore, the copyright information should be placed near the bottom of the page and in a font size that's noticeably smaller than the Web page's body text. Most people realize that your site is copyrighted. They'll scroll down if they need more specific information about the copyright holder.

## Privacy Policies

Privacy policies are the slightly newer kids on the Web text block. As everyone on the Internet knows, security is one hot topic. We've all downloaded security patches to our browsers and operating systems, and privacy is a recurring theme. Therefore, to help alleviate visitors' concerns, if you gather any information from your visitors—including e-mail addresses—you should include a privacy policy that states your rights as well as your visitors' rights.

To see privacy policies in action, surf to almost any major corporation's Web site, scroll down, and click the privacy policy link. You'll find that many privacy policies are filled with legalese. Many corporate legal departments quickly took privacy issues under their wings.

If you're writing a privacy policy for your own Web site, you can keep yours fairly simple. Some privacy issues you might consider addressing include:

- Copyright and fair use policies
- Contact information (a mailing address, and an e-mail address or phone number) for copyright, permissions, and privacy issues

- Reason(s) the site gathers visitors' names, e-mail addresses, and other information
- Way(s) in which gathered information is used
- Description of any other information being gathered
- Steps used to protect information (including using HTTPS, which is the secure version of the HTTP protocol)
- Indication of whether information will be provided to others
- Ways to remove information from the compiled data

In addition to privacy policies, you should always include a statement on forms you use to gather information that you respect your visitors' privacy. The form shown earlier in Figure 2-6 includes a statement that indicates visitors' privacy is respected. Figure 2-7 shows a very simple sample privacy policy (also available online, at www.creation-guide.com/privacy). We grant you, as a reader of this text, the right to copy the sample privacy policy text for use on your own Web site until you create a custom policy.

**Figure 2-7**  *A sample privacy policy*

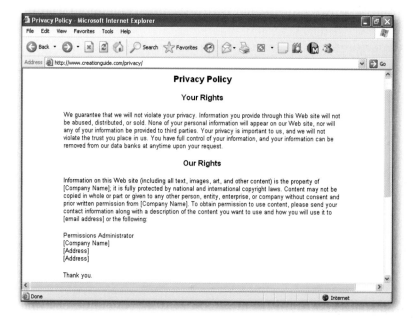

As you can see in Figure 2-7, a privacy policy can be quite simple. For most Web sites, the main goals of a privacy policy are to:

- Reassure visitors that you won't breach their trust regarding information they provide.
- Assert your copyright and permissions policies.

Of course, if you're conducting some serious market research, data mining information for resale, or using information in ways unrelated to the implied usage, you should certainly have a lawyer draft a privacy policy that covers all the necessary legal angles. Better safe than sorry in those situations. Besides, by contracting a lawyer to write your policy, you'll make a lawyer's day!

Now that we've touched on the basic textual elements of Web pages, you're ready to shape and write Web content.

> **tip**   If you use a logging utility to gather Web site traffic information, as discussed in Chapter 5, "Considering Tools and Stockpiling Goods," you should include a privacy policy. Logging utilities use computer domain addresses to compile many statistics.

## Writing for the Web

As we mentioned earlier in this chapter, good Web writing shares some basic similarities with well-written printed text. For example, Web text should be clear, grammatical, and well formulated, and it should be written for a specific audience. But Web text requires some unique considerations that don't crop up when you're writing for another medium. One reason Web text requires this unique approach is because the Web is *nonlinear*. Users don't often methodically read through a Web page or Web site as they would a novel, nor do they "watch" a Web site in the way they would a scripted TV show. Instead, Web surfers scan a page, read a couple snippets of text that interest them, click a link (you hope), possibly read a paragraph or two in depth, check out a picture or other multimedia element, and then click again to access another page or site. Therefore, you need to form and mold your text (and page design) to cater to the desires and habits of Web surfers.

## Organizing Web Text

Writing Web text requires you to take a new approach to wordsmithing—specifically, when writing for the Web, you need to think *topic*, not *document*. At the highest level, you use topical text keywords to frame and organize your site. We discuss using text to frame a Web site in Chapter 6, "Planning Your Attack." This chapter focuses on the writing and organizing processes involved in writing for the Web.

Fortunately, you can effectively shape your Web text by using a combination of methods, including:

- Using the classic *inverted pyramid methodology* used by journalists (described next) whenever possible

- Using headings, subheadings, boldfacing, and hyperlinks effectively

- Streamlining your paragraphs and body text to about 50 percent of printed content

- Using an active voice and the language of "you" (which means telling readers why "you want to read this Web site and what's in it for you" as opposed to "here's a bunch of information about me me me!")

The next few sections detail how you can implement effective writing techniques for the Web.

## Web Text Attracts Users' Attention Before Graphics

Here's yet another reason to take your Web text seriously. According to Jakob Nielsen, author of *Designing Web Usability* (New Riders, 2000) and an early pioneer of Web page usability, Web text frequently grabs a reader's attention before graphics do. As Nielsen reports, "It is almost twice as common for users to fixate on the text as on the images upon their initial visit to a page. In general, users were first drawn to headlines, article summaries, and captions, often not looking at the images until the second or third visit to a page." Other usability experts have conducted studies that reinforce the "text first" approach to Web content.

## Inverted Pyramid Methodology

Many Web professionals liken Web content to newspaper text. And to an extent, the analogy works, although we believe Web text also incorporates some marketing traits. First, let's analyze the news text approach. Like news text, Web text should fundamentally take the classic inverted pyramid form. An inverted pyramid approach places the most important information at the beginning of a story, including stating the conclusion up front (usually in the heading). In traditional news writing, a good story answers the questions *Who? What? Where? When? Why?* and *How?* as rapidly and succinctly as possible in order of importance. For example, a news report on a freeway car fire would probably first answer the question *What?*—a car fire—and then quickly answer the questions *Where?*—on the freeway—*When?*—during rush hour—and *Why?*—overheated engine. Of course, if the burning car belonged to the president, the story's *Who?* element would jump to the top of the pyramid. After the key points are stated in an inverted pyramid story, the remainder of the article serves to fill in the details and wind down to the least important information at the end.

As we said, you should also generally take an inverted pyramid approach when you're writing for Web sites, especially if your site contains substantial textual content. A number of online news sites effectively use a modified approach to the inverted pyramid setup. For example, look at any one of the big news sites, such as Reuters (www.reuters.com), Associated Press (www.ap.org), CNN (www.cnn.com), and MSNBC (www.msnbc.com), or access a few news sites at once on a news portal, such as iWon (www.iwon.com).

Most news sites use a clear-cut variation of the inverted pyramid. On iWon, for example, the home page shows links similar to the hierarchy displayed on the following page.

**try this!**

To see a large collection of examples of manipulating text online, visit news sites such as USA Today, CNN, MSNBC, and so forth. To see samples of newspapers from around the world, visit the Internet Public Library, at www.ipl.org/div/news, a comprehensive collection of links hosted by the University of Michigan School of Information.

```
Top News
            Headline
            Headline
              •
              •
              •
Sports News
            Headline
            Headline
              •
              •
              •
Business News
            Headline
            Headline
              •
              •
              •
Entertainment News
            Headline
            Headline
              •
              •
              •
Technology News
            Headline
            Headline
              •
              •
              •
```

**note**  To help speed up the trickle-down informational process, you can also click a headline on the iWon home page to display the full story of any headline that immediately captures your interest. Also note that iWon has been successfully implementing the modified pyramid style for years; in fact, we discuss this setup in the first edition of this book, which was written in 2000 and published January 2001. This methodology clearly stands the test of time.

Using the preceding setup, users can click a main heading (such as Top News, Sports News, Business News, Entertainment News, or Technology News in the preceding example) to view the first few lines of each headline's story. For example, let's say you click the **Top News** link. You would then see the following layout (see Figure 2-8):

```
Top News
            Headline
                        A few lines of text providing the main gist of the story
            Headline
                        A few lines of text providing the main gist of the story
            Headline
                        A few lines of text providing the main gist of the story
```

At this point, you could click a headline to read the full version of any story that interests you (see Figure 2-8). Notice the trickle-down effect of the information: headline, headline with a short synopsis, and headline with the full story. Imagine if a news site's home page contained every full news story of the day—readers would flee from the text-packed site quicker than the page could download.

Although the news site setup described here is highly effective, it's probably much more complex than your Web site needs to be. (We're pretty sure you're relieved to hear that!) The setup of the iWon site provides a good example of the inverted pyramid methodology.

On your site, you'll be more concerned with ensuring that your most important points (the key points in an inverted pyramid) are displayed quickly and "jump out" at readers. You can achieve this effect by employing a few key techniques, including using headings and hyperlinks wisely and streamlining your text for Web use.

## Brainstorms, Headings, Hyperlinks, and Boldfacing

Now that the theory of serving the best information first is firmly in place, you're ready to start thinking about actual content. When it comes to creating text, some people have a hard time getting started. Therefore, we suggest a popular, freeform approach to creating your Web text—brainstorming with a pencil, pen, or keyboard. To effectively brainstorm text for a Web page, follow these steps:

1 Sit down with a pad of paper (or your laptop), create a mental picture of what you want to communicate, and then jot down every concept and idea that you want to include on your Web page. Don't worry about organization or wording. The goal here is to get your ideas out of your head and onto paper (or screen).

2 After you have all the topics that you want to include on your Web page in front of you in hard-copy form (print your electronic notes, if necessary), write a *keyword* next to each topic. You might find that multiple topics can be associated with the same keyword. That's fine—in fact, that will help you group your information later. Again, don't overanalyze the details; you're working on big umbrella concepts at this point.

> **lingo** A *keyword* is a word or phrase that succinctly summarizes the overall essence of a concept or topic. Frequently, a keyword also serves as a main idea that encompasses a group of related concepts.

3 Review each keyword, and determine which keywords deserve to be headings and which should be hyperlinks. A heading calls attention to a brief amount of information on an existing page; in contrast, a hyperlink indicates that you have enough related text to create a separate Web page from existing information or point to a major section in a long document.

Figures 2-2 and 2-3, provide an ideal end result of effective brainstorming for a single Web page (as opposed to a site's organization). As you can see, Figure 2-2 displays a large block of text—essentially an information brain dump; Figure 2-3 shows where keywords (formatted as headings) come into play to point out the main facts included

**tip**   To deter-
mine whether key
topics should be
hyperlinks on your
Web page, visualize
each page as a
table of contents
that summarizes
the Web site's main
ideas and points
users to each area
of the site. (See the
*Space Camp for
Kids* home page,
shown earlier in
Figure 2-4, and the
*Cosmic Creepers!*
home page, shown
in Figure 2-9.) In
most cases, every
Web page should
lead to related Web
pages; Web pages
that don't provide
links to other pages
are rare and often
referred to as *dead
ends*.

in the text. If you were brainstorming about alien ants, you might come up with the paragraph in Figure 2-2. Then when you reviewed your paragraph, you would come up with the heading topics shown in Figure 2-3.

Remember—clearly calling attention to key points for users is critical. Not only is reading online more arduous than reading printed text, but millions of Web pages are also vying for users' time and attention.

To illustrate how brainstorming can organize a Web *site* as well as a Web *page*, let's view the *Cosmic Creepers!* navigation bar, shown in Figure 2-8. By looking at the navigation bar's hyperlinks, you can instantaneously see that the Cosmic Creepers! site includes a home page and three outer-space species pages. You can almost visualize exactly how the site's brainstorming session might have progressed— the types of alien bugs emerged as the big ideas (thereby necessitat- ing hyperlinks and a separate Web page for each species), and the main facts about each type of species served to create headings on the topical Web pages (such as Habitat, Threat, Quick Facts, and so forth, as shown in Figure 2-3). Brainstorming—the first step before fram- ing, outlining, or flowcharting a Web site (as discussed in Chapter 6, "Planning Your Attack")—helps you visualize your approach to your Web pages and Web site, which in turn helps you write clear, topic- driven text.

**Figure 2-8**   *The Cosmic Creepers! navigation bar, which clearly defines the site's organization*

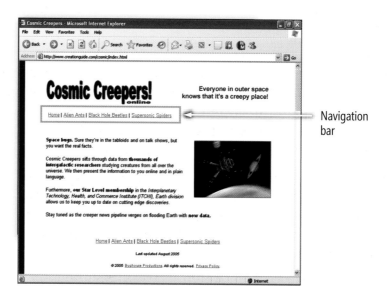

Navigation bar

## Body Text

At this point, you should have a fair idea of the information you want
to include on your Web page as well as the logical headings. You
should also have a feel for possible ancillary (linked) pages. You're
now ready to begin molding the freeform ideas you jotted down into
user-friendly text. In other words, it's time to write.

---

**try this!**   As mentioned earlier in this chapter, readers scan a page and then skim for emphasized words
and phrases. A quick test will show you if you're emphasizing the proper words and phrases on a Web page.

To perform the test, copy the emphasized words or phrases on your page into a makeshift paragraph on a
separate page. Then read the paragraph, even though it will be filled with incomplete sentences. Does the
paragraph accurately create an impression of your Web page's content? If so, you've chosen your emphasis
well, and skimming eyes will quickly grasp meaning from your page.

To see this test in action, view the Cosmic Creepers! home page shown in Figure 2-9, or look at the page
online, at www.creationguide.com/cosmic. Copy the emphasized words and phrases into a paragraph to
determine if the words and phrases accurately tell you about the Web site.

---

# Copyrights and Web Text   Because you'll be creating and pub-

lishing text on the Web, you should know a little about copyright laws. Copyright
laws protect intellectual property. Under the Berne Convention, authors and copyright
owners in 159 countries are entitled to protection of their literary and artistic works.
Among other countries, most of Europe, Canada, Japan, and the United States are
members of the Berne Union, and they adhere to the rulings of the Berne Convention,
which initially laid the groundwork for copyright issues in 1886 and has since passed
through a number of revisions.

According to current Berne Convention guidelines, a writer of an original work
automatically holds the work's copyright (unless the writer specifically waives
that right) for life plus 50 years at a minimum. Some countries guarantee a longer
copyright—for example, the United States grants a copyright for life plus 70 years after
death. Furthermore, the Berne Convention rulings stipulate that a copyright is granted
automatically, without any paperwork or other required formalities.

Keep in mind that the copyright laws protect the actual words used to express an
idea—not the idea itself. Therefore, you shouldn't copy text off the Web and paste it
into your site. Instead, if you want to include information you found on another site,
you should paraphrase relevant text and reference the original source or provide a link
to the original source's Web page.

> **note**   In the next section, we describe how to streamline your Web text, so if your paragraphs run a little long at this stage, don't sweat it.

Fortunately, you don't need to stall yourself at this time by fixating on finding the perfect words (which don't actually exist) or devising precise sentence structures. Right now, simply formulate your message in rough-draft form by following these steps:

1 Use the inverted pyramid style to organize your brainstormed ideas for the Web page you're writing.

2 Cut to the chase and display your main topics first.

3 Convert your brainstormed ideas into readable sentences and clear headings.

4 Always keep in mind that readers scan and skim before they read, so begin to implement or at least think about visual cues—such as headings, sidebars, boldfacing, and formatted typography. (In Chapter 4, "Mastering Web Design Basics," we describe how to use page-layout elements that can add to your page's scannability and skimmability as well.)

That's a lot to keep in mind. To help simplify this stage, the opposite page contains a checklist of considerations you can refer to as you write text for Web pages.

---

**Try This!**

If you're facing a bout of writer's block and are having trouble settling into the "inverted pyramid" mindset, try this. Write down (or type) a list of all the nouns—persons, places, and things—that draw mental pictures of what you want the current Web page to cover. Your list of nouns doesn't have to be in any logical order whatsoever; you might even set a time limit—say, 10 minutes—for yourself to help you write the first nouns that come to mind. Next write down adjectives to modify each noun. Then come up with verbs to go with the nouns and adjectives. Follow up with some adverbs if you're still stuck, and add a few prepositions to create complete sentences. If necessary, combine some of your sentences into logical paragraphs.

At any time during this process, you might start to see main ideas and organizational patterns emerging. You'll start to get a feel for what you want to say and how you're going to say it. You might draft an entire section without realizing it or outline a clear presentation format. If you make it all the way to combining sentences into paragraphs and still feel like you're floundering, put your work down for a while to let your mind mull over the information. Return to your writing later for a fresh start. Sometimes, when you step away and return to your writing, you can more readily see the progress you've made, which should inspire you to forge ahead.

---

## Writing Effectively for an Online Audience

You've organized your information by topic, written paragraphs, added bulleted lists, inserted headings, and indicated which key points will be formatted as hyperlinks or in boldface. Your Web text

# Checklist: Web Page Writing

Also available online, at *www.creationguide.com/lists/writing.html*.

❑ Introduce one idea per paragraph.

❑ Keep sentences short without dumbing down, but make sure to vary sentence lengths to avoid putting readers to sleep. (Language has a rhythm; use it to your advantage.)

❑ Use simple sentence structures. Avoid compound sentences and unnecessary introductory and subordinate clauses.

❑ Think about how you can draw attention to keywords and key phrases later during the design phase (such as by inserting hyperlinks or using color, boldfacing, or typeface variations, as shown in Figure 2-9).

❑ Aim to limit paragraphs to approximately 75 words or fewer, if possible. In Figure 2-3, the "Recent Research" paragraphs are all 55 words or fewer.

❑ Use bulleted lists whenever possible.

❑ Use numbered lists only when you're presenting a sequential series of steps.

❑ Insert informative headings and subheadings to break up text and highlight key points.

❑ Keep headlines simple and direct, use active verbs, choose meaningful over clever, and use keywords to aid search engines–a reader who skims only a Web page's headlines should leave the page with at least some valuable information.

❑ Ensure that the hierarchy of the headings is clear, both editorially and visually. In other words, make sure your main headings follow a logical system of subordination and are displayed uniquely, such as by formatting main headings larger than subheadings or differentiating them by color or typeface.

❑ Separate paragraphs within a section by using *white space* (space without any content, either textual or graphical). As you'll see in Chapters 3 and 4 (and beyond), white space is your friend.

❑ Avoid having too many hyperlinks in body text. Don't embed hyperlinks within paragraphs unless the hyperlinks add extremely pertinent information to your content and you're sure readers will return to your page after clicking the embedded link.

**tip**   To test whether your headings are doing their job, write or type them on a separate page without any other text, graphics, or formatting. Read the headings and have a couple other people check them out as well. You'll know you're on the right track if your headings provide a good idea of your Web page's content.

**tip**   To quickly count the number of words in a paragraph, copy the paragraph into a Microsoft Word document, select the text, and then on the **Tools** menu, click **Word Count**.

should be shaping up nicely by now, but the actual wording probably still needs some attention. As with all good writing, you're not finished with the process until you've polished and streamlined your text (as well as read and revised it at least a million times!). One way to fine-tune your text is by looking for and avoiding specific types of writing weaknesses. The number-one way to streamline Web text entails strengthening your sentences.

### Word Workout: Building Strong Sentences

Never fear—you won't need steroids or garlic to create strong sentences. Strengthening your sentences merely involves packing as much meaning into each word or clause as possible. As we discussed earlier in this chapter, because you want to limit the number of words you use to convey your Web page's information, you need to make the most out of the words that make the cut.

On Web pages, conciseness is the key (so if you're a Dickensian writer, you'll face a greater challenge than the minimalists out there). To strengthen your text, go through your copy word by word and line by line to ensure that the text implements the following techniques as much as possible:

**Precise words**    Your text should use clear, easily understood words. If you mean

> *Haight & Ashbury*

don't write

> *The intersection at which Haight Street crosses across Ashbury Street.*

In addition, opt for shorter words over longer words. For instance, choose *use* instead of *utilize*, *chew* instead of *masticate*, *lie* instead of *prevaricate*, and so forth.

**Strong verbs**    Whenever possible, your sentences should use short, solid verbs. Additionally, single-word verbs work better than multiple-word (phrasal) verbs. For example, instead of writing

> *This page serves to explain...*

simply write

> *This page explains...*

Also, replace *to be* verbs (*is, are, was, were*—you get the idea) with more specific action verbs whenever possible. For example, instead of writing

> *The TV is on in the background, and it is loud.*

replace both instances of *is* with one strong verb:

> *The TV blares in the background.*

When you use strong verbs, you add life to your text and frequently reduce sentence lengths.

To practice reworking sentences, surf the Web for a while. When you see passive text or weak verbs (and there are lots of examples out there), stop and consider how you could modify the text to be more concise, precise, and active.

**Active voice**   When you use active voice, your sentences clearly show who or what performs the action. Active voice *shows* instead of *tells*; it engages people's senses and focuses on more specific ideas. Using active voice works hand in hand with implementing strong verbs. To illustrate, here's a passive-voice sentence:

> *Many homes were destroyed by the tornado.*

Notice that the tornado performed the action (destroyed), yet the word *tornado* appears dead last in the sentence. To make the preceding sentence active, move the word that's performing the action closer to the beginning of the sentence and change the verb, as follows:

> *The tornado destroyed many homes.*

Notice how the active sentence imparts a much stronger sense of the tornado's damaging effects.

**Clear antecedents**   Frequently, writers insert pronouns—such as *it, he, she, they*, and so forth—and readers are left wondering just what the pronoun refers to. You can easily eliminate antecedent problems

> **tip**   Obviously, writing clearly and concisely helps visitors who speak the language used to build a Web site. As an added bonus, simple and clear writing also aids people who view your Web site in other languages. Translators and translating services have a much easier time translating clear text than complex prose. And as we all know, the Web is truly an international medium.

> **tip**   One key idea to keep in mind while you write is that you're ultimately creating a Web site for other people; otherwise, you'd just write in your personal journal. In visitors' minds, your site isn't all about you (even if it is!)—they're looking to find what's in it for them. Therefore write in the language of "you" as much as possible.

**tip**  If you need to brush up on your grammar skills, we highly recommend that you snag a copy of *When Words Collide: A Media Writer's Guide to Grammar and Style*, by Lauren Kessler and Duncan McDonald (Wadsworth Publishing, 2003, now in its sixth edition). Because the guide targets media writers, you'll find word usage help, such as differentiating between eminent and imminent, and tips for streamlining your text.

by replacing all unclear pronouns with specific text. (Hint: When in doubt, replace the pronoun; better to be overly clear than even slightly vague.) A key antecedent tip is to limit the use of the word *it*, and especially avoid starting sentences with weak "crutch" constructs such as *It is*. For example, the following sentence is grammatically correct but not very strong: *It is common for cats to sleep all day while you work to put food in their bowls.*

You can strengthen this sentence simply by eliminating *It is*, as follows: *Commonly, cats sleep all day while you work to put food in their bowls.*

You should also avoid starting your sentences with *There is* and *There are*. Both constructs are weak and almost as often overused as *It is*.

### Spelling and Grammar

After you streamline your text, the final stage of writing involves checking your spelling and grammar. This step has few gray areas, so we'll put it simply:

*Always, always, always run your spelling checker on your Web site's copy. Then print out your text and read it from the hard-copy version–out loud!*

## Some Things That You Can Do to Keep Things Clear of Extra Stuff

*Things*, *stuff*, and *that*–somehow those words work their way into perfectly nice sentences when they have no business being there. First and foremost, watch out for all variations of the word *thing*–the term frequently weakens otherwise strong sentences and headings. To quickly eliminate this vagary from your text, use your word processor's Search feature to find each instance of *thing*. (Some writers might be surprised to see how often the term pops up.) Replace the word with more specific terminology whenever you can. Likewise, *stuff* can almost always be replaced with a more descriptive word. Even borderline-vague words like *items* or *topics* give your readers more to work with than *things* and *stuff*. Finally, that's right–*that*. Don't tell us that you can't live without that! Or better yet, *Don't tell us you can't live without that!* Notice how removing the word *that* after *Don't tell us* in the second instance doesn't change the sentence's meaning at all. On the Web, conciseness and clarity count. Most of the time, you won't need that extra *that*. Now, how about if you rewrite this sidebar's heading for us? It's driving us crazy!

Reading your copy out loud slows down your perception of the text so that you can see misspellings as well as hear when your grammar takes a nosedive. If you change your text significantly during your hard-copy read-through, make the changes to your Web text, save the changed text, print it out, and read it aloud again. At this point, you might even consider having a friend or professional read over your text to gain the benefit of a "second pair of eyes." Finally, when you think you have your text just right, put it down for a couple hours (or longer). Then return to the hard copy with fresh eyes and ears, and read it aloud one last time.

Our recommended polishing process might sound time-consuming and possibly annoying to anyone sitting in your general vicinity, but it's well worth it. (And if you're concerned about wasting paper by repeatedly printing your modified Web text, cross out the old text and print the revised edition on the page's flip side.) Almost no other Web

## We're Not the Only Ones...

*Writing is rewriting.* Oh sure, you might easily dismiss that little statement because you've heard it before. Therefore, to add a little weight to this sentiment, here are a few more quotes about rewriting and revisions extracted from a list originally compiled by Diana Hacker for *The Bedford Handbook*, Instructor's Annotated Edition (Bedford/St. Martin's, 1998), and also displayed online, at www.bedfordstmartins.com/hacker/quotes3.htm#revision:

- Good writing is essentially rewriting. *Roald Dahl*
- I have never thought of myself as a good writer. . . . But I'm one of the world's great rewriters. *James Michener*
- I have rewritten—often several times—every word I have ever published. My pencils outlast their erasers. *Vladimir Nabokov*
- I can't write five words but that I change seven. *Dorothy Parker*
- I can't understand how anyone can write without rewriting everything over and over again. *Leo Tolstoy*
- The best writing is rewriting. *E. B. White*

Now when you rewrite, you'll know you're in good company.

site design error erodes your credibility faster than misspellings and incorrect grammar on your Web pages.

### Proofreading Online Text

Misspellings, bad grammar, and typographical errors steal your online credibility. Therefore, you should take polishing your Web text seriously. You'll find a list of sure-fire techniques that you can use when you proofread your online text at www.creationguide.com/lists/proofreading.html.

## Treating Text as a Design Element

**see also**  You can find the Proofreading Checklist online at www.creationguide.com/lists/proofreading.html as well as some tips on using text as design at www.creationguide.com/lists/textdesign.html.

As you know, text on a Web page informs as well as adds to a page's overall design (see, for example, Figure 2-4). In Chapter 4, "Mastering Web Design Basics," we talk about combining Web text with Web art to create attractive and effective layouts, but you should start to mull over basic text design issues while you're pulling your text together. You'll find a list of tips for using text as a design element at www.creationguide.com/lists/textdesign.html. We'll also consider this issue when we discuss Web page layouts in more detail.

Finally, as a parting text tip after all the dos and don'ts outlined in this chapter, we want to suggest that you have fun with your Web site's content. The Web grants you the freedom to quickly and creatively impart information in new ways. Think about what you want to say, and then write the parts of your message as clearly and actively as possible. Once you start to write strong concise sentences, you'll be hooked.

# check it

- Users scan and skim Web pages instead of reading them linearly.
- Titles, contents, hyperlinks, logos, WordArt creations, graphical text elements, forms, menus, navigation options, last-modified dates, copyright information, and privacy policies represent typical uses of Web text.
- The text on a Web page attracts users' attention before the graphics do.
- Web text organization should loosely emulate the traditional inverted pyramid news-style writing methodology.
- Brainstorm to clarify your Web pages' and Web site's main points, headings, boldfacing, hyperlinks, and organization.
- Write clear, strong, active sentences and well-formed, concise paragraphs.
- Keep headings and hyperlinks clear and descriptive.
- Use bulleted lists, boldfacing, color, and a heading hierarchy to help readers quickly identify key points.
- Cater to all users by including important information as text.
- Spell-check, spell-check, and then spell-check again.
- Check your grammar.
- Print and read the text aloud.
- Start to think about text design elements, including typographical formatting, color, and graphical text elements.
- Most of all, after taking into account the strengths and limitations of Web writing, allow the writing experience to be an enjoyable and creative process.

# creating and
## using art on the web

# CHAPTER

# 3

Ever try to give directions without gesturing? Amazing how a few good hand signals can clarify 10 minutes of rambling. Web graphics offer the same benefit (with the added bonus of vibrant colors) as gestures do—a few good graphics and well-placed design elements can transform hard-to-read, text-laden pages into highly communicative and effective works of Web design.

# Welcome to Web Graphics

In this chapter, we simplify the topic of Web graphics. In a perfect world, we'd dedicate hundreds of pages to the nuances of using graphics on the Web (mostly because we like graphics), but then you'd never get to the rest of the book. Our main goal here is to eliminate the mild anxiety pangs experienced by people around the world whenever the topic of using Web graphics arises.

As you might have discovered, you can easily find an overabundance of information about advanced graphics by looking on the Internet and in bookstores everywhere. Fortunately, you can use Web graphics effectively without immersing yourself in gamma theory and rasterizing. Therefore, we've opted to take the practical approach of presenting what we deem to be the most significant and fundamental information about Web graphics. Think of this chapter as your personal crash course in Web art. By the time you reach the "check it!" section at the end of this chapter, you'll have plenty to think about, a few tricks up your sleeve, a cocktail party quip or two, and a number of places to turn to during your search, acquisition, creation, and preparation of Web art.

# Mechanics of Web Graphics

Before you start flipping through this chapter to check out the pictures and unearth the addresses to our online examples, you really need to read this section to make sure you understand a few key Web graphics issues. As you know, Web graphics look similar to printed graphics, but some Web-specific factors come into play when you're creating and using graphics on the Web. Specifically, online graphics require you to consider color limitations, file formats, and file sizes, as well as possible transparency, downloading, and animation issues. Acquiring an awareness of three main factors—colors, file types, and file sizes—enables you to begin using graphics on your Web sites and provides a jumping-off point for further graphics study and experimentation. Therefore, the overall plan of attack here is to tuck some Web graphics fundamentals into a cranial corner or two before opening your mind to the more creative (and fun) prospects of using, gathering, and creating Web graphics. Let's get started by looking at how graphics display color.

## Pixels, Palettes, and Colors

First and foremost, every online graphic consists of a bunch of tiny colored squares working together to form an image. In a way, online graphics emulate a painting technique called *pointillism*. Pointillism, introduced by French painter Georges Seurat (1859–1891), is the art of painting pictures one dot (or tiny brush stroke) at a time. Through pointillism, Seurat broke down each image on his canvas into tiny dots of color. When you look closely at a pointillist painting, you can see each dot. As you move away from the painting, the dots blend together to create a picture. Computers display pictures using a technique similar to pointillism, except that instead of painted dots, computers divide pictures into colored squares, called *pixels*. For example, take a look at the cherries in Figure 3-1. (You can view this graphic online, at www.creationguide.com/cherries.) Figure 3-1 could be any graphic displayed on your screen. As you can see, the graphic looks like most other pictures online (or in printed material, for that matter), and there are no blatant signs of dots, squares, or pixels.

**lingo** A *pixel* is one square on a grid of thousands of squares that are individually colored to create an image.

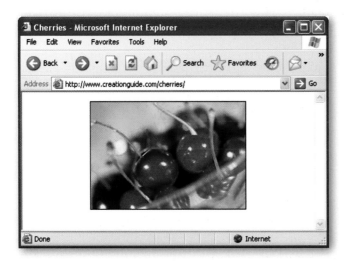

**Figure 3-1** *A typical graphical image (also available online, at www. creationguide.com/cherries)*

Now let's look at the graphic a little more closely. If you open the cherries picture in a graphics editing application (for quickest results, drag the image from www.creationguide.com/cherries into a graphics editing program, such as Paint Shop Pro, Adobe Photoshop Elements, or Microsoft Paint) and then dramatically magnify the image, you'll be able to see the actual squares (pixels) that make up the picture, as shown in Figure 3-2. If you magnify the cherries on your monitor, you'll see that the picture's colors and shades vary from pixel to pixel, or square to square.

**Figure 3-2** *The same graphical image shown in Figure 3-1 magnified 5,000 percent to show the image's pixels*

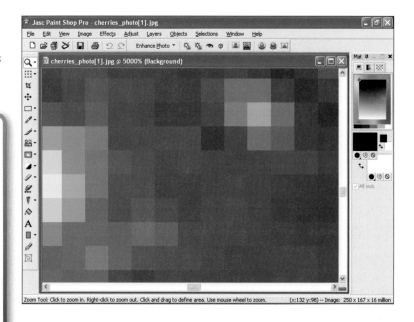

**tip** If you don't have a graphics editing application on your system or if you want to test-drive a popular "full-service" graphics editing application, you can download a free tryout version of Paint Shop Pro (www.corel.com) or Photoshop Elements (www.adobe.com).

We have more to say about graphics editing applications later in this chapter and in Chapter 5, "Considering Tools and Stockpiling Goods."

**lingo** A *palette* holds the set of colors used in a graphic.

Now that you know about pixels, we can talk a little about *palettes*. A palette is simply the table of colors used in a graphic. Some Web graphics—namely, graphics saved using the Graphics Interchange Format (GIF), as described in the next section—use a limited collection of colors. You can assign a palette to an image, or you can let your graphics program generate a palette automatically as you create and edit an image. A GIF palette can hold up to 256 colors, but many images use fewer colors than that. For example, the cherries graphic shown in Figure 3-3 uses 9 colors, and the grapes graphic shown in Figure 3-4 uses 128 colors. Notice the pictures' sizes—the cherries graphic is 7 KB (pretty small), and the grapes graphic is 17 KB (also on the small side). You can view both images and their palettes online, at www.creationguide.com/palettes_samples.

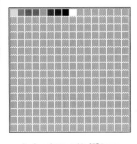

9-color palette used in GIF image

GIF (9 colors): 7 KB

**Figure 3-3** *The cherry image's palette (very small)*

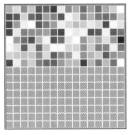

128-color palette used in GIF image

GIF (128 colors): 17 KB

**Figure 3-4** *The grape image's palette (small enough for quick downloading)*

Generally, most graphics applications enable you to view the colors included in a GIF graphic's palette. Further, you can reduce the size of a GIF image by reducing or limiting the number of colors in the picture's palette. And, as you probably know, smaller file sizes equate to quicker download times on the Web.

**try this!**

To view a color palette, go to www.creationguide.com/palettes_samples, and display either the cherries or grapes GIF image in your graphics editor (as described in the previous Try This! sidebar). To display the image's palette in Paint Shop Pro, on the **Image** menu, click **Palette**, and then click **Edit Palette**. In Photoshop or Photoshop Elements 3, on the **Image** menu, click **Mode**, and then click **Color Table**. (We realize that every graphics package has its own menu options; we provide the preceding commands to give you an idea of the types of commands you should look for in your graphics application.)

**try this!**

To illustrate this section's pixels discussion firsthand, display www.creationguide.com/cherries in your browser. Right-click the cherries graphic, and then click **Copy**. (If you'd like to save the graphic on your desktop instead of copying it, click **Save Picture As** on the shortcut menu.)

Next open your graphics program—such as Paint Shop Pro, Paint, or Photoshop Elements—and then paste the copied graphic into your program (or, if you saved the file earlier, open the file in the application). You can also avoid using menu commands by simply dragging the picture from your browser window into your graphics program window.

To view the image's pixels, enlarge the picture by using your graphics program's zoom tool or magnifying glass. To further illustrate how pixels work, incrementally decrease the image's view (or "zoom out") to a slightly more viewable size, as shown here:

If you zoom out slowly, you can see how the pixels start to blend to create a clear image.

**lingo**  In some Web graphics applications and documentation, a palette is also referred to as a *color lookup table* (CLUT) or simply a *color table*.

As we just mentioned, palettes come into play when you use GIF images. We realize we haven't defined GIFs yet—or any Web-friendly image formats for that matter. Now that you have a feel for the nature of pixels and palettes, let's move on and discuss graphics file formats that you can use on the Web. We'll talk more about palettes when we discuss GIFs later in this chapter. Palettes are also discussed in Chapter 4, "Mastering Web Design Basics," when we talk about choosing colors for your Web site.

## Graphics File Formats

As you might recall, in Chapter 1, "Demystifying Your (Future) Web Site," we said that every graphic on a Web site is stored as a separate file. As a refresher, look at Figure 3-5, which shows the names of two of the images used on the Space Camp for Kids home page.

index.html
(Home page)

ribbon.gif

p_astronaut_th.jpg

**Figure 3-5** *GIF and JPG files used on a Web page*

The small blue ribbon figure's file name ends with a .gif file extension (ribbon.gif), and the other figure's file name ends with a .jpg file extension (p_astronaut_th.jpg). Graphics file extensions work on the same principles as other file formats. For example, if you see a file on your desktop named gift_list.doc, you know by the .doc extension that the file is probably a Microsoft Office Word document, and you'll want to open the document in Word (especially if you suspect that you're one of the people listed on the gift list!). Similarly, if you see a file on your desktop named bills.xls, you know the .xls indicates a Microsoft Office Excel document, so you could open the file in Excel (although you might want to avoid files named *bills*). As for Web graphics, your Web pages can include graphics images that use the .gif and .jpeg (or .jpg) file extensions, because Web browsers can display GIF and JPEG (Joint Photographic Experts Group; pronounced "jay-peg") files.

**tip**  You might wonder why we named the JPEG image in this sample site p_astronaut_th.jpg. We actually have a method to our madness (in this case at least!). We follow a number of naming conventions to keep our graphics organized. In this file name, the **p** indicates that the file is a photograph, ***astronaut*** refers to the photo's subject matter, and **th** tells us that the image is a thumbnail picture (which links to a larger version of the same picture). When you begin to collect and name pictures, you might want to come up with some organizational schemes of your own. We show you some more of our methods in the walkthrough chapters in Part Two, which you're more than welcome to adopt.

## GIFs

GIFs are the most widely supported graphics type on the Web (which means that almost all browsers—old, new, and in-between—can display GIF images). *GIF* stands for *Graphics Interchange Format.* CompuServe created this format in the 1980s as an efficient means to transmit images across data networks. The GIF format's main strength is that GIF images are usually small, which means that they can be downloaded and displayed quickly.

As we mentioned earlier in this chapter, GIF images use palettes and support up to 256 colors (which makes them 8-bit graphics). Because GIFs support a limited number of colors, you should use GIFs for flat color areas, logos, line art, icons, cartoonlike illustrations, buttons, horizontal rules, bullets, backgrounds, and other graphical elements that require few colors. Figures 3-6 and 3-7 show examples of GIF images. To see the GIF images in Figure 3-6 online, go to www.creation-guide.com/gif_samples, and to see the ExtraCheese Web site online, go to www.creationguide.com/extracheese.

**lingo**  *GIF* (Graphics Interchange Format) is a graphics file format used to create images for use on the Internet. GIF images can contain up to 256 colors, support transparency, and provide simple animations.

**Figure 3-6**  *Line art, horizontal rules, buttons, bullets, and graphical text examples of GIF files (also available online, at www.creationguide.com/ gif_samples)*

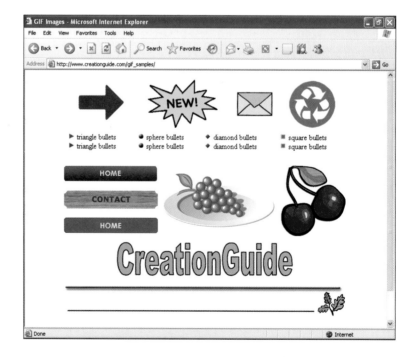

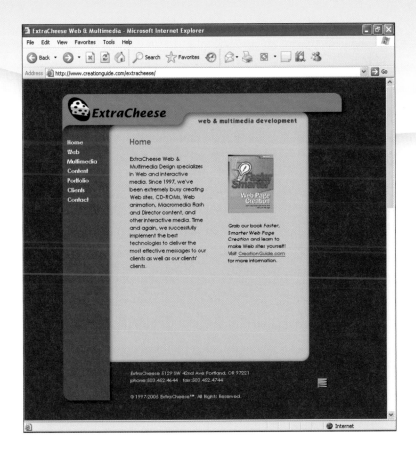

**Figure 3-7** *GIF images used for large, flat color areas (also available online, at www.creationguide.com/ extracheese)*

In addition to being palette-reliant, small, and efficient, GIFs perform three special tricks—interlacing, transparency, and animation.

## Interlaced GIFs

Normally, a GIF image appears on-screen row by row, from top to bottom of the image, like pulling down a window shade. If you want to, you (as a Web page designer) can change how a GIF downloads onto viewers' monitors by saving your GIF file as an interlaced GIF file. An interlaced GIF graphic is displayed on users' screens as blurred or jagged at first and then gradually becomes clearer. Figure 3-8 shows an interlaced GIF in the midst of downloading. The figure on the left shows the image before it's fully downloaded, and the figure on the right shows the fully downloaded image. To view the interlaced GIF online next to a noninterlaced version of the same image, visit www.creationguide.com/interlaced_sample. Keep in mind that if you have a fast connection, you won't see any difference in the downloading processes.

**Figure 3-8** *Downloading an interlaced GIF on a slow Internet connection (also available online, at www.creationguide.com/ interlaced_sample)*

**note** If you're using a fast Internet connection, such as a cable modem, you won't see the effects of interlacing.

Interlaced GIFs are good to use when you want to transmit an image's main idea to readers while they wait for the complete download. The drawback of interlaced GIFs is that they have slightly larger file sizes than conventional (noninterlaced) GIF images. Therefore, for buttons, icons, and small graphics, you're better off sticking to the conventional GIF file format.

### Transparent GIFs

**note** If a GIF's background color matches your Web page's background color—such as an image with a white background on a Web page with a white background—you automatically achieve the illusion of transparency.

Transparent GIFs (GIFs that use the GIF89a format) enable you to design icons, logos, and other elements that appear to be "cut out," thereby allowing the Web page's background to show through areas of the image. For example, as you can see in the right side of Figure 3-9 (and online, at www.creationguide.com/transparency), the purple background shows through in the transparent GIF to create the illusion of a nonrectangular image.

When you create a transparent GIF, you essentially specify a unique color in your image to serve as your transparent color. For example, you could color the background of your picture hot pink and then assign hot pink to be the picture's transparent color—just make sure hot pink doesn't show up elsewhere in your image or you'll create unwanted transparent spots. When a browser encounters the transparent color, the browser doesn't show any graphics information in the color's area, which enables the Web page's background to show through.

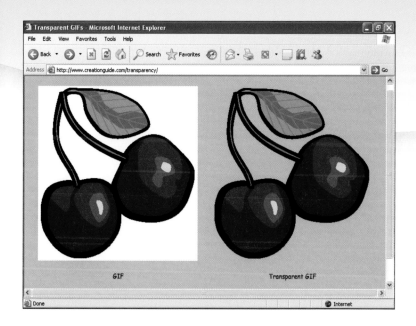

**Figure 3-9**  *Comparing a standard GIF with a transparent GIF (also available online, at www.creationguide.com/transparency)*

## Animated GIFs

The last GIF "trick" involves animation. Using GIF animation tools and graphics editing programs, you can layer GIFs and save the layers in a "stack" to create simple animations. When a browser displays the stacked GIF images, it displays each image one after the other. This technique is similar to the old flipbook "movies" that were popular long before most of us were born. Moving icons, rollover buttons, and some banner ads are prime examples of animated GIFs. Figure 3-10 illustrates the theory behind animated GIFs. To see the smiley animation in action, along with a few other examples, visit www.creationguide.com/animated_gifs.

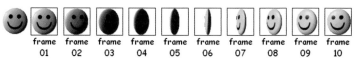

**Animated GIF:** Uses layers of GIF images to achieve animation.

frame 01  frame 02  frame 03  frame 04  frame 05  frame 06  frame 07  frame 08  frame 09  frame 10

**Figure 3-10**  *The GIF images used to create a spinning smiley face animated GIF (also available online, at www.creationguide.com/animated_gifs)*

> **tip**   The clip art in recent versions of Microsoft Office includes animated GIFs as well as transparent GIFs that you can use in your Web sites. To identify a clip art item that's an animated GIF, look for a gold star in the lower-right corner of the thumbnail image in the Clip Art task pane. To identify a clip art item that has a transparent background, look for items that appear to be "cut out" in the Clip Art task pane. You can test an image's transparency by inserting the image into a Word document that has a color background. In the section "Adding Transparency to an Image," later in this chapter, we show you how to apply transparency to a GIF image.

## JPEGs

> **lingo**   *JPEG* (Joint Photographic Experts Group) is a graphics file format used to display photographic-quality and other high-color images on the Internet. The JPEG file format can support millions of colors.

In addition to GIF graphics, your Web site will probably include JPEG images. The *JPEG* image file format was created by and named after the *Joint Photographic Experts Group*. This image format supports millions of colors, and JPEGs are almost universally supported by browsers. (Technically speaking, JPEGs support 24-bit color, which is also referred to as *full color* or *true color*.) Because JPEGs can contain millions of colors, JPEG graphics frequently display photographic images.

When you're working with JPEGs for your Web pages, you can specify whether you want to save your JPEGs as *standard* or *progressive*:

- **Standard**   When you save an image as a standard JPEG file, the image loads line by line from the top of the screen down, similar to how GIFs download by default.

- **Progressive**   When you save an image as a progressive JPEG file, the image first appears blurry and then becomes more focused as the image data is downloaded (similar to interlaced GIFs). With fast Internet connection speeds, the progressive rendering might not be readily apparent to viewers; instead, after a delay, the image will seem to "pop up" on the screen. In our experience, progressive JPEGs seem to create smaller file sizes and are downloaded slightly quicker than standard JPEG files.

# "Safe" Colors for the Web   As you know, all computer systems are not created equal. Many people have a heck of a time keeping up with the computer industry's rapid pace of hardware development. Therefore, when you design Web sites, you should keep in mind that not all people will be able to access your pages

if your pages require the latest and greatest display hardware. In fact, a very small percentage of Web surfers using computers are still restricted to viewing Web pages in 256 colors (although most new systems display millions of colors, so the 256-color design issue will probably soon be a design consideration of the past for Web browsers). But more and more people are starting to view Web content on handhelds and cell phones—those technologies aren't quite up-to-speed as far as showing millions of colors. So for the next few years, when you design your Web sites and create GIF images, you might consider relying most heavily (although not necessarily exclusively) on colors that 256-color systems can display without a hitch. The universal colors are referred to as the *Web-safe* or *browser-safe* colors. If your Web page uses colors other than Web-safe colors, systems that support only 256 colors will resort to dithering the nonstandard colors.

*Dither* refers to the random dot pattern that results when colors are approximated by mixing similar and available colors from a limited palette. To avoid dither, stick to the 216 Web-safe colors. (The other 40 colors out of the 256 colors are reserved for the computer system's use.) The Web-safe color palette is shown here:

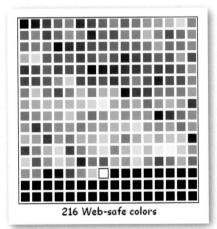

216 Web-safe colors

> **lingo** *Dither* refers to the random dot pattern that results when colors are approximated by mixing similar and available colors from a limited palette. Special types of dithering techniques—such as diffusion, pattern, and noise—can be used to simulate continuous tones in images that use a restricted palette (such as GIFs).

Graphics editing programs usually provide a Web-safe palette that you can load when working with GIF images, or you can copy the palette shown here off the Web (at www.creationguide.com/palettes) and create your own Web-safe color palette based on the Web image. For example, open the color palette image in Paint Shop Pro, and on the **Image** menu, click **Palette**, and then click **Save Palette**.

Another JPEG configuration parameter that you can use to your
advantage is *compression*. Compression is a process that reduces
an image's file size by throwing out some color information. JPEG
compression is called a "lossy" compression scheme because once
you compress an image, the deleted information is lost. Fortunately,
if you're careful, people viewing the image online can't easily discern
the information loss.

Keep in mind that the more you compress an image, the smaller the
image's file size becomes, but the resulting image won't be as sharp
as a less compressed image. Therefore, you should experiment with
various compression settings when configuring JPEG images for your
Web pages. In most cases, you should limit compression to 50 percent
or less. We usually stick to around 40 percent compression for Web
graphics, although sometimes we compress up to 80 percent for large
Web graphics.

At this point, you should be comfortable with the idea of progressive and compressed JPEG files, but we haven't yet explained how to
configure these types of settings for a JPEG image. Fortunately, most
image editing programs make specifying JPEG file parameters fairly
easy. To access JPEG file settings in Paint Shop Pro, follow these steps:

1 Open your JPEG image in Paint Shop Pro. (Feel free to practice
  with any of the fruit.jpg images shown at www.creationguide.
  com/jpeg_samples.)

2 On the **File** menu, click **Save As** to display the **Save As** dialog
  box.

3 Ensure that **JPEG** appears in the **Save As Type** box, type a new
  file name, and then click **Options** to access the **Save Options**
  dialog box, shown in Figure 3-11.

**try this!**

To view online images using standard and progressive rendering as well as to compare compressed images, visit www.creationguide.com/jpeg_samples, also shown here:

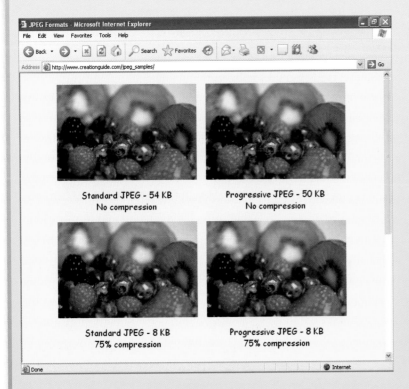

If you're using a slower connection, watch the page closely as the pictures are downloaded, and notice which image is displayed first. Also notice the quality and size of each JPEG image. (If you're using a fast Internet connection, you might not see a speed difference.) Also notice that at 75 percent compression, the file sizes are much smaller and yet the image quality remains good enough for displaying on the Web.

**Figure 3-11**  *Configuring JPEG compression and rendering settings in Paint Shop Pro*

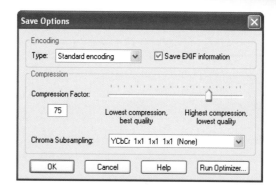

4 Specify an encoding option (**Standard** or **Progressive**), select a compression setting (**Compression Factor** is the compression percent), click **OK**, and then click **Save**.

To configure JPEG settings in Photoshop Elements, follow these steps:

**tip**  You can specify JPEG settings before you save a file in Photoshop Elements by opening the file and then clicking **Save For Web** on the **File** menu.

1 Open your JPEG image in Photoshop Elements. (Feel free to practice with any of the fruit.jpg images shown at www.creationguide.com/jpeg_samples.)

2 On the **File** menu, click **Save As**.

3 Enter a file name, and then click **Save**. The **JPEG Options** dialog box opens, as shown in Figure 3-12. Specify compression settings by moving the **Quality** slider, and then click **OK**.

**Figure 3-12**  *Configuring JPEG compression and rendering settings in Photoshop Elements*

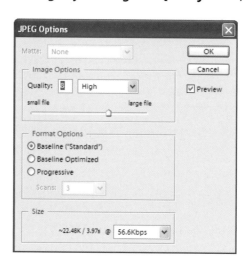

## PNGs

The third (and final) graphic type we address in this chapter is the PNG (pronounced "ping") file format. *PNG* stands for *Portable Network Graphics*. Similar to GIFs, PNG files are small, they load quickly, and they support transparency. Similar to JPEGs, PNGs can display millions of colors. The main drawbacks of PNGs are that only the newer browsers support them and they don't handle animation as well as GIFs.

Initially, the PNG file format was devised because Unisys, the makers of the GIF compression algorithm, decided to enforce the patents for that algorithm—meaning that software vendors had to pay to use it. But the patents have expired, and you really don't need to know the details about the PNG vs. GIF debate anyhow. Just know that newer major browsers (including Microsoft Internet Explorer 5 and later) can display PNG images, but most Web designers don't use PNGs yet in deference to users who surf the Web with older or less technologically advanced browsers. At this point, your Web pages probably shouldn't use an overabundance of PNGs either.

> **lingo** *PNG* (Portable Network Graphics) is a graphics file format designed to replace GIF images on the Internet.

> **note** Internet Explorer for Microsoft Windows began to incorporate some PNG support in 1997 and began providing PNG support in Macintosh versions of Internet Explorer in 2000. As you can see, the PNG file format is taking a while to catch on, partly because developers know that all users don't have access to the most up-to-date or most technologically advanced browsers, so they don't bother to use PNGs. From a developer's perspective, there's currently no strong reason to risk losing viewers by using a PNG file format when the GIF file format is readily available, just as easy to use, and widely recognized in almost all browsers (regardless of version).

## Size Matters

The last major "technical" Web graphics consideration that we cover in this chapter is file size, which is directly related to download speeds. As a Web surfer, you've probably caught yourself drumming your mouse impatiently while waiting for pages that take longer than 6 or 7 seconds to be displayed (or, even more likely, clicking away before the slow page ever fully displays). As a Web designer, you need to hold on to that impatient feeling. When you design Web sites and use Web art, you should always keep one eye on your design and another eye on the user's perspective. (That almost sounds painful!)

When you use Web art, you can take advantage of a few techniques that will help keep your file sizes manageable. We already covered a few key topics earlier in this chapter that can help to reduce file sizes and speed download times, including these:

- Avoid dither in GIF images by using Web-safe colors whenever possible, especially in large, flat color areas, unless of course you want to create a dithering effect. (Just think—before reading this chapter, this sentence wouldn't have made a bit of sense to you!)
- Configure JPEG images to be rendered progressively.
- Compress JPEG images to reduce file sizes.

In addition to using the three preceding graphics file techniques, you can control download speeds by:

- Resizing images.
- Cropping images.
- Using thumbnails.

We briefly describe each technique in the following sections. Please keep in mind that the actual mechanics of accomplishing certain tasks vary among graphics editing tools.

### Resizing images

One of the best ways to conserve download time is to physically resize your images in a graphics editor. Note that we're talking about resizing the image, not simply changing your view. Zooming in and out changes your view of an image, but it doesn't affect the file's actual size or dimensions. Try to size your images to the approximate sizes you want them to be displayed on your Web page. Figure 3-13 shows the Resize dialog box you use in Paint Shop Pro to resize an image. (To access this dialog box, open the image, and then click **Resize** on the **Image** menu.)

**Figure 3-13** *Resizing an image in Paint Shop Pro*

**tip**   Usually, you'll want to ensure that the **Maintain Aspect Ratio** option (or its equivalent in your graphics program) is selected when you resize graphics; otherwise, you could distort your images.

Keep in mind that smaller images result in small file sizes, which result in quicker download times.

**try this!**

To experiment with resizing images, open a JPEG image in your graphics editor, and then change the image's width or height setting. You can use the apples image stored at www.creationguide. com/sizing/apples.jpg. Save the JPEG image, and then repeat the process a number of times using various measurements, renaming each version with a unique meaningful name (such as apples400w.jpg for a picture that's resized to 400 pixels wide). After you've created a few variously sized images, view the images locally in your browser window—that is, either navigate to the figures by using your browser's Address bar or drag the JPEG images' file name icons into your browser window.

# Sizing Images Just Right—A Quick Trick

When you first start to design Web pages, you might not know what sizes your graphics should be. Some graphics programs, like Photoshop Elements, includes a Save For Web tool that lets you view your images while you resize and compress them. You can also use Web editors to help you pin down the sizes of your graphics. For example, you can use a Web editing program, such as Microsoft FrontPage.

To determine the optimal size for a Web graphic, follow these steps:

1 Insert the graphic into a blank Web page in FrontPage (for example), and resize the graphic by dragging the image's selection handles.

2 After the image is sized to your liking, display the image's properties (in FrontPage, right-click the graphic, and then click **Picture Properties** on the shortcut menu), and note (and then write down) the image's height and width parameters.

3 Reopen the image in your graphics editing program, and then resize the graphic by entering the numbers you copied from FrontPage (or other Web editing program) into the appropriate dialog box. For instance, in Paint Shop Pro, you open the **Resize** dialog box by clicking **Resize** on the **Image** menu, and in Microsoft Paint, you open the **Attributes** dialog box by clicking **Attributes** on the **Image** menu.

## Cropping images

**lingo** *Cropping* refers to cutting off a part of an image, such as unnecessary portions of a graphic.

In addition to resizing an image, you can *crop* an image to reduce its size. When you crop an image, you cut out the portion of the image that you don't want to use. Cropping is frequently used to remove any unwanted or unneeded portions of a photograph. For example, you might want to crop the apples.jpg image shown in Figure 3-14 to show a close-up of the green apple amidst the red apples in the colander. The image on the left in Figure 3-14 shows crop lines (the dashed lines that surround the portion of the image you want to retain) in the apples.jpg image, which is 50 KB, and the image on the right shows the result of cropping apples.jpg. The cropped version is only 6 KB.

**Figure 3-14** *Crop marks indicating the portion of an image that you want to use as a Web graphic, and the cropped image*

## Using thumbnails

After you master the art of resizing and cropping images, you're ready to use *thumbnails*. A thumbnail is a small picture that links to a larger image. (The larger image is usually the same as the thumbnail, but we've seen some creative uses of thumbnails in our day.) When you use thumbnails, viewers can choose to view the small image and be done with it, or they can click the thumbnail to view the larger image. In other words, when you use thumbnails, you grant viewers the option to download large images if they're willing to endure the longer download times.

**lingo** A *thumbnail* is a miniature version or small portion of a graphic. Frequently, on Web pages, thumbnail graphics are hyperlinked to larger versions of the graphic.

**try this!**

To crop an image, follow these steps:

1. **Open an image in your graphics editor.**
2. **Click the selection tool (which usually looks like a dashed rectangle or square in the application's toolbar).**
3. **Click and drag in your image to outline the area of the image that you want to retain. If you outline the wrong area, press ESC and try again.**
4. **After you have an area selected, on the Image menu, click Crop To Selection (in Paint Shop Pro) or Crop (in Photoshop Elements), or choose a similar command in your graphics editing program.**

**tip**    You can view thumbnails in action by clicking the thumbnails at www.creationguide.com/sizing.

The trick to using thumbnails is to create two graphics with different names. Usually, you use the same image for both graphics, and you make one image small with a quick download time and the other image (while optimized to the best of your ability, of course) larger with a longer download time. Then you display the small image on your Web page, and you link the small image to the larger image. (We show you how to link images in the walkthrough chapters.) Figure 3-15 shows two thumbnails. The left thumbnail displays the entire linked image, and the right thumbnail shows a cropped portion of the linked graphic. Figure 3-15 also shows the larger graphic that's linked to the thumbnails. By clicking either thumbnail shown in Figure 3-15, you can open a window displaying a large view of the apples.jpg image.

**Figure 3-15**    *Thumbnails that link to a full-size version of the apples.jpg image (also available online, at www.creationguide.com/sizing)*

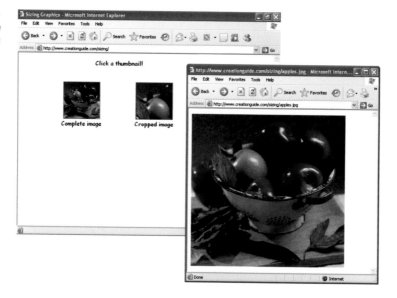

## Art of Using Web Graphics

Now that we've gotten the technical aspects of graphics out of the way, let's talk briefly about graphic design. The overriding premise of Web graphics is that your Web page's graphics should serve two masters—aesthetics and utility. Ideally, every piece of art on your Web page should contribute to both causes by looking good and serving a purpose. Therefore, this chapter helps you to brush up on the various

# Top 10+1 Tips for Great Photos

Also available online, at www.creationguide.com/lists/greatphotos.html.

To get the best advice, ask the best in the business. When it comes to photography, John Phillips knows what he's talking about. John is an internationally recognized photographer for the Black Star Photo Agency (www.blackstar.com) who has snapped thousands of photographs for numerous publications, including Arizona State University's award winning *Research Magazine*. In fact, if you pick up any issue of *Research Magazine* published within the past 15+ years, you'll find John's remarkable handiwork. (As a side note, John is also an accomplished folk musician; you can learn more about his musical talents at www.phillipstunes.com.) To aid you in your photographic endeavors, John generously passes along the following top 10+1 tips for designing great photos:

- **Vertical, horizontal, or square**   Choose your orientation beforehand, and then compose your shot according to the following tips.
- **Rule of thirds**   Place strong horizontal or verticals along lines bisecting a third of the frame. Put important subject matter, like people's faces, at or near the intersection of these lines, as shown in this sample image, originally shot for *Newsweek* magazine:

photo credit: John Phillips

- **Leading lines and patterns**   Occasionally use objects like fences, sidewalks, and so forth to create lines leading into your photo. Also, look for and use repeating patterns in your subject. For example, the sample image uses the pillars to lead viewers back into the shot.
- **Foreground and background**   If possible, consciously have a foreground and a background in your shot.

- **Depth of field**    *Depth of field* is a term for how much of your photo, from front to back, is in focus. Portraits of people usually have a shallow depth of field. The subject is in focus and the background is out of focus. The portrait mode on many digital cameras will automatically create this effect for you. Wide-angle lenses in bright light will give you a large depth of field. Most of the photo, from front to back, will be in focus

- **Dramatic light**    Use strong light from either the right of left for dramatic effect. Also look for interesting kinds of light, particularly one hour after sunrise and one hour before sunset. Strong shadows can also add drama to your photo.

- **Closeups and Viewpoints**    Most of the time, getting closer to your subject will improve your photo. You can use macro mode on many digital cameras for very close detail. Or move around. Get higher or lower. A change in perspective can make a big difference.

- **Vibrant or unusual color**    Look for unusually strong or vibrant color to add an element to your shot. A black-and-white photograph with strong elements can also have the same effect.

- **Fill flash**    Using the flash in brightly lit outdoor scenes with people will eliminate strong shadows on faces and improve your photos.

- **Communicate**    Your photo should quickly convey a message about your Web site or the particular page it's on. For example, the individual in the sample photo is the dean of architecture, planning, and landscape architecture at University of Arizona in Tucson, and the pillars help place him in context.

- **Plus 1: Be there!**    You can only get a few good shots while sitting on your couch. Go out and be there!

types of aesthetically appealing and useful graphics that you should start to consider for your Web pages, including these:

- Photographs and illustrations
- Buttons and logos
- Icons, bullets, and horizontal rules
- Graphical text
- Backgrounds

In the next few sections, we'll take a quick look at each of these graphical elements.

## Photographs and Illustrations

We won't dwell too long on photographs and illustrations given our extended discussion of image formats earlier in this chapter. As we've mentioned numerous times, the key to using photographs and illustrations is to keep the file sizes as small as possible so that they can be downloaded quickly. Furthermore, you should ensure that your photographs and illustrations add to your page's content instead of detract from your message. Imagine waiting patiently for a movie review Web page to download only to find that the page contains a few links to reviews and a large picture of the Web designer's dog wearing sunglasses. Without a second thought, you'd probably dash off to find a faster, more useful movie review site for future reference. Taking great photographs takes practice and know-how, but to help you lean toward better picture taking, we invited a professional photographer to provide his top 10+1 list of tips for taking great photos.

Finally, one use of photographs and illustrations that we haven't mentioned yet is *image maps*. Images maps are graphics that have clickable areas that enable you to visit various Web pages. Quite possibly, you've clicked your state or country on an online map to get local information. If done properly, image maps represent a good mix of aesthetics and utility, but they should be used judiciously. Image maps involve mildly complex Hypertext Markup Language (HTML) coding, plus you need to ensure that you don't create an image map with a graphic that takes forever to download. You also need to keep in mind ways to cater to people who don't view graphics online. To help you cover all your bases, we show you how to create an image map in Part Two of this book.

## Buttons and Logos

Buttons and logos are a Web site's bread-and-butter graphics. No doubt you've clicked a countless number of buttons and caught sight of more than a few logos. Thus, you're well aware that buttons help you to navigate around a site and logos brand a Web site as well as provide a quick link to a site's home page. The MSN logo in Figure 3-16 (and online, at www.msn.com) is easy to spot, appears consistently on every page, and serves as a reliable hyperlink to the MSN home page.

**more info** Later in this chapter, in the section "Acquiring Art," we describe ways in which you can acquire photographs.

**lingo** An *image map* is a graphic that's formatted so that various areas of the graphic serve as hyperlinks to related Web pages. For example, an image map made out of a solar system graphic might allow visitors to click a planet to access a related Web page that contains details about the clicked planet. We show you how to create image maps in the walkthrough section of this book, in Chapter 11, "Going All Out with FrontPage."

MSN logo

**Figure 3-16** *The MSN logo, which appears on every page in the site*

**more info**  Look for a 10+1 Tips sidebar in Chapter 4 that describes the steps you can take to create a great logo.

On your Web pages, the key to successfully using graphic buttons and logos is consistency. If you're using a logo, ensure that the logo is instantly identifiable and easily visible on every page. For example, your logo should use the same colors throughout your site and appear in the same area on every page. (We talk more about page and site setup in later chapters.) Your logo should also link to your site's home page in every instance. If you're using custom buttons, use the same buttons on every page in your site and position them in the same location on each page, if possible.

**more info**
Later in this chapter, in the "Acquiring Art" section, we show you a quick way to create simple custom buttons using Word.

Consistently displaying buttons and logos adds an overall feeling of unity to your site and speeds the downloading process. Once a viewer downloads your home page, your button and logo graphics will be stored in the *temporary cache* of the viewer's machine. If the same button and logo images appear on your Web site's ancillary pages and are referenced with the same file names, the browser won't have to redownload the button graphics because the graphics will already be stored on the computer. In turn, less downloading means quicker page displays. Kind of a sneaky design tactic, but it's great for reducing download times.

## Icons, Bullets, and Horizontal Rules

Icons, bullets, and horizontal rules help draw attention to elements on your Web pages as well as quickly communicate information in place of text. But tread lightly when you use these elements. A fine line exists between clarifying and cluttering. When used sparingly and with discretion, icons, bullets, and rules can add a professional look to a page. When overused, these elements can make your page look amateurish and bury your message in visual mayhem.

Icons are small graphics used to call attention to a particular feature or to communicate a brief message. For example, you might use a graphic icon that looks like an envelope on your Web site to quickly identify a link to an e-mail form that visitors can use to send feedback to you. To get a feel for the effective use of icons, surf around a few on-line auction sites (such as Amazon and eBay), and you'll see all sorts of icons. Notice how each icon is a simple graphic that clearly denotes a particular message.

Bullets are small graphics added at the beginning of entries in a list or series. When you add graphical bullets to your Web site, make sure that the graphics you use draw attention to your lists and not to the bullets themselves. For example, any of the small bullets shown in Figure 3-17 (and online, at www.creationguide.com/bullet_samples) are effective bullet graphics. In contrast, spinning, rainbow-colored, bouncing bullets will drive most users away from your site before they even attempt to read your content.

Horizontal rules denote sections in your Web pages. You can insert a graphical rule (as shown in Figure 3-17), or you can use HTML to create standard horizontal rules and bullets, as described in the following Try This! sidebar. You can further modify standard HTML rules and bullets by using *cascading style sheets*, as you'll see in the walkthrough chapters in Part Two, particularly in Chapter 8, "Demystifying Basic CSS and XHTML." In our opinion, you should limit your use of horizontal rules that span entire pages. Wide horizontal rules tend to chop up pages (thereby making them harder to

**Lingo** The *temporary cache* is a portion of your hard drive that's set aside in accordance with your browser's settings, and its main job is to temporarily store copies of the Web pages and images you view. To view your temporary cache settings in Internet Explorer, click **Internet Options** on the **Tools** menu, and on the **General** tab, click the **Settings** button in the **Temporary Internet Files** section.

**tip** You can combine icons and button features to create picture buttons. For example, you might use a small picture of a house to serve as your Home button.

read), and 9 times out of 10, a little white space or a heading will serve your needs better than a wide horizontal rule. Used appropriately, horizontal rules can be useful, especially in long, text-heavy pages.

**Figure 3-17**  *A sampler of bullets and rules (also available online, at www. creationguide.com/bullet_samples)*

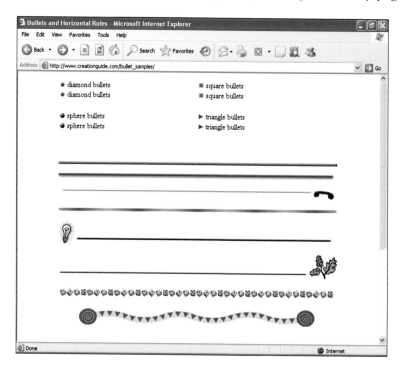

**try this!**

You can add bullets and rules to your Web site without creating graphics. To create a standard bulleted list in HTML, you use the following tags:

&lt;ul&gt;    Identifies the beginning of a bulleted "unordered" list

&lt;li&gt;    Marks the beginning of each list item

&lt;/li&gt;    Marks the end of each list item

&lt;/ul&gt;    Identifies the end of the list

To create a horizontal rule, you use the &lt;hr /&gt; tag.

To see HTML bullets and rules in action, open a blank Notepad document, and type the following:

```
<html>
<head>
<title>
Bulleted Lists and Horizontal Rules
</title>
</head>
<body>
<h1> Fruit </h1>
<ul>
     <li> Grapes </li>
     <li> Kiwis </li>
     <li> Watermelon </li>
</ul>
<hr />
</body>
</html>
```

Save the file as test.html, and then open the document in your browser. Your bulleted list and horizontal rule should look similar to those shown here in Microsoft Internet Explorer:

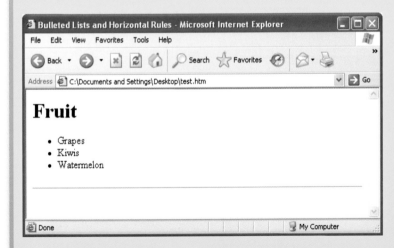

By the way, as you might've noticed, we snuck in the <h1> heading tag just for fun.

## Graphical Text

As you might know, browsers display text differently based on the browser's make, model, and year. But sticking with standard text when designing a Web site is rarely exciting or desirable. Fortunately, graphics provide a livable workaround for occasional variation. Basically, *graphical text* refers to text elements that have been created and then saved as a GIF, JPEG, or PNG image that you can insert into your Web site as a picture. Graphical text includes titles, headings, and page banners. (A *banner* is generally a rectangular graphic that blends art and text, and usually runs across the top or down the side of a Web page.) Using graphical text, you can customize text without relying on fonts that might or might not be installed on users' computers. Figure 3-18 (also available online, at www.creationguide. com/graphicaltext_samples) shows some text that can be imported into a graphics editing program, cropped, and used as graphical text on a Web site. Notice that the bottom entry in Figure 3-18 is another example of WordArt.

**Figure 3-18**   *Samples of graphical text (also available online, at www.creationguide. com/graphicaltext_samples)*

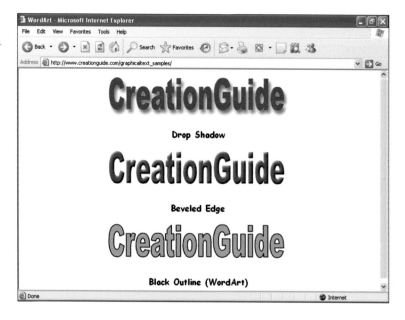

# Backgrounds

You can modify your Web site's background in two ways—by coloring the background or by displaying a graphic beneath your Web page's contents. The key to using backgrounds is to ensure that together your content and the background create a striking contrast. Above all else, your content must be easy to read. If your background makes your page hard to read, lose the background (no matter how cool the color or pattern). Showing low-contrast, hard-to-read text on a dark or busy background is usually a sure sign of an amateur Web designer.

Adding background color to a Web site simply entails adding an HTML or CSS instruction that tells browsers which color to display. When you add a background image, the image is displayed repeatedly across and down a user's screen (in a pattern called *tiling*) to create the illusion of a large graphical background. We cover background commands, colors, and images throughout Part Two. In the meantime, Figure 3-19 shows some sample background images. You can visit the background samples online, at www.creationguide.com/bg_samples. Click any sample to see a Web page filled with the background image.

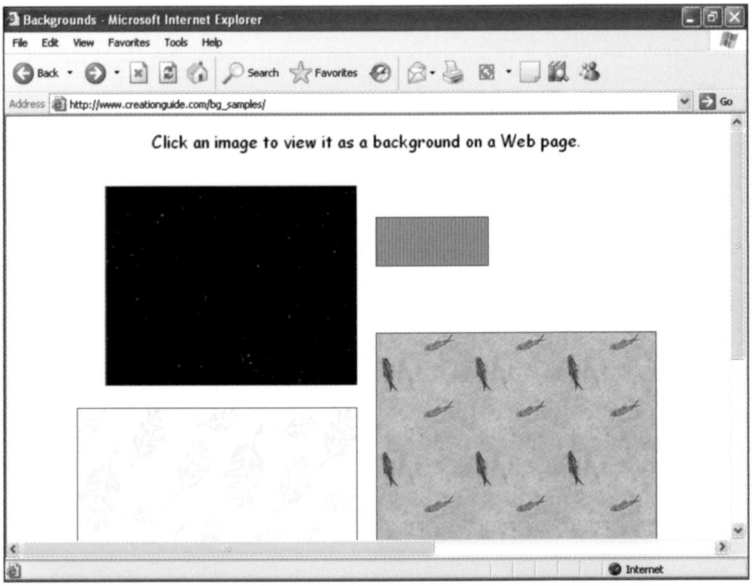

**tip** You can find lots of free background patterns on the Web. For starters, visit our online resources page, at www.creationguide.com/resources. Some Web page editor programs, such as Microsoft FrontPage, also provide a selection of background patterns.

**Figure 3-19** *Sample background images (also available online, at www.creationguide.com/bg_samples)*

**tip**   As you acquire and create images for your Web site, keep the files stored together in a folder on your desktop and give each graphic a unique, clearly identifiable name. You'll thank yourself later if you start organizing your images now.

**note**   When you save Web graphics from the Internet for your own use, make sure the artwork is truly freeware; otherwise, you might violate copyright laws. If you're unsure about whether a graphic is free for use, send an e-mail message to the site's Webmaster and ask permission to use the artwork.

# Acquiring Art

Now that you're on top of some of the *what* and *how* of graphics, you're ready for the *where*—as in, *where* are you going to find graphics for your Web site? Years ago, when we first started designing Web sites, we asked ourselves the same question. Today, we're more interested in where we can store all the graphics we've collected! Fortunately for you, acquiring graphics nowadays is pretty easy. Therefore, in this section, we briefly describe where you can find graphics as well as introduce you to the art of creating your own graphics. Specifically, we talk about acquiring prepared art, creating custom art, and gathering photographs.

## Prepared Art

Prepared art is plentiful—you just need to know where to look. You can obtain Web graphics from a number of resources, including these:

- **Clip art**   You can buy clip art CD-ROMs wherever software is sold, or you can use the clip art that comes with applications, such as Microsoft Word.
- **Free online art**   Many Web sites provide art for free (making the art *freeware*) from their Web sites. You simply use the "right-click and save" method to copy the images to your disk.
- **Online art vendors**   A number of major vendors sell artwork online.
- **Graphic designers**   If you have a specific need and want a professional product, you can hire computer artists and graphic designers to create custom art for you.

## Custom Art

Sometimes, Web sites cry out for custom art. You can pay a designer to create the custom art (as mentioned in the preceding section), or you can try your hand at creating your own art (which we recommend in most cases). Creating custom art isn't as difficult as some people believe. Like any endeavor, the more you work at it, the better your results. But we're not here to give you a pep talk, so instead, let's focus on how you can create your own custom art.

At this point, the most useful types of custom art that you can create are graphical text elements (such as title text and banners) and buttons. Fortunately, you can create custom art in almost any graphics editor as well as in desktop applications, such as Word. To ease you into creating your own art, we've put together a couple mini-projects that you can complete in Word. First, we show you how to create a button, and then we give you a quick lesson in adding transparency to an image.

**tip** You can find a few links to free art and art vendor Web sites by visiting our resources page, at www.creationguide.com/resources. One resource we highly recommend is iStockphoto (www.istockphoto.com). iStockphoto is a royalty-free photography and illustration community where you can search and download over 350,000 images starting at just $1 each.

## Creating a button in Word

We provide this exercise simply to make sure you know that you truly can create custom art. If you like the buttons you create, you should save them for later. In Part Two, we show you how to insert and link buttons into your Web sites. Further, you can easily modify the buttons you create in this exercise by changing the color, text, AutoShape, or other design attributes.

1 Open a new document in Word.

2 Display the **Drawing** toolbar (if necessary) by pointing to **Toolbars** on the **View** menu and clicking **Drawing** on the submenu. (By default, the **Drawing** toolbar appears docked at the bottom of Word's window when you start Word.) Figure 3-20 shows the **Drawing** toolbar in Word.

**Figure 3-20** *Word's Drawing toolbar, which contains all the tools you need to design a Web button*

3 On the **Drawing** toolbar, click **AutoShapes**, point to **Basic Shapes**, and click **Rounded Rectangle**, as shown in Figure 3-21.

4 Click on the blank Word document, and drag to create the button's outline. (Don't worry about the size—you'll adjust that next.)

5 Double-click the AutoShape you just drew to open the **Format AutoShape** dialog box, and then click the **Size** tab.

**Figure 3-21** *Selecting a shape for your button*

**tip** You can hover the mouse pointer over a button or graphical menu option to see the name of the button or option. For instance, to see the names of the AutoShapes, position the mouse pointer over the small illustration of the AutoShape on the menu.

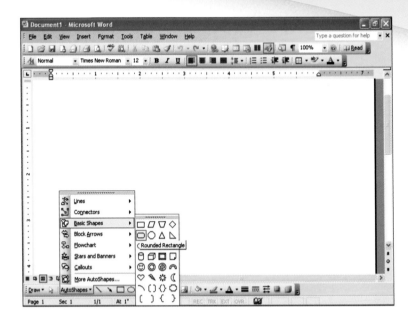

**6** In the **Height** box, type **.35**, and in the **Width** box, type **2.15**, as shown in Figure 3-22.

**Figure 3-22** *Drawing and sizing your button*

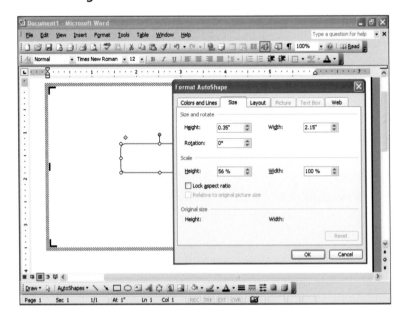

**7** Click the **Colors and Lines** tab in the **Format AutoShape** dialog box.

**8** Click the **Color** down arrow, and then click **Fill Effects**. The **Fill Effects** dialog box opens.

**9** In the **Colors** section on the **Gradients** tab, click **One color**, and in the **Color 1** palette, click **Blue-Gray**, as shown in Figure 3-23. Then click **OK**.

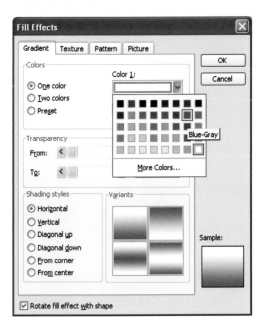

**Figure 3-23** *Working with the Fill Effects dialog box*

**10** In the **Format AutoShapes** dialog box, click **No Line** in the **Line Color** list, as shown in Figure 3-24, and then click **OK**. You should now have a rectangle shaded with a lovely blue-gray gradient.

**Figure 3-24** *Removing the outline from the AutoShape*

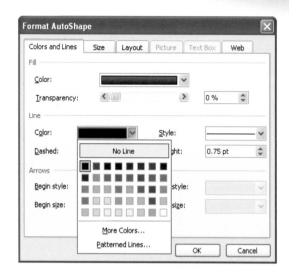

11 Right-click the button you created, and click **Add Text**. Your AutoShape is converted to a text box.

12 Before typing button text, use Word's **Formatting** toolbar to format your font as Century Gothic, 12 pt, bold, centered, and light yellow. After your font settings are in place, type **HOME**, as shown in Figure 3-25.

**Figure 3-25** *Adding formatted text to your button*

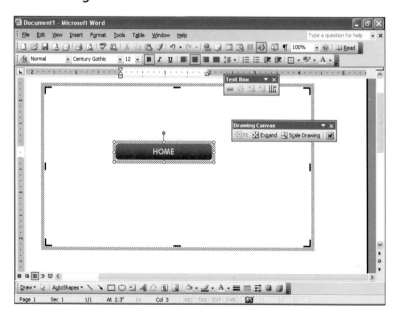

To save your button as a GIF image, you'll need to copy your button into a graphics program, such as Paint Shop Pro, and save the image as a GIF file.

13 Copy the button you created (select the button in Word, and then click **Copy** on the **Edit** menu, or right-click the button's edge and click **Copy**). Open your graphics program, and paste the button into the program as a new image.

14 On the **File** menu, click **Save As** to open the **Save As** dialog box. Save the button using GIF as the image's file type.

Now that your button is saved as a GIF, the image is ready to be used as an image button in Web sites. We show you how to insert buttons into Web sites and add hyperlink properties to buttons in Part Two.

### Adding transparency to an image

In this section, we present a quick exercise in transparency. Many readers have asked us how to apply transparency to images to create "cut-out" graphics on their Web pages, so we think you might appreciate this quick rundown. Although images are generally formatted in graphics programs, you can add transparency to a GIF in Office applications (including Word, Publisher, FrontPage, Excel, and PowerPoint) as well. Furthermore, numerous clip art images in Office are already formatted as transparent GIFs, so in many cases, you can simply insert clip art that's already formatted as a transparent GIF onto a Web page. You'll hear more about Clip Art in the walkthrough chapters in Part Two, particularly Chapter 9, "Diving into Design with Publisher Templates."

To apply transparency manually to a graphic in an Office program, you insert the picture and then assign transparency to the color of your choice. For this example, you apply transparency to an image in Word, but you can follow along using the same steps in Publisher, FrontPage, Excel, or PowerPoint if you prefer.

First you need to obtain a GIF file that doesn't contain transparency. For this exercise, you can copy the newsguy picture from www.creationguide.com/newsguy, shown in Figure 3-26.

**note** To view a sample of the finished button, see Figure 3-6, shown earlier in this chapter. The figure includes three buttons. The top button is the button described in the preceding steps; the middle button (the Contact button) is the same button with a different font color, background, and AutoShape applied; and the third button is the same button with a flat blue-gray color instead of a gradient fill effect.

**tip** After you create one button in Word, you can use the existing button as a template to create similar buttons with different text, as shown in Figure 3-6.

**Figure 3-26** *Adding transparency to a GIF image (also available online, at www.creationguide.com/ newsguy)*

To use the sample image:

1 Display www.creationguide.com/newsguy, right-click the GIF image with the orange background, and click **Copy**.

2 Open a new document in Word, and click **Paste** on the **Edit** menu (or press CTRL+V, or right-click and click **Paste**) to past the image of the newsguy into your document. (If you're working with your own graphic, insert your graphic by clicking **Picture** on the **Insert** menu and then clicking **From File**.)

In the sample graphic, you're going to designate the orange color to be your transparent color.

3 If necessary, click the newsguy picture to display the **Picture** toolbar, and then click the **Set Transparent Color** tool, as shown in Figure 3-27.

**Figure 3-27** *Using the Set Transparent Color tool*

4 In the picture, click the orange background. The orange background is set as the transparent color, and all portions of the image containing the color you clicked will appear transparent.

In this section, we've obviously barely skimmed the surface of creating custom art, but as you can see, custom art provides a lot of leeway for creativity. In addition to using Word, Paint Shop Pro, and Photoshop Elements, you can use other Microsoft Office programs and graphics packages, as described in Chapter 5, "Considering Tools and Stock-piling Goods," as well as scan hand-drawn art pieces for use in your Web site.

## Photographs

Thanks to your parents (or grandparents), you probably have at least one boxful of prime Web art resources lying around your home—photographs. You can use new and old photographs to add art to your Web site. The trick is getting the hard-copy picture turned into information your computer can understand. To do that, you can use any of the following options:

- **Scanners** Basically, a scanner takes a picture of your photograph and saves the picture information as a file on your computer. After you have a scanned picture, you can manipulate the file just as you manipulate other graphics files. You can use any flatbed scanner on the market to create Web graphics. You don't need to get a top-of-the-line machine, either. We use moderately priced scanners to scan most of our pictures. If you don't have a scanner and you aren't planning to purchase one, you can pay others to scan your pictures for you. For example, many copy centers also scan pictures for a small fee.

- **Film developers** Remember film developers? Now that so many people have digital cameras, film developers have expanded to do much more than develop film. Many film developers can develop your film on CD, post your pictures to the Web, send your pictures through e-mail, create quality prints from digital pictures, and provide numerous other digitizing services. For a list of links to online photo services, visit www.creationguide.com/resources, and click **Online Photo Services**.

- **Digital cameras** A third option for obtaining photographic images is to use a digital camera. Digital cameras enable you to snap a photo and then instantly send the picture into your computer.

**caution** If you click the background color of an image and it doesn't turn completely transparent, your background might consist of more than one color. For best results, you should use an image that has a solid, single-color background when you're creating a transparent GIF. In many cases, you can recolor a background as a solid flat color before you apply transparency—if you do this, ensure that the color you choose for your solid background color doesn't appear in the image; otherwise, you'll have transparent spots in your image.

**lingo**   A *mega-pixel* refers to one million pixels, and it's a term used in reference to the resolution of graphics devices, such as scanners, digital cameras, and monitors.

**see also**   www.creationguide.com/lists/digitalcameras.html

**tip**   To help manage your photos, consider using a photo management application, such as Microsoft Office Picture Manager, Google's free Picasa software (www.picasa.google.com) or Apple's iPhoto (www.applice.com/ilife/iphoto).

If you're thinking about buying a digital camera, here are a few issues to consider:

- **Cost**   Know your budget before you shop—most people don't need a top-of-the-line digital camera to get the job done. If you're buying a camera only for Web pictures, you can get away with a 1-*megapixel* camera, but if you want to use your pictures online *and* in print, you should get a 2-megapixel or 3-megapixel camera. Higher-megapixel cameras generally create better-quality pictures, provide more area for you to crop when you modify your images, and enable you to print quality pictures at sizes larger than snapshot size.

- **Automatic vs. manual**   Digital camera features run the gamut, but if you're a beginner, make sure your camera has automatic and manual features.

- **Battery types and life**   Cameras can burn through batteries. Make sure you understand the type of batteries required by the camera and the typical battery life before you buy.

- **Shutter lag**   Most basic digital cameras require you to wait after each shot while the camera processes the image, especially when you're using automatic features. To avoid unnecessary frustration, make sure the camera you purchase doesn't require too much time to process images.

- **Weatherproof**   Last but not least, remember that digital cameras are basically handheld computers. If you're going to be taking pictures under all sorts of circumstances and conditions, make sure you choose a camera that's built to withstand the torment..

All in all, regardless of how and where you obtain your Web site's graphics, remember to optimize your images and save them as GIF or JPEG files. Make sure your images file sizes are as small as possible without compromising quality. Furthermore, store your images in a central location on your computer, and don't forget to give every graphic a unique and meaningful name.

# check it!

- Online graphics are made up of pixels.
- Browsers fully support GIF and JPEG (or JPG) images. PNG images are steadily gaining widespread support.
- GIF images are small, limited to 256-color palettes, and quick to download.
- GIFs can be interlaced, transparent, or animated.
- JPEG images can contain millions of colors and are frequently used to display photographs.
- By default, GIFs and JPEGs are displayed line by line from the top down, but you can change the default by creating interlaced GIFs or progressive JPGs.
- The JPEG compression scheme enables you to reduce the size of JPEG images, but the compression is "lossy," so compress with care. (Remember, the more you compress, the lower your picture quality.)
- Size graphics in your graphics editing program to help make your Web site's graphics files as small as possible.
- Cropping images reduces file sizes as well.
- Consider using thumbnails to link to large online graphics.
- Graphical Web elements include photographs, illustrations, buttons, logos, icons, bullets, horizontal rules, graphical text, and backgrounds.
- You can acquire Web graphics from clip art collections on CD-ROMs, online freeware, online art vendors, and graphic designers.
- You can create custom art by using various software programs as well as by scanning hand-drawn art.
- Photographs can be converted to image files via scanners, film developers, and digital cameras.

#99CC33 #FFFF33 #FF9900
153 255 255
204 255 153
51 51 0

#FF6600
255
102
0

#009933 #FF6633
0 255
153 102
51 0

#CC0000
204
0
0

#660000 #660099
255 0
102 102
0 153

primary colors

secondary colors

Navigation Bar

Classes bar (links to course-related pages)

New Frontiers for Learning in Retirement

NFLR | Calendar | Photo Gallery | Contact Us

Classes

Learn, Socialize and Grow!

Body text

# mastering
# web design basics

# CHAPTER

# 4

Given an instrument and some sheet music, a musician can perform the music, modify the music by adding personal flair, or ditch the music and use the instrument and standard musical guidelines to compose an original work. Likewise, given Web elements, you can create a Web site by using a tried-and-true layout, modifying a version of a standard design, or using design theory and custom elements to create an original site.

# Before You Design

You read about Web text in Chapter 2, "Composing and Shaping Web Text," and looked over Web graphics in Chapter 3, "Creating and Using Art on the Web." Now you're ready for some Web design theory. And that's what this chapter's all about—successfully blending Web text and graphics to create appealing and usable Web pages and Web sites. But before we dive into the mechanics of Web design, we can't resist mentioning a couple planning issues. (Think of this section as preparation for Chapter 6, "Planning Your Attack," which discusses planning Web sites in detail.)

Understandably, planning affects design in a few major ways. Specifically, before you design for the Web, you should consider your audience and define your site's structure, *home page* layout, and *subpage* layout (if you're planning to expand your home page into a larger *Web site*).

> **lingo**  A *Web page* is a single page that is displayed in your browser, a *Web site* is a collection of related Web pages, a *home page* is the main page (which usually serves as a table of contents or an introductory page) in a Web site, and *subpages* are pages linked to the home page in a Web site to help organize and present additional information.

## The Audience Reigns Supreme

Most likely, you're creating a Web presence because you have information to impart, a message to pass along, a service to provide, a group to keep organized, or entertainment to offer. But before you state your piece by creating a Web site, you should answer at least four audience-related questions:

- What is the purpose of my site?
- Who is my audience?
- Who am I?
- How will my audience view my site?

Let's take a closer look at each question.

### What is the purpose of my site?

You need to clearly define the goal of your Web site to yourself. Whether you're planning a one-page site or a multilayered site, you need to know the overriding purpose for your Web presence. For example, determine whether the purpose of your site is to:

- Inform.

- Entertain.
- Serve as a Web portal, such as a search site or a directory of links.
- Address a specific community, such as hobbyists, activists, employees, customers, and so on.
- Present an artistic expression.
- Provide a personality profile, such as a personal page or résumé.
- Fulfill another specific purpose.

After you define the overall goal of your site, refine your site's topic. For example, let's say you decide to create an informational site. You then decide to inform people about pets. You chose an informational topic—"pets"—that's a start, but it's a little broad. You could then further refine your goal by deciding to provide information about caring for pet lizards, and even more specifically, iguanas. Notice how creating an *informational site about pet iguanas* seems much more focused and doable than creating a *site about pets*.

## Who is my audience?

After you state your site's purpose, analyze who will be viewing your pages—corporate clients, cartoon-watching kids, local artists, armchair athletes, your extended family, and so forth. Be as specific as possible. Then think of a particular person—a *real* person—to represent a typical audience member that you can keep in mind while you design. For example, let's say you're creating a fan site for a basketball team. When you design this site, you should imagine the one friend, relative, neighbor, coworker, or acquaintance who proudly owns a full spectrum of team shirts, refuses ever to miss a game, and regularly yells at the TV set throughout the season. If you don't have one of those types around (you're definitely an anomaly!), you could focus on a well-known sports analyst (Jim Rome comes to mind), a sports-driven TV sitcom character, or even a character from a novel or movie as your ideal audience member. In this example, to create a dynamic well-focused site, you should design your site with a clear picture in mind of a particular sports fan—you should not design your site with the vague notion that you're creating a Web site for anyone who has ever watched a basketball game.

**tip**   Designing without an audience in mind leads to aimless design decisions. In contrast, pinpointing your audience provides recognizable boundaries and enables smart design choices.

At this point, you might be muttering, "What's the big deal about designing for a *real* person?" We have an answer for that. When you pick a person, you take a big step toward creating a strong *voice*. Yes, that's the same *voice* your English teachers begged you to consider. With a person in mind, you'll automatically tend to design and write in a consistent way that's appropriate for communicating to that person. Conversely, if you design for a vague, homogenous group, you'll find your focus and voice shifting every two minutes and day to day as you envision different group members. Even worse, you'll dip into that cold gravy bowl of platitudes and stereotypes in an attempt to "please the masses." Of course, we're talking about selecting a real-person audience for your site's foundation design and content creation—later, we show you how to refine your Web site's structure and design so that it appeals to all types of audience personalities in terms of navigation and information processing.

One caveat before we move on—you might not want to tell the person who's serving as your "ideal audience member" that you're using him or her as a design tool!

### Who am I?

Now that you've thought about who "they" are, determine who you are. Define how you want to present yourself to your target audience and consciously choose how you want to communicate to your audience—casually, formally, professionally, comically, creatively, seriously, and so on. Creating a perspective (or a persona) for yourself can keep you from straying toward inappropriate design decisions, such as including an adorable picture of your nephew at his first birthday party on your company earnings page.

The persona you define for yourself combined with your target audience further clarifies and defines your site's voice.

### How will my audience view my site?

After you identify your purpose, audience, and persona, you need to consider the technical capabilities of your audience. After all, you *are* designing for the Web. Basically, you need to think about how a typical person in your audience will most likely access your site. If your site is targeted to on-campus university faculty members, you probably won't have to worry about bandwidth, because most universities have high-bandwidth networks. On the other hand, if you're designing pages for your friends who relocated all over the country (or the world) after graduation, you should create pages that can be downloaded reasonably quickly to accommodate dial-up modem connections.

As mentioned earlier, Chapter 6 covers Web site structure, planning, and audience analyses in greater depth, but your answers to the preceding four questions should give you a good foundation for audience considerations. And as you'll soon see, knowing your audience comes into play when you make some of your design decisions. For example, we redesigned the New Frontiers for Learning in Retirement (NFLR) Web site to serve as a case study for this chapter. The site's main audience is the retirement community—a group of people who generally access the Internet at typical dial-up modem speeds (as opposed to high-speed cable, *DSL*, or *T1* lines). Therefore, when we redesigned the NFLR site, we kept the retirement community and their dial-up connections in mind.

> **lingo** *DSL* (digital subscriber lines) and *T1* lines are types of high-speed communications lines that can provide Internet access at the rate of up to 1.5 megabits per second (Mbps) for DSL and 1.544 Mbps for T1.

## Framing and Storyboarding Your Web Site

After you identify your audience but before you start to create your Web pages, you should sketch your home page's layout as well as any relationships among ancillary pages—this visual representation is called *framing* and *storyboarding*. You don't have to be an architect to frame your site or an artist to create storyboards for your Web pages. In fact, one of our favorite ways to sketch a site is on napkins at a nearby Italian restaurant. As with our preceding "consider your audience" chat, framing and storyboarding Web sites is also covered in more detail in Chapter 6. At this point, we simply mention sketching out your site's hierarchy (if you plan to include more than one page in your site) and page layouts as a design step.

> **lingo** *Framing* refers to representing a Web site's organization by using words and lines that illustrate relationships among the pages that make up a site.

Simply put, *framing* entails using words (and maybe boxes) and connecting lines to show a tree or framework view of your Web site. When you were thinking about text in Chapter 2, you might have come up with some site organization ideas based on your brainstorming results. You can use the organization ideas to help build your site's framework. Figure 4-1 shows the framework we created for the NFLR Web site.

**Figure 4-1**  *Framework for the redesigned NFLR Web site's page relationships*

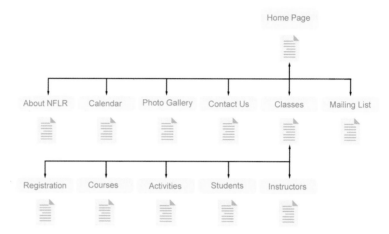

*Storyboarding* moves from site organization to page organization. Storyboarding a site means that you sketch the relationships among elements on your home page as well as subpages. Often, a home page has a slightly different design than subpages. Keep in mind that at this point, you're focusing on *structure*, not the finer aspects of your content. Figure 4-2 shows the storyboard we drew for the redesign of the NFLR home page.

Now that you've at least briefly considered the concept of audience and site planning, let's move on to discuss how to best assimilate Web text and Web graphics into well-designed Web pages and Web sites. First we look at Web *page* design issues. Later in this chapter, we address Web *site* design considerations.

**lingo**  *Story-boarding* refers to sketching the layout of a Web page to show where various page components will be displayed. After sketching rough page layouts, you can **mock up** your page layouts in a graphics program before you build so that you can further analyze your design decisions.

## Web *Page* Design Rules That Won't Let You Down

Before you can create a Web site, you have to build a Web page—even if your site consists of only a home page. Regardless of the number of pages in your site, you can take advantage of some tried-and-true Web

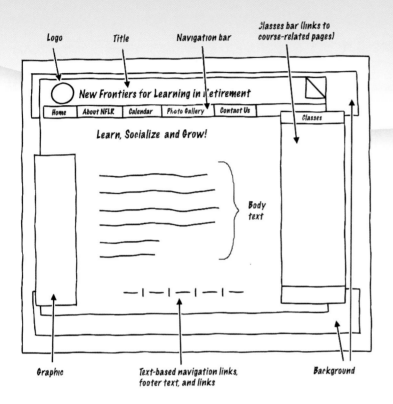

**Figure 4-2** *Sketch of the redesigned NFLR home page*

design tips. In this section, we address key Web page design issues and proven tactics. But we also have a small disclaimer, because first and foremost, Web design is a creative endeavor. We have no desire to take away a drop of your creativity—we'd much rather spark your imagination. The parameters we outline in this chapter (as well as throughout this book) are merely guidelines. We hope you'll experiment with your Web designs in a number of ways not mentioned in this text. We highly encourage you to do so, and in the walkthrough projects in Part Two, we suggest various ways you can customize the projects. The information in this chapter will provide a strong foundation for you—a good base for custom designs. If you follow the advice in this book, you'll be able to create clean, attractive, and easy-to-navigate Web sites. Then you can take the fundamentals to new creative heights (and e-mail us when you do, because we'd be happy to review your Web site for posting to www.creationguide.com/readerpages.html).

**tip**   Keep in mind that most good *page* design theories carry over to good *site* design practices.

For discussion purposes, we've divided Web page design fundamentals into the following topics:

- Web page dimensions
- Page layout issues
- Color
- Navigation tools and hyperlinks
- Standard credibility components
- Text
- Graphics

## Web Page Dimensions

**try this!**
Let us know what type of computer setup you're using and see what other readers are using. Vote in our Browser Version and Screen Resolution polls, at www.creationguide.com/2cents. As always, your vote is anonymous, and we provide the polls for interest, entertainment, and unscientific information gathering purposes only.

Theoretically, Web pages are infinitely long and infinitely wide because they aren't bound by the size of cut paper. Of course, designing your pages with measurements such as "infinity by infinity" in mind doesn't help you or your page's visitors. So let's look at a more reasonable way to select Web page boundaries. The best way to narrow down a page's parameters is to consider the browser window real estate on a lowest common denominator machine. In other words, you need to think about the amount of viewable content in the browser window of the user who has the most limited browser capabilities.

For Web page design purposes, the lowest monitor resolution out there these days displays 800 × 600 pixels at a time. Further, various browsers tend to show even less area than 800 × 600 pixels because of the browser's setup (including toolbars, scroll bars, status bars, Favorites or Bookmarks, task panes, and so forth). For example, if you measure and compare the viewing areas of Microsoft Internet Explorer version 6 for PC, Firefox version 1 for PC and Macintosh, and Safari version 1.3 for Macintosh, you'll find that the smallest viewing area is 779 × 458 pixels, or 775 × 450 if you round down. (We tend to round down a little further and design with a 750 × 450 pixel limit in mind.) We call this common-denominator viewable area the *safe area*.

When you design your Web pages (particularly your home page), you should keep the safe area measurements in mind and, as we describe next, make sure that your page's most important information appears within the safe area boundaries to accommodate the largest number of visitors.

## Screen Resolutions—Then and Now
In the past, we recommended determining the safe area by using 640 × 480 pixel screen-resolution measurements. Technically speaking, the smallest monitor resolution setting is 640 × 480 pixels, but very few people use that setting these days. In fact, in our experience, visitors viewing Web sites at 640 × 480 account for less than 1 percent of the total viewing population. For example, the following graphic shows the screen resolutions used by visitors to the CreationGuide.com site:

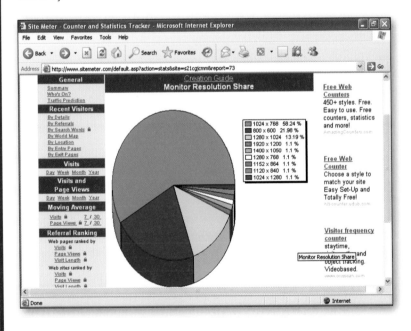

In addition, TheCounter.com (www.thecounter.com/stats) published the following global screen-resolution statistics on September 30, 2005:

| | | |
|---|---|---|
| 1024 × 768 | 37,538,307 | (56 percent) |
| 800 × 600 | 15,492,946 | (23 percent) |
| 1280 × 1024 | 8,923,471 | (13 percent) |
| 1152 × 864 | 2,214,736 | (3 percent) |
| Unknown | 1,840,062 | (2 percent) |
| 1600 × 1200 | 501,100 | (less than 1 percent) |
| 640 × 480 | 273,040 | (less than 1 percent) |

Incidentally, notice that both in the worldwide statistics and on the CreationGuide.com tracking page, 1024 × 768 (bright green on the CreationGuide.com chart) leads the pack, with 800 × 600 (dark blue on the CreationGuide.com chart) coming in second. Also notice that 640 × 480 comes in last in TheCounter.com stats and doesn't even appear in the CreationGuide.com chart.

Using statistics, then, we can deduce that the safe area for 800 × 600 screen resolutions makes sense for the majority of visitors. Of course, if you know your viewers will be viewing your site at 640 × 480, you should design accordingly, and keep your safe area limited to about 600 pixels across.

**note** Keep in mind that, while you should design for as many browsers as possible, over 80 percent of Internet visitors currently use Internet Explorer 6, even though the Internet supports a variety of browsers and display settings.

With safe area measurements and Web site statistics under your belt, you still have one more Web page dimension to consider—namely, people don't always maximize their browser windows, especially if they're using large monitors. Thus, even when you're designing for 800 × 600, you won't be able to control exactly how people will size and view your pages. To counter the unpredictability of your page's presentation, we show you how to create *liquid pages* in Part Two of this book, as in the walkthrough project in Chapter 8, "Demystifying Basic CSS and XHTML." Liquid pages automatically resize to a browser window as much as possible without losing the page's overall structure. Your other option is to create fixed-width pages that are centered or sometimes left-aligned in the browser window. Both liquid and fixed layout options are widely accepted, and we'll show you how to create both so that you can build sites to suit your preferences.

Given all these "unknowns" associated with Web page dimensions, you might be wondering if there's any hope for successfully designing a page that can be viewed by the masses. Of course there's hope—after all, you've surely seen a number of well-designed sites online. Basically, when it comes to online page dimensions, your goal is to ensure

**try this!**

If you have a fairly modern (Microsoft Windows 98 or later) computer system, you can see the effects of viewing Web pages at various screen sizes. To do so, follow these steps:

1 Right-click a blank area on your desktop, and click **Properties**.

2 In the **Display Properties** dialog box, click the **Settings** tab.

3 On the **Settings** tab, drag the slider control in the **Screen Area** or **Screen Resolution** section to change the screen setting to **800 × 600**, click **Apply**, and then click **OK**. (Your screen might go blank for a moment or two while it readjusts the screen area.) Click **Yes**, and then click **OK**.

4 View www.creationguide.com/nflr-new in your browser, and then minimize your browser window.

5 Repeat steps 1 through 3, changing the **800 × 600** setting to **1024 × 768** (the most common screen area setting).

6 View www.creationguide.com/nflr-new with the new settings, and then minimize your browser window.

7 Repeat steps 1 through 3 using the **1280 × 1024** setting, view www.creationguide.com/ nflr-new, and then close your browser window.

As you worked through the preceding steps, the NFLR site should have gone through a metamorphosis similar to the changes shown here:

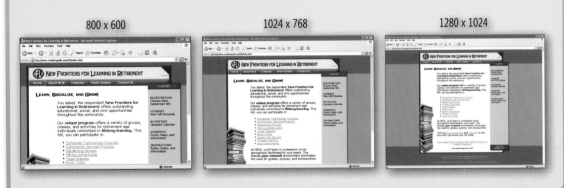

800 x 600     1024 x 768     1280 x 1024

that your important information appears in the minimum safe area zone. Further, you should create liquid pages or center your fixed-width pages if possible. And most of all, preview your site while you work in various resolutions. (See the following Try This! sidebar.)

## Page Layout Issues

Now that we've pinned down a target page size, let's look at page layouts. For the record, we'd like to state that just because the Web provides almost carte blanche publishing freedom, you can't get away with simply uploading text and images willy-nilly—unless you don't care whether anyone visits your page long enough to read or even glimpse your content. A more successful approach—one that we highly recommend—involves following some basic rules for laying out pages.

### Templates

The number-one layout rule is to apply basic template principles. A *template* (as you might know from hard-copy page design) is a grid that you can use as a guideline to lay out your page's elements. Although current limitations make it difficult for you to adhere to strict page layout rules and regulations for your Web pages as consistently as for printed text, numerous Web pages follow loosely defined templates to help contain the flow of information. For example, Figure 4-3 shows the very basic template we used to create the NFLR site. Every page of the NFLR site adheres to the simple, straightforward template shown in Figure 4-3.

**lingo**  A *template* provides basic layout guidelines for the placement of page elements. Using a template helps you to keep spacing, buttons, margins, footers, and other design elements consistent throughout your site. This consistency adds a professional polish to your site as well as improves your visitors' experiences because they know where to look to find particular site elements. You can build your own templates, as we describe in Part Two, and you can find numerous free templates online.

Creating and using templates enables you to align elements and create consistent external and internal spacing between and around elements. When you devise templates, keep in mind that people generally scan Web pages in the way most familiar to their native reading patterns. For example, people who speak and read English scan pages from left to right and top to bottom—so design accordingly. The sites we design in this book cater to people who read from left to right across and down a page. Therefore, according to recent studies, our primary design area is the upper-left corner, across the page, and then down the left side. (See Chapter 2, "Composing and Shaping Web Text," for more information about usability studies.) This reading pattern very nicely brings our discussion back to the "safe area" topic.

Logo area    Title area    Navigation bar    Subpage links

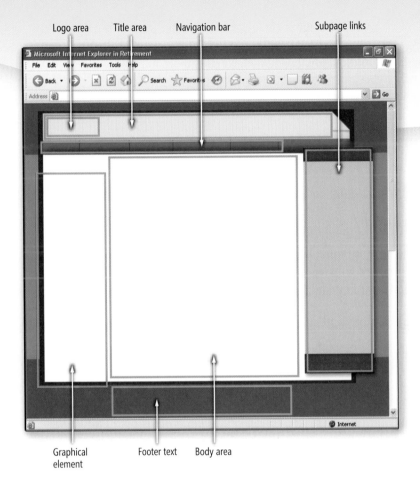

**Figure 4-3** *The NFLR site template*

Graphical element    Footer text    Body area

## Safe area

As we mentioned earlier, you can count on an area of 750 × 450 pixels as your safe area when your page is loaded into any browser. For the most part, users are willing to scroll down but not across. Therefore, when you create a Web page, stay within the width limitations as much as possible, but don't become overly concerned if your page flows below the safe area's height limitation.

## Upper-left corner

Now here's an even bigger tip:

*The choicest spot of all within the safe area is the upper-left corner.*

**tip** When you design Web pages, you should view your pages using various screen settings, color settings, and browsers to ensure that your page is displayed correctly for the majority of people. For instance, you should perform the steps in the preceding Try This! sidebar to view your Web pages' development at various sizes. Then experiment with various sizes in other browsers and with other color settings.

Why? For a couple reasons. First, it's the place people's eyes go to first to verify that they're on the correct, or at least a desirable, page. Second, no matter how much a visitor resizes the browser window, the upper-left corner remains in view (or, in worst-case scenarios, it's the last area to go if window resizing gets completely out of hand). Therefore, the upper-left corner is prime property—the ideal place for you to insert your logo or other key information.

### Above the fold

After the upper-left corner, the next-best area on your Web page is what journalists refer to as "above the fold." Newspapers carry the day's most notable news stories above where the paper folds so that when the paper appears on newsstands, passersby will see the top news stories and be tempted to purchase the paper. Obviously, users can't fold their monitors (not yet, at least), so your design "fold" is the bottom edge of the safe area. When you lay out your page's information, make sure that the most significant and eye-catching information appears in the opening view. Further, if your page scrolls below the fold, ensure that your design lets viewers know that the page continues beyond the initial display. Otherwise, users might not scroll at all. You can indicate that a page continues by avoiding obvious page breaks, such as a large space between paragraphs, at the safe area's bottom limit.

Finally, you should include your site's main navigation links, such as a navigation bar, menu bar, or buttons, within the page's safe area—preferably along the top or left side of the viewable area. The redesigned NFLR site uses the very common top navigation bar setup. Secondary links align along the page's right edge.

### Fundamental page elements

In addition to using templates and designing within the safe area, you should incorporate fundamental Web page elements into your pages, as shown in Figure 4-4. Most pages contain title bar text, a title area, a logo, navigation links, body content, and footer text. You'll find numerous combinations and positioning of these elements, but the basic elements generally appear on most home pages in some manner.

Logo    Title bar text    Title area    Navigation links

**Figure 4-4** *Incorporating basic page elements into your Web pages*

Footer text    Body    Sublinks

## Basic "good design" principles

The remaining page layout considerations we want to impress on you encompass universal "good design" practices. Here are some common design principles that you should keep in mind and on-hand. (Notice that we've ordered the following principles in alphabetical order to avoid implying importance; this list is also available online, at www.creationguide.com/lists/goodpage.html.)

- **Blinking text and gratuitous animation**   Avoid blinking text and unnecessary animation; many people find these effects annoying and meaningless. On the other hand, many people appreciate a slick yet simple rollover effect for buttons, such as the effect used on the redesigned NFLR site (www.creationguide.com/nflr-new).

- **Competition**   Search similar sites to see what's out there, and then make your site unique. By viewing similar or related sites, you can also get ideas of topics that need better coverage or that you've forgotten to address on your page.

- **Content**   Keep content fresh, simple, and smart. Further, aim to use at least 80 percent of your page to present your content (especially if you plan to use advertising on your page), and restrict navigation elements to 20 percent or less of your page area.

- **Cutting-edge technology**   Avoid using too many high-tech features, or you'll lose the majority of your viewers. Most people don't want to download a plug-in (which is a small "helper" application that works with a browser to run a specific file type) just to view a Web page. Further, when you do use more advanced technology, make sure you know what your page looks like to visitors who don't have the plug-in installed.

- **Download speed**   Ensure that your page is downloaded as quickly as possible; you have about 10 seconds max before viewers itch to surf elsewhere.

- **Frames**   Please do not use frames. Or, if you do, use them sparingly. Frames are tricky to implement properly and sometimes hard for users to navigate. Essentially, frames are used to divide the browser window so that users can view multiple pages at once. Frames can be useful for sites that include many links, but you have other options, which means *not* using frames shouldn't pose a problem.

- **Functional design**   Opt for function over form—every design element should also serve a purpose. If you're not sure whether a design element is functional, temporarily remove the element from the page and analyze the page without it. If your page works as well (or better) without it, the element is more ornamental

**tip**   To learn more about available browsers, review the Web browser comparison offered by Wikipedia, the free online encyclopedia at en.wikipedia.org/wiki/Comparison_of_web_browsers.

than functional and should be dropped. Keep in mind that including an element to create a good design counts as functional. For example, the small page tab in the upper-right corner of the revised NFLR site visually represents turning the corner of a page down to save a spot in a book. This complements the stack of books image, sends the message to bookmark the page, and directs the visitor's eye back into the body of the page.

- **Important elements**   Size elements in proportion to their importance. Bigger means more important and draws attention quicker, whereas smaller equates to lesser importance.

- **Moderation**   Avoid using too much of any element or technique, including links, colors, scrolling, and so forth. Remember, too much emphasis results in no emphasis at all.

- **Sound files**   Don't automatically enable sound files. If you must include sound, provide an option to play an audio file. Most people don't like to listen to background sounds, and many people keep their speakers turned down or off, which means that extraneous audio files only serve to slow download speeds considerably for no purpose. One way you can add sound if you're determined to do so is to add it in subtle ways, such as playing a short sound when viewers click a hyperlink.

- **The kitchen sink**   Don't get crazy and overload your home page (or any page, for that matter). If you have more than enough information for your home page, expand your page into a Web site by dividing information into logical chunks and placing each chunk on a separate subpage. Also, you don't have to use all your text and graphics just because you have the information on hand. Remember that the Web is dynamic, which means that you can selectively update and modify information on a regular basis, so opt to show pertinent information in a timely manner. For example, if you want to publicize your city's charity events, consider showing just the current month's events and updating the events list monthly.

- **Visual appeal**   Verify that your page looks good in Internet Explorer and Firefox (at a minimum) at various resolutions on Windows and Macintosh systems.

● **White space**   Create eye relief and visual space with strategically placed blank areas (white space), as described toward the end of the next section.

## Color

After page dimensions and layout, you should consider your color scheme. A *color scheme* refers to your site's interface elements (not necessarily the colors used in images), such as title graphics, buttons, background, text, and so forth. Some tips for creating a good color scheme include the following (also available online, at www.creation-guide.com/lists/colorschemes.html):

● Limit the number of colors used in your main color scheme to three or four complementary colors. If you're unsure of complementary color combinations, use a color wheel. Figure 4-5 shows a very simple Web-safe color wheel, which is also available online, at www.creationguide.com/colorwheel. Color wheels are designed to help people combine colors into winning combinations. Notice that the redesigned NFLR site uses the primary colors yellow, blue, and red, as identified on the color wheel.

**Figure 4-5**   *Viewing complementary colors on a color wheel (also available online, at www.creation-guide.com/colorwheel)*

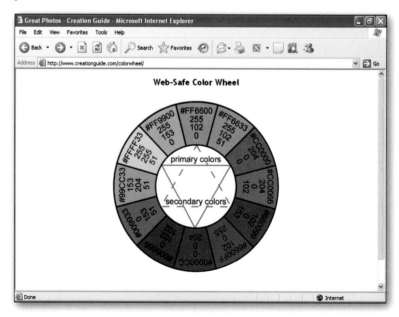

- Use contrasting colors, especially if you're using a colored background.

- Keep your colors appropriate for your message. For example, if you're creating a mountain ski resort site, opt to use icy cold blues and purples to convey great winter conditions instead of reds and oranges, which bring to mind sunshine and melting snow.

- Consult the Web-safe color palette discussed in Chapter 3, "Creating and Using Art on the Web." Whenever possible, opt to use Web-safe colors to avoid unnecessary dithering. For example, the redesigned NFLR site's darker blue at the top is #336699 (RGB 51 102 153), and the lighter blue in the middle is #6699CC (RGB 102 153 204). (You can find the colors used on the NFLR page on the Web-safe color palette shown in this book's Appendix and available online, at www.creationguide.com/colorchart.)

- If you can't decide which colors will work best for you, go for black text on a white background—the standard black-on-white combination is pretty much bulletproof when it comes to readability and design sense.

**tip** You can purchase digital color wheels that let you experiment with color combinations. For example, Color Consultant Pro (www.code-line.com/software/colorconsultantpro.html) is a popular tool used for the Macintosh, and Color Wheel Pro (www.color-wheel-pro.com) and ColorImpact (www.tigercolor.com) are popular Windows programs.

**try this!**

To experiment with various background and text colors, visit a Web color selection page, such as those shown at www.creationguide.com/colortest.

In addition to using a color scheme for your interface, you can use colors to call attention to certain content items on your page. For example, if you have a store site and you're running a special, you could highlight the information by placing a color background behind the text advertising your sale.

Overall, you should use your color scheme to create balance and unity throughout your site, but you should also use colors to draw attention to specific areas of the page, including links, titles, logos, key points, items of interest, and so forth.

**try this!**

To compare a site that uses Web-safe colors with one that doesn't, follow these steps:

1 Right-click a blank area on your desktop, click **Properties**, and then click the **Settings** tab in the **Display Properties** dialog box.

2 On the **Settings** tab, click the **Colors** or **Color Quality** drop-down arrow. (Note your current setting so that you can return to it in step 5.) If you're using Microsoft Windows 98, Windows Me, or Windows 2000, click **256 Colors** in the drop-down list, click **Apply** (your screen might go blank for a moment), and then click **OK**.

If you're using Microsoft Windows XP, a **256 Color** option isn't provided by default. You can view this example by clicking the **Medium (16 Bit)** color setting on the **Settings** tab to get some idea of color differences, or you can dredge up a 256-color setting. To access a 256-color setting in Windows XP, click the **Advanced** button, click the **Adapter** tab, click **List All Modes**, and select a monitor setting that uses 256 colors. Then click **OK**, click **Apply**, click **Yes**, and click **OK** again.

3 Open www.creationguide.com/nflr-old in your browser. Notice the dithering that occurs on the Web page's background.

4 Now open www.creationguide.com/nflr-new in your browser. As you can see, the page's colors appear clear and crisp, without dithering, because the colors used to create the page are included in the Web-safe color palette.

5 Close your browser, right-click on your desktop, and return your color display to the previous setting.

Complementary to colors is *white space*, which we've already introduced a couple times in this book (including earlier in this chapter). As we mentioned in Chapters 2 and 3, white space isn't necessarily white—white space is an area without any content. The concept behind white space is to provide visual relief. You use white space to create visual space between and around images and body text. In essence, white space frames and draws attention to your content.

## Navigation Tools and Hyperlinks

Navigation tools and hyperlinks include buttons, clickable logos, text links, and graphical links—basically, all the elements you provide on your Web pages that enable users to find additional information easily.

Effective navigation elements tell users where they are, where they've been, and where they can go next. Therefore, all successful navigation tools and hyperlinks must use meaningful descriptors, whether the descriptors are graphical, textual, or both.

To further clarify how to effectively use navigation tools, the following sections offer some rules of thumb for designing navigation elements.

### Buttons

If you create a navigation bar that uses buttons, keep the buttons consistent on the current page (same dimensions, color schemes, and so forth) and display the same group of buttons on every page. You can easily confuse viewers by offering different sets of buttons on various pages. To ensure consistency, we almost always recommend using templates that include the navigation links and other universal Web site information (such as copyright information). Also, ensure that buttons are named so that they clearly indicate where viewers will go after they click a particular button. Finally, consider slightly modifying navigation buttons to display the current page's button differently—such as slightly darker or a different color—so that viewers instantly know which page they're on by looking at the navigation bar. We show you how to use navigation buttons effectively in Part Two's walkthrough projects.

### Logos

If you include a logo on your Web site, ensure that your logo is a high-quality Graphics Interchange Format (GIF) graphic that uses Web-safe colors. You want your logo to look great, regardless of a user's system capabilities. Ideally, you'll want to show your logo on your home page in the upper-left corner, a little larger than the logo's display on subsequent pages, and surrounded by a light padding of extra white space to ensure that your logo stands out. Then on all ancillary pages, link a smaller version of your logo (also slightly padded by white space) to your home page. That way, users can easily access your home page from anywhere within your site, while you reinforce your logo identity.

**tip**   As we mentioned earlier in this chapter, remember to restrict your use of navigation elements so that they account for less than 20 percent of your Web page's area if possible. (At times, they might require more space—perhaps you're creating a site or page that consists mostly of hyperlinks, or possibly you're creating a site with very little content and you want to visually balance the site.)

**Logo Design**    If you're designing a logo, keep in mind that logos are usually used in a variety of situations and sizes. One mistake that many people make when they create their first logo is that they make it too complex. Complex logos become blurs and blobs when they're reduced to small sizes for business cards or other marketing materials. So keep it simple. Further, ensure that your logo appears sleek and legible in black-and-white as well as in color. You don't want to be disappointed when your logo, which looks so beautiful on your Web page, looks like an ink splotch when it appears in your newspaper advertisement. A great way to test your logo's durability is to resize your graphic to an inch or two, print your logo, and then fax it to yourself. A good logo will be able to withstand this abuse and arrive intact after all's said and done.

For more tips about creating a great logo, see the "Top 10+1 Tips for Great Logos" sidebar below, presented by Sarah Spencer, a professional graphic artist and successful identity and product brand designer.

## Top 10+1 Tips for Great Logos

Also available online, at www.creationguide.com/lists/greatlogos.html.

*Sarah Spencer* earned her BFA from Rochester Institute of Technology in 1993. She worked for award-winning graphic design firms for eight years before starting her own design business. After developing many successful identities and product brands for clients, Sarah established 26 Letters (www.26-letters.com), based in Phoenix, Arizona, to express her own ideas and provide an outlet for her illustrating and writing talents. To aid you in creating your own logo, Sarah generously passes along the following top 10+1 tips for designing great logos:

- **Gather ideas.**    Take some concentrated time, be it an hour or several hours spread over days, to write down thoughts about your company. If you've chosen a name, consider images that can accompany the name to clarify the purpose of the business. Don't reject any ideas at this point.

- **Refine your thoughts.**  Reexamine the ideas from your brainstorming session and consider how each image might affect customers. If your customers are conservative, eliminate off-the-wall suggestions. If your customers expect whiz-bang, get rid of the ideas that seem old or stodgy.

- **Set the direction.**  Once you narrow down the names and images to accurately represent your company's ideals and products or services, make a list of the items for reference. Use this list as a guide to stay on track with decisions made about the logo.

- **Keep it simple.**  The golden rule for an effective logo is to keep the design simple. Choose a limited color palette and steer away from intricate shapes, patterns, and typefaces.

- **Choose a logo type.**  When choosing a typeface (or font) to represent your company, consider what your company does. If your product or service is for the corporate sector, a more formal typeface will project a sense of responsibility and longevity. If your company provides personal products or services, you have more flexibility to use a font with some flair.

- **Design a logo mark.**  Not every corporate identity has a logo mark (a graphic representation of the corporate identity), but having one often helps to define what the company does and provides instant recognition that transcends language barriers. The most important aspect of a logo mark is that it should be relevant to the core business. Second, it should be designed simply so that it's memorable, like the Nike swoosh or MSN butterfly.

- **Pick logo colors.**  The fewer the colors, the greater the impact. The colors you use depend on the desired image of your company. Financial institutions might need subdued colors to represent trustworthiness, while technology companies (often working at the cutting edge of their industry) might want bright colors that represent movement and newness.

- **Select orientation, vertical vs. horizontal.**  Ideally, you should design a logo so that it's just slightly horizontal, keeping the height and width in close proportion. If your company name is long, consider stacking the words. If you have a logo mark, place it where it balances the logo type.

- **Strengthen your brand with collateral**. Consider logo applications to media other than business cards and Web sites, such as T-shirts, brochures, banners, vehicles, and so forth. Remember that your business's colors, those chosen for your logo, should be the first used on your collateral. All additional colors should not overpower, either by amount or hue, your business's colors.

- **Trademark your logo.** Once you design your logo, protect it by attaching a small *TM* to indicate a trademark. Often this appears in the upper-right corner of the logo. For detailed legal information about trademarks, visit the United States Patent and Trademark Office Web site, at www.uspto.gov.

- **Plus 1: Tear it apart.**     To get great impact on a Web site design, tear the logo to shreds (figuratively) and incorporate the lines, dots, curves, and so forth in other areas of the site. For instance, the bar along the left side of the page might resemble a curve found in one of the logo letters, or the background pattern might be a portion of the logo mark. Get creative!

## Text links

As mentioned in earlier chapters, you should always provide text links for all graphical links (including buttons, logos, and linked images). Doing so ensures that everyone—even those who opt to hide graphics in their browser window—can navigate within your site.

Colorwise, you should generally use standard hyperlink colors (you can change link colors by using cascading style sheets or HTML code) when you use hyperlinks embedded in text. Visitors have grown accustomed to clicking blue underlined text. But in some designs, you might want to use custom hyperlink colors. When you do, ensure that you assign specific colors to nonvisited and visited hyperlinks, and keep the colors consistent throughout your site. Usually, sites use brighter colors for nonvisited links and darker colors for visited links. We talk more about formatting hyperlinks in Part Two. Viewers frequently use visual cues to help them keep track of their online travels, so you should help them along whenever possible.

Finally, on long pages, include a "Back to the Top" or "Home" link after long sections or at the base of the long page. And don't forget your bottom-of-the-page text-based navigation links, Webmaster e-mail link, and copyright notice.

**try this!**
To see links that take you to another part of the same page, visit www.creationguide.com/resources. Each categorical group of links on the resources page is followed by a Top Of Page link. Clicking a Top Of Page link returns visitors to the list of resource categories displayed at the top of the page.

## Graphical links

On some sites, graphical elements, such as images, serve as hyperlinks. For example, a site might display thumbnail images (as explained in Chapter 3) that link to larger images. The redesigned About NFLR Web page includes a thumbnail picture of the organization's president that links to a larger image. Many Web surfers are used to clicking images for more information, so you generally don't need to format your image to look like a link. With that said, graphical links are often accompanied by text links to make the association clear on retail sites—we highly recommend this practice in those instances. For example, on a retail site, you might see a clickable picture of a coffeemaker accompanied by text link stating the brand and model of the coffeemaker below the picture. In this setup, users can click either the linked image or the text to view detailed information about the coffeemaker.

## Standard Credibility Components

Often when you view a Web page, you have no idea where the page's files are located, who created the page, or where the information you're reading came from. Anyone can post a Web site, and you shouldn't automatically believe everything you find on the Web—but you already know that! With that in mind, you should strive to make your Web site as credible as possible. You can do that in a number of easy ways:

- **Attribution**  Give complete attribution, credits, bylines, and references for any quotations, graphics, or statistics you use on your Web page. Attribution gives credit where credit is due, and it strengthens your site's trustworthiness.

- **Contact information**  Make it easy for visitors to contact you and obtain more information through e-mail, mailing lists, telephone numbers, physical addresses, and so on. One of the Web's biggest draws is its interactive appeal, so take advantage of this unique communication channel.

- **Copyright notice**  Include a copyright notice on your Web site to show that you care enough about your Web site to take ownership of your content.

**tip**  Above all else, avoid the cardinal Web page sin of providing *dead links*. To prevent this problem, check your links and run your site through an online validation service. A number of validation sites—including validator.w3.org, www.htmlhelp.com/tools/validator, and www.craigcecil.com/checkyoursite.htm—will check your Web page's links and HTML code for free. Other fee-based validation services are also available online, such as www.netmechanic.com, among others.

- **Current content**   Keep your content up-to-date and modified regularly. If you show readers that you're serious about your site, they'll be more likely to take an interest in it.

- **Last updated**   Include text that shows when the site was last updated so that viewers know they're reading current information and to reassure them that you haven't abandoned the site.

- **Personal information**   Provide information about yourself or a prominent person associated with the site (such as the club president); include your name (or the prominent person's name) and possibly a picture.

- **Privacy policy**   If you collect information from visitors, such as their e-mail addresses, include a privacy policy that reassures them that you won't use their information for nefarious purposes. You can also protect the rights to your content in your privacy policy.

- **Special interests**   State your point of view if your page presents commercial interests or advocacy issues.

- **Spelling and grammar**   Check your spelling and grammar religiously. Not to sound preachy or melodramatic, but typos and grammatical errors are frequently construed as highly unprofessional, and they almost instantaneously jeopardize your credibility.

- **Webmaster link**   Provide an e-mail link to the Webmaster in case viewers have problems or questions.

**tip**  Just as you use standard credibility components on your Web pages and Web site, you should look for these components on Web sites you visit to verify their credibility.

## Text

In Chapter 2, we looked at how to write effective Web text, and in Chapter 3, we reviewed how to use text in graphical elements, such as title bars and buttons. In this section, we review effective ways to format nongraphical text.

As you know, text is used to present content and create hyperlinks. As a Web designer, you have the power to control your text's size, color, formatting, and style. A variety of thoughts are bandied about when it comes to text rules, but for your benefit, we've consolidated the basic premises that the majority of Web designers support, including preferences for font size, font style, and font formatting.

## Font size

Almost universally, Web designers recommend that you use the default font size for body text. This allows viewers to choose the font size via their browser's default settings. For special text, such as copyrights and other footer information, text-based navigation bars, and so forth, you can specify smaller font sizes to avoid disrupting your page's focus on the content. If you want to display larger text, such as headings, you should use the HTML default heading tags and cascading style sheets (CSS), as described in Part Two, instead of simply increasing the body text's font size.

## Font style—serif vs. sans serif

Even though thousands of font styles exist, all font styles can be categorized as either *serif* or *sans serif*. Serif fonts, such as **Times New Roman**, use "hooks," or short lines, on the ends of letters, whereas sans serif fonts, such as **Arial**, use plain-edged letters. On the whole, the Web design community voices a mixed response to the use of serif and san serif fonts online. Personally, we generally prefer to use sans serif fonts rather than serif fonts when creating Web pages, because we find sans serif fonts easier to read online as well as more visually appealing.

In the past—when monitor resolutions left much to be desired (and were generally alien-glow green)—sans serif fonts were overwhelmingly recommended for on-screen text because serifs helped only to blur the

**caution**   You should avoid displaying your text—both serif and sans serif—too small. A common (and slightly disturbing) trend seems to be emerging in which sites containing numerous links display the links in tiny font sizes. This setup can make the links illegible as well as hard to click. Clarity becomes even more of an issue when a serif font is used to display the tiny text. On the flip side, some Web developers assert that once you capture a visitor's attention, you should display text smaller to encourage the person to read more text. This thinking is a newer idea, and we haven't seen enough support research to convince us that smaller text keeps people on pages longer.

text into further illegibility. Nowadays, monitors are much improved, so accounting for the blurriness factor doesn't hold much water (unless you opt to use very small text, which we don't recommend). But you're not off the hook—you still have other font-related design decisions to address. For example, the NFLR site uses Verdana—an easy-to-read sans serif font—for the body text to present clear letters to accommodate viewers with low vision.

If you've worked with print text, you might know that a common serif-related design technique is to use sans serif fonts for headings and serif fonts for body text. If you want to blend serif and sans serif text online to differentiate body text from headings, you can do so, but we recommend that you reverse the standard print practice. In other words, try using serif fonts for headings and sans serif fonts for text. Although you might feel odd at first when you reverse the age-old print standard, you'll most likely get over it quickly when you see that your headings stand out nicely with serifs and your sans serif body text is easy to read.

### Font families

Next, regardless of your serif preferences, you should stick with cross-platform fonts to ensure that users see your text similar to how you designed your page. Specifically, cross-platform fonts are common fonts that willbe displayed on most Macintosh and PC computers as well as in Internet Explorer and Firefox browsers. Cross-platform fonts include the following:

Arial

**Arial Black**

Comic Sans MS

Courier New

Georgia

**Impact**

Times New Roman (or Times)

Trebuchet MS

Verdana

# Graphics

In the previous chapter, we took an in-depth look at Web graphics. For Web graphics and page design, you should adhere to the following four practices in addition to the techniques discussed in Chapter 3:

- Avoid large graphics that seem to take days to download on dial-up modems.

- Steer clear of meaningless graphics. If a user has to wait to see a graphic, make sure that the graphic contributes positively to the user's experience.

- Ensure that every graphical link has a text link equivalent.

- Include an ALT tag for every graphic. *ALT* stands for *alternative*, as in text that serves as an alternative for a graphic. An ALT label provides the pop-up text when you position your mouse pointer over a graphic, as shown in Figure 4-6, and is displayed in graphical placeholder areas when graphics are turned off, as shown in Figure 4-7. ALT tags also provide text for page reader tools, which read content to visitors with low vision.

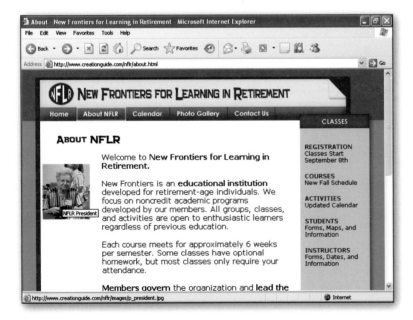

**Figure 4-6**  *An ALT label displaying image information in a pop-up window*

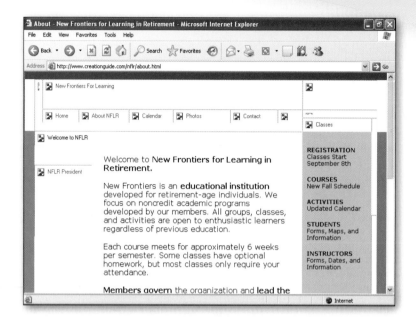

**Figure 4-7** *ALT labels displayed in graphic placeholders when graphics are turned off*

# Web *Site* Design Rules to Live By

Now that you've been inundated with good Web *page* design tactics, let's take a quick look at good Web *site* design techniques. Fortunately, good Web site design mostly involves applying good Web page design tactics across the board. Therefore, make sure that you use the following two Web site design theorems in conjunction with the numerous Web page design techniques presented earlier in this chapter.

As far as Web site design goes, our goal is to have you leave this section with two main Web site design concepts painlessly emblazoned in your mind—consistency and structure.

## Consistency

Web site consistency means that when visitors move from page to page throughout your site, they can visually see and intuitively grasp that they remain within your site. Viewers should recognize instantly when they've surfed to a page that's not yours. To create consistency, you use common design elements throughout your Web site, such as similar title bars, a consistent navigation bar, a universal color scheme,

**tip**   Remember, you should use templates and style sheets to help achieve consistency throughout your Web site, enabling users to gain an overview of the Web site as well as access to every link in the site. To see a site map in action, visit www.creationguide.com/sitemap.html.

standard graphical text styles, consistent body text fonts, and so forth. Most important, users should be able to find your pages' navigation tools and logo in approximately the same area on every page in your site.

As you can see, if you create solid home page and subpage templates, achieving site consistency is a snap; you've already taken care of all the "hard" work, such as devising color schemes, creating navigation bars, customizing title bars, and so on. The site simply needs to mold the template to your content's needs on each page.

## Structure

Similar to consistency is a site's structure. And one of the most important points about site structure is to have one! In other words, you should outline your site's structure up front (as described earlier in this chapter when we discussed framing and storyboarding) and stick to your building plans so that visitors won't get lost and turned around within your site. When creating structure, keep the following points in mind:

- Create a clean, logical structure. For most sites, you can aim to keep your site three clicks (or three levels) deep or less. (For example, see the framing example shown in Figure 4-1.)

- Ensure that your navigation links clearly outline your site's hierarchy. On larger sites, consider including a *site map*. Frequently, we click site map links whenever we visit a new site to quickly see what's offered. Ideally, your site should be so well-designed that visitors won't look for a site map, but a site map serves multiple purposes. Namely, a site map gives visitors a one-page table of contents, and it gives search engines a number of keywords to use to classify your Web site.

- Use page titles on every page. Further, make the home page's title text larger and ancillary page's titles slightly smaller to visually indicate the page's hierarchy.

Finally, before you test your site design knowledge, Kevin Martonick has generously summarized keys to good Web site design.

**tip**   A highly effective way to keep users informed of their location within your site's structure is to display title bars on each page that depict the page's content and to slightly modify navigation bar buttons to indicate the current page. Figures 4-9 and 4-11 in the next section show examples of modified buttons and page titles.

**lingo**   A *site map* is a Web page that shows all the links in a site in a hierarchical structure, enabling users to gain an overview of the Web site as well as access to every link in the site.

# Top 10+1 Tips for Great Web Design

Also available online, at www.creationguide.com/lists/greatwebdesign.html.

*Kevin Martonick* is a talented professional animator who has spent years creating artwork for online and digital media. Currently, Kevin is an animator at Cartoon Network, working his magic for the popular cartoon *Foster's Home for Imaginary Friends*. Before animating for television, Kevin created numerous online artwork and interactive pieces for online educational products and software. Based on his education and experience, Kevin has compiled some tips to pass along to you regarding what you can do to help create a visually effective and appealing Web site, especially in relation to effectively using graphics and buttons:

- **Draw from content.**   Content has a powerful influence on the look of your overall design—graphics and buttons included. After you decide on your content, draw from it for design ideas.

- **Organize by topic.**   Content decided on, pick an overall topic that everything else in your site relates to. Each page of the site should then hit on different aspects of the main topic. It might help to think of navigation buttons as a table of contents or an index that takes visitors to different pages of a book or more specific tables of contents.

- **Research successful designs.**   Look at other Web sites that you like or Web sites that have been nominated for design awards. What is it that you like about their graphics and buttons? How are they placed? Do they relate to the content and serve a purpose? Also research other media, such as CDs and record albums, books and magazines, to see how their designs work together as a cohesive whole.

- **Choose an overall theme.**   Content helps you to come up with an overall theme. This theme should act as a guideline for designing site elements, including buttons and graphics.

- **Design buttons and graphics wisely.**   Buttons and graphics contribute to the overall look of a site, so they must match the rest of the design. Decide on a color scheme for the buttons and their text as well as a background or border for pictures, drawings, and other graphics. If you decide to use two shades of the same color for a duotone look, or a gradient look, make sure that the colors come from your color palette. Another good way to think about buttons and graphics is to imagine them as a frame around a painting. In the same way you don't want the frame to overpower the artwork, you don't want the buttons and graphics to overpower your information—unless, of course, the buttons and graphics are the main point of your Web site.

- **Match design to function.**   Buttons and graphics should serve a purpose. In most cases, a close-up picture of Saturn's rings wouldn't quite suite a site about trees. And a button labeled Video Clip should take the user to a movie file, not a still image or a page of text.

- **Keep it simple.**   Keeping your site simple and avoiding clutter makes it easy to understand. Button titles should be short and descriptive. Display only the necessary information for each page that relates to its button's title. In the same way, use only graphics that are necessary and serve the purpose of the content.

- **Organize navigation from general to specific.**   Buttons that lead visitors from general subjects to more specific subjects are very helpful. A home page should have general buttons that send visitors to pages where they will find more specific links. For example, if you're creating a site to display a portfolio, you might start with a home page containing the buttons Résumé, Examples Of Work, Recommendations, Awards, and so forth. Each button might then take visitors directly to a page or subdirectory with content and links to more specific information.

- **Choose easy-to-read fonts.**   In most cases, fonts on buttons and under pictures should be easy to read and easy on the eyes. If you choose color fonts, make sure the color contrasts strongly with the background. Because of the many formatting options you have with fonts—such as boldface, italics, size, width, and color—you should keep to a minimum of two or three font families throughout your site. This will make it easier to keep everything related to your content and keep the user from being overwhelmed. In addition, if more than one font is used, make sure that the difference between the fonts is obvious to avoid confusion.

- **Test your work.**   *Always* test your work, and if you have really patient friends, have them test it as well. The creation process in Web production (much like all creative processes) is a matter of trial and error. If one idea doesn't work, try another. Often the best answer is the most simple and obvious one.

- **Plus 1: Be patient.**   Every problem has a solution. Sometimes it just takes time to figure out the answer; it could just be a matter of going off and doing something else for a while to clear your mind.

# Case Study

To wrap up this chapter, we present the original and redesigned versions of the New Frontiers for Learning in Retirement (NFLR) home page. (You can see online versions of this page and an About page at www.creationguide.com/nflr-old and www.creationguide.com/nflr-new.) The figure below shows the original and redesigned NFLR home pages. Compare the two pages, and identify the Web page and Web site design issues and modifications addressed in this chapter.

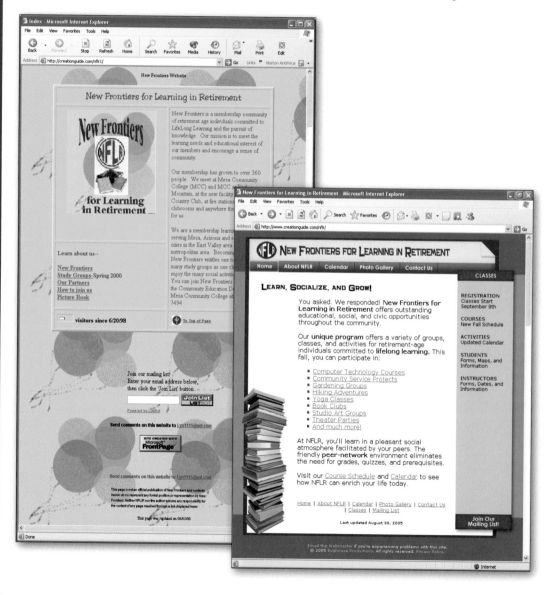

# check it!

- Remember that the audience reigns supreme—always design with a specific audience member in mind.
- Frame your site to show relationships among your Web pages—think structure, not content details.
- Storyboard your home page and subpages—think general layout.
- Keep the 800 × 600 computer screen resolution "safe area" in mind.
- Use templates, grids, and style sheets to guide your layout.
- Reserve your Web site's upper-left corner for your most important information.
- Display main concepts "above the fold."
- Include navigation links within the safe area.
- Incorporate a title area, a logo, navigation links, body text, and footer text into each Web page consistently throughout your site.
- Implement a color scheme, preferably limited to three or four colors. (Refer to a color wheel to find complementary colors.)
- Employ white space for visual relief and to draw attention to main elements on your page.
- Keep your navigation tools easily accessible, clearly defined, and consistent throughout your site.
- Link your logo to your home page throughout your site.
- Build credibility by providing contact information, channels of communication, and supplying attribution, credits, references, and a privacy policy.
- Use the default font size for body text, and stick with cross-platform fonts whenever possible.
- *Never* underline nonlinked text.
- Include ALT tags with every pertinent graphic.
- Create consistency throughout your site by repeating your color scheme, title text, navigation tools, and other page layout elements on every page of your site.
- Ensure that users can easily identify a clear and logical structure for your site.

# considering tools
## and stockpiling goods

# CHAPTER

# 5

Picture scoops of vanilla ice cream. One scoop is placed right into your hands without any utensils or toppings. The other scoop comes in a bowl with a spoon, some hot fudge, a sliced banana, a dollop of whipped cream, some sprinkles, and even a maraschino cherry to top it all off. Same ice cream—completely different dessert experience. All you need to create a satisfying dessert—or a Web site, for that matter—are the proper tools, a few supplies, and a little creativity.

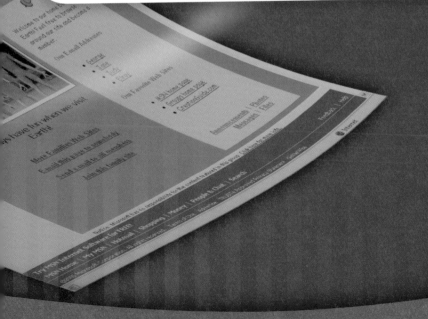

## Tools of the Trade

When you create a Web site, you need to have at least a couple (probably more) tools on hand. Mind you, we're not talking hardware—we're sure you've realized the importance of having a computer as well as possibly having access to a scanner, printer, and camera. In this chapter, our focus falls on the array of software that you can use to create, edit, and manipulate Web elements. As you'll see in Part Two, "The Walk—Creating Web Sites," you can create, edit, and publish Web sites by using a number of software applications and tools—we find that we frequently mix and match our weapons of choice. Likewise, knowing your choices will help you create a working environment that best suits your needs and personal style.

To get started, let's look at two of the most basic "tools" you'll need during your Web creation endeavors—an Internet connection and server space.

## Internet Connectivity and Server Space

No matter how astounding the Web site you've developed on your computer, it will live in virtual anonymity if you can't connect to the Internet and transfer the site's files to a server. (Recall from Chapter 1, "Demystifying Your [Future] Web Site," that a *server* is a powerful computer that is connected to the Internet's backbone data lines, stores Web files, and responds to users' requests to view the stored Web files.) You must be connected to the Internet or have access to an Internet connection before you can achieve an online presence. Granted, you can *create* most Web sites without an Internet connection, but you'll be dead in the water when it comes time to make your pages available online.

> **tip**   If you use your computer to surf the Web, rest assured—you have an Internet connection. Using a standard dial-up Internet connection, you can copy Web files from your computer onto a server that's connected to the Internet.

In addition to the basic prerequisite of Internet connectivity, you might need to pay for some space on a server for your Web files. We say *might* because, in a lot of cases, server space is freely given away or provided in addition to other paid services. For example, your Internet service provider (ISP) might give you 30 MB (give or take 20 MB) of free server space in addition to your Internet connection. The notion of *free server space* catches many people by surprise—but it's out there, and it's a thriving online practice. Not surprisingly, however, you'll find benefits in purchasing server space as well as using free space.

## Free Space Online

It's true. You can create and display a Web site at this very moment for free—as in no cost whatsoever. All you need to spend is a little time and creative effort (and we'll make your task even easier by showing you how to get your own blog started on MSN Spaces in Chapter 7, "Posting a Web Site Within an Hour [or So]"). You don't need any additional software or Internet accounts—nothing but your text and a few pictures, if you want to include them. Of course, you face a couple minor limitations when you take this approach (such as a long Web address, limited space, advertisements, and limited page-layout options), but depending on your ultimate goal and the free service you choose, the limitations might not affect you all that much. So consider yourself informed—free Web space is readily available; we run into more than a few people who are amazed to discover this fact.

The number-one way to become the proud owner of a free Web page is to turn to *blogging* (short for We*b* *logging*) sites and *online communities*. Blogging sites offer Web-based tools that help you publish a Web site instantly, and online communities are areas on the Web where people share information, often organized by topic. One of the benefits of creating a blog or joining an online community (other than the "free" factor) is that most blogging sites and online communities enable you to create Web sites by using templates and wizards. A couple popular free blogging sites are:

- Blogger (www.blogger.com).
- MSN Spaces (spaces.msn.com).

Some popular online communities include:

- Lycos Tripod (www.tripod.lycos.com).
- MSN Web Groups (groups.msn.com).
- Yahoo! GeoCities (geocities.yahoo.com).

As mentioned, in Chapter 7, we show you how to get started on the MSN Spaces blogging site so that you can create your own free Web site in a matter of minutes. Figure 5-1 shows the MSN Groups home page, which is another way you can build a Web presence online for free. Notice the partial categories list along the left side of the page.

**Figure 5-1**　*The MSN Groups home page*

The biggest drawbacks of blogs and online communities are that your Web address might be fairly long (for example, the address for the family group site shown in Figure 5-2 is groups.msn.com/TheVisitingFamily), you generally have a limited amount of server space, your choices of page layouts are usually limited or highly controlled, you'll have advertisements on your site, and if you don't want to use the templates, customizing your site can be tricky or not permitted.

Similar to online communities, another free way to get on the Web is to create site-specific pages. During your surfing, you might find that some Web sites offer free Web space to registered members. For example, you can create an About Me page on eBay (www.ebay.com) if you're a registered site participant. The purpose of eBay's About Me pages is to introduce eBay users to other people who visit eBay.

In addition to blogs, communities, and site-specific pages, you can get free space from numerous free hosting providers. As you might imagine, using a free hosting provider has benefits and drawbacks.

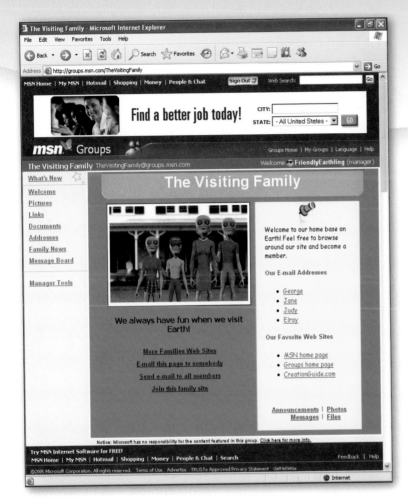

**Figure 5-2** *An MSN family group site*

The main benefits of free hosting providers are that they're inexpensive (free), they're quick and easy to use, they cater to all experience levels, and they provide just enough space for a basic site. Common drawbacks of free hosting providers usually are that they offer little or no support, they use overcrowded servers (which can cause slow downloads or server crashes that make your site temporarily unavailable online), they offer limited long-term reliability and fewer features (such as no e-mail addresses), and they post advertisements on your site. With that said, free hosting often provides a good way for you to practice setting up your first Web sites or short-term Web sites.

Yet another type of "free" online Web space—which technically isn't free—is Web space that you get from your ISP. Because you most likely cut a check to your ISP on a regular basis (or at least record an automatic payment), we can't exactly label ISP server space as free; it's more like prepaid, available space. When you signed up with your current ISP (assuming you have one), they probably informed you in an excited voice or a sentence ending in an exclamation point that you get "*X* megabytes of free server space!" At the time, you probably didn't know what that meant or didn't care, so you might have just thought "Oh, that's nice" and moved on to the next detail. Now that you're thinking of creating a Web site, you should revisit the "free server space" component of your ISP agreement. Most likely, you'll find that you have 10 MB to 50 MB of server space at your disposal.

The upside of ISP server space is that you're already paying for it, so you might as well use it. Another advantage that ISP server space has over blogging sites and online communities is that you generally have greater freedom regarding how you create and display your site (which, of course, could also be a disadvantage if you prefer to work with the preconfigured templates). The downside of ISP server space is that you'll probably have to live with a cumbersome Web address, similar to online community Web addresses. For example, a couple of our ISPs (we have several) grant "free" server space, but the Web addresses' formats are *www.ISPdomainname.com/~username/filename.html* and *members.ISPdomainname.net/username/filename.html*. For most people, the preceding naming formats are a little long and not easy to remember.

All in all, the main point about free online sites is that Web space is instantly available to you. And as long as you don't mind a longish Web address, some design limitations, and possibly advertising, free space is a great way to initiate yourself on the Web.

## Purchasing Server Space

In contrast to using free Web space, you can shell out a few clams for a Web site that uses the Web address of your choice as long as someone hasn't beaten you to the name. When you take this route, you have two main considerations—choosing and registering a Web address

**try this!**
To find free Web space, type **free "Web space"** in any search engine—you'll be rewarded with a slew of sites offering to host your page. Or check out the 100 Best Free Web Space Providers Web site, at www.100best-free-web-space.com. This site provides reviews and site rankings, which makes it a great resource for locating and reviewing free Web hosting services.

name (such as creationguide.com), and signing up with a provider that will host (or store) your Web site (unless you're going to run your own server—but that topic is best saved for more advanced books). Let's look at how to register a Web address and obtain a hosting service.

### Registering a Web address

Before we go any further, let's nail down some simple vocabulary. In particular, instead of *Web address*, we really should say *domain name*. Loosely speaking (very loosely), a domain name is a Web address. As you might know, all Web addresses are actually groups of numbers (called *Internet Protocol*, or IP, numbers) that serve as Internet addresses. Being a human, you probably also know that, for most people, remembering a meaningful name is much easier than remembering a series of numbers divided by dots. Therefore, the *Domain Name System* (DNS) came into existence. Fundamentally, DNS simply assigns textual names (such as creationguide.com) to numbered Internet addresses (such as 207.155.248.5). Thus, to appear as if you know what you're doing, you should use the term *domain name* in place of *Web address* when you're referring to a Web site.

When you're ready to obtain your own domain name, you can pick a domain name (such as creationguide.com—although we can tell you right now that the name is already taken), see whether it's available, and if it is, register the domain name as your very own for a nominal annual fee. By nominal, we mean anywhere from the price of a cheap meal or slightly more per year.

Choosing and registering a Web domain name is straightforward after you access a legitimate registration site. Fortunately, InterNIC (which is under the umbrella of the U.S. Department of Commerce) hosts a Web page that lists all the acceptable domain name registration Web sites. Many hosting sites also offer name registration services (as we'll discuss in the next section). To see the official list of domain name registrars, visit www.internic.net/alpha.html.

While visiting the InterNIC site, check a few registration sites to review their pricing schedules and policies (or visit www.creationguide. com/resources, and we'll link you to a couple of our favorite hosting services, which will register as well as host your site for you). When you've found a site you like, you can generally type your proposed domain name in a text box, and the site will then inform you whether the name is available. If it is, you work out a payment arrangement (usually by credit card), and the site registers your domain with InterNIC. Your next step is to find an ISP that will host your domain name and Web site.

## Finding space for your domain

If you don't run your own server—and most people don't—your next step is to find an ISP or a hosting service that's willing to provide a home for your domain name, if you didn't complete this step during your domain registration process (as described in the preceding section). You can find numerous hosting services online—type **Web hosting** in any search engine, and you can have a field day researching various Web hosting providers. Or better yet, visit hostindex. com, a comprehensive site devoted to providing information about numerous aspects of hosting services, including a monthly list of the top 25 hosts. Finally, as mentioned a moment ago, you can visit www. creationguide.com/resources for links to hosting services and domain name registrars.

Regardless of how you conduct your research into finding server space, remember to check a few key facts, including fees, network configuration, Microsoft FrontPage Server Extensions (if you're using FrontPage features, as discussed in Chapter 11, "Going All Out with FrontPage"), and reliability. On average, basic Web hosting services charge a nominal fee along with a one-time setup fee. (See each hosting service's Web site for specific prices.) Unless the rates seem outrageous, don't let the fees rule your decision. Before signing on with a Web hosting service, find out how the host handles the following features:

- **Bandwidth**   Most hosting companies are connected to the Internet by T1, T3, or OC3 (optical carrier) lines; anything less than a T1 and you might as well choose another company. Basically, a T1 line can carry up to 1.544 megabits of data per second (Mbps), a T3 line can carry 43.232 Mbps, and an OC3 line can carry 155 Mbps. For general Web browsing, hundreds of users can easily share a T1 line comfortably, but if all the users are all downloading MP3 or video files simultaneously, higher speed lines like T3 and OC3 would be more effective.

- **Clients per server**   In addition to Internet connection lines, you should check to see how many clients are hosted on each machine. If a hosting service overloads its machines, performance will be slow despite high-speed connection lines.

- **Space**   When you sign up for Web hosting services, ISPs and hosting companies assign you a certain amount of server space (just as your computer has a certain amount of disk space that you can use to store files). Most ISPs and hosting services offer more space on their servers than you'll need (at least initially). However, you should get at least 10 MB of server space. Most hosts provide at least 25 MB.

- **Support**   Technical support is an important element when you're choosing a Web hosting company—if you run into problems, you'll want to be able to turn to someone who can help. The most basic support consideration you should look for is the number of hours per day the technical support staff is available. Many sites offer 24 hours a day, seven days a week support, so look for round-the-clock support when you're weeding out potential companies. Round-the-clock support is important because you'll most likely be updating your pages during off-hours, so off-hours are the times you'll probably need support the most. Also see whether the site publishes its support response rate. Finally, check to see whether you can readily identify the avenues of support the company offers, including phone numbers (look for toll-free numbers), fax numbers, e-mail addresses, online informational reports, and a snail-mail address.

- **Extras**   You might want to check to see what "extras" each company offers to entice customers. For example, most hosting services provide e-mail accounts you can use with your domain name (such as mm@creationguide.com or jc@creationguide. com). You can generally set up anywhere from 5 to 40 or more e-mail accounts with a single Web hosting agreement. Other features you might check out include the cost of adding space to your site, in case your site grows larger than your originally allotted space; the cost of upping your traffic quota, in case more people visit your site than you anticipated; whether FrontPage Server Extensions (if you're using FrontPage) and streaming media are supported; and available add-on services, such as chat groups, e-commerce features, and site search features.

Now that you've considered your domain name, hosting services, and basic Web site options, we're ready to move closer to home and talk about desktop applications. In the next section, we look at software applications you can use on your system to create, edit, and publish Web sites.

## Web Site Creation and Management Tools

**tip**   You can download many of the applications (or demos of the applications) mentioned in this chapter from shareware sites such as www.tucows.com or www.shareware. com. *Shareware* can be best summed up as "try before you buy." When you download a shareware program, you try it out for a while for free. If you like it, you send the developer the requested fee. Too bad all merchandising isn't so user friendly!

In this section, we outline the types of tools you might need to create Web sites, name a few applications we've found helpful, and point you down the path of finding other utilities that best suit your needs. As you might imagine, because of the Web's booming popularity, lots of software vendors have created Web publishing tools. In this chapter, we introduce many tools (but nowhere near all the available utilities), and in Part Two, "The Walk—Creating Web Sites," we show you how to use some of them to create complete Web sites. Ultimately, though, you have the pleasure of choosing the software that feels most comfortable for you.

To simplify our approach in this chapter, we've divided basic Web page development tools into the following four main categories:

- Templates
- Web editors
- Graphics applications
- File Transfer Protocol (FTP) utilities

### Templates

If you create a Web presence using a blogging site or an online group, you'll most likely start by using templates to set up your site. A template is a preformatted page layout that incorporates graphical components, font styles, colors, and other design elements. Figure 5-3 shows the theme and layout templates you can choose from when you create an MSN Spaces blog. Templates are also available online and with software applications that you can use to design your Web pages. We introduce you to a few templates in Part Two.

Themes        Layout

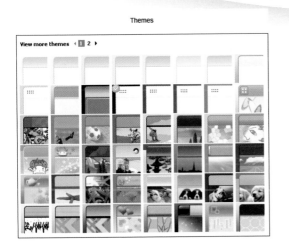

**Figure 5-3** *Using templates to select a theme and page layout style for an MSN Spaces blog*

## Web Editors

Overwhelmingly, when you create Web sites, you'll be spending the greatest amount of time interacting with a Web editor. You use Web editors to create Hypertext Markup Language (HTML) files, Extensible Hypertext Markup Language (XHTML), cascading style sheets (CSS), Extensible Markup Language (XML) documents, and other files that contain display instructions for Web browsers and provide content for your Web pages. When you use a Web editor, you have the option of working with a basic editor, in which you enter code manually; using a midrange editor that provides slightly more advanced Web development features; or using an advanced WYSIWYG (what you see is what you get—pronounced *wizzy-wig*) editor, which creates HTML code for you while you type text, insert images, and drag elements around in a Web design layout view. We take a quick look at all three types of editors in the next few pages.

**tip** You can search online to find hundreds of Web site templates, many of them free. Even if you don't use templates, you should spend some time looking at what's available. By perusing Web templates, you'll be able to see color combinations, page layouts, font styles, graphics, and design elements that you like (or don't like), which will help you make better design decisions when you create your custom designs.

## Basic Web editors

A basic Web editor is a text editor. When you use a text editor to create a Web page, you type in all the HTML commands and your Web page's text into a blank document. The most basic of the basic text editors is the Notepad application that comes with the Microsoft Windows operating system. Figure 5-4 shows Notepad containing some HTML text.

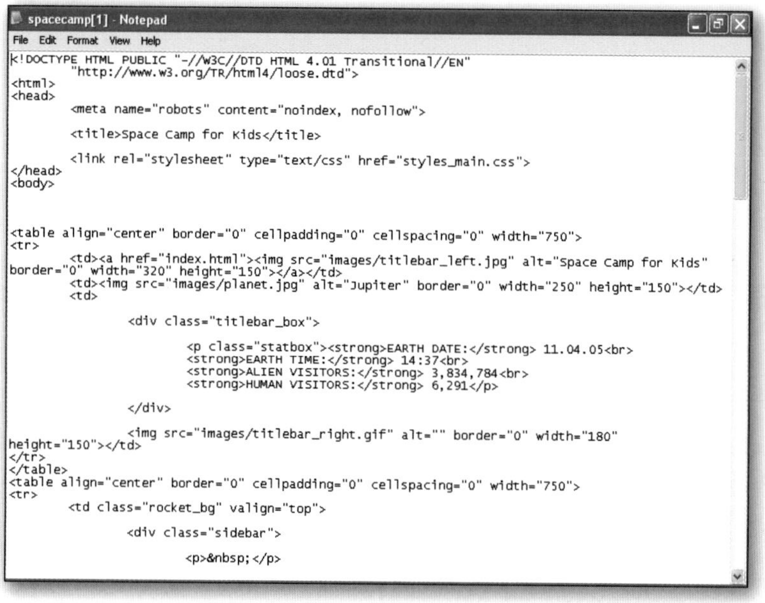


```
<!DOCTYPE HTML PUBLIC "-//W3C//DTD HTML 4.01 Transitional//EN"
        "http://www.w3.org/TR/html4/loose.dtd">
<html>
<head>
        <meta name="robots" content="noindex, nofollow">

        <title>Space Camp for Kids</title>

        <link rel="stylesheet" type="text/css" href="styles_main.css">
</head>
<body>


<table align="center" border="0" cellpadding="0" cellspacing="0" width="750">
<tr>
        <td><a href="index.html"><img src="images/titlebar_left.jpg" alt="Space Camp for Kids"
border="0" width="320" height="150"></a></td>
        <td><img src="images/planet.jpg" alt="Jupiter" border="0" width="250" height="150"></td>
        <td>

                <div class="titlebar_box">

                        <p class="statbox"><strong>EARTH DATE:</strong> 11.04.05<br>
                        <strong>EARTH TIME:</strong> 14:37<br>
                        <strong>ALIEN VISITORS:</strong> 3,834,784<br>
                        <strong>HUMAN VISITORS:</strong> 6,291</p>

                </div>

                <img src="images/titlebar_right.gif" alt="" border="0" width="180"
height="150"></td>
</tr>
</table>
<table align="center" border="0" cellpadding="0" cellspacing="0" width="750">
<tr>
        <td class="rocket_bg" valign="top">

                <div class="sidebar">

                        <p> </p>
```

**Figure 5-4** *Using Notepad as a basic Web editor*

You might wonder why Web developers would opt to manually code their Web pages. The answer varies, but for the most part, Web developers hand-code their Web pages for any of the following reasons:

- **Control** Hand-coding enables you to use the codes you want instead of the codes a WYSIWYG editor inserts. For example, you might want to use two blank line breaks, but a WYSIWYG editor might insert a paragraph marker. Furthermore, some WYSIWIG editors create "messy" code; hand-coding can keep code orderly and easy-to-read, with code alignment set to the developer's preferences.
- **Quick fixes** Knowing how to manually create and modify HTML, XHTML, CSS, and XML code enables Web designers to make quick changes to a Web site, regardless of how the Web

site was initially created. For instance, if you want to update your site's copyright date or title bar text, you could update and save the change in a text editor in less time than it would take to simply open the page in a WYSIWYG editor.

- **Code cleanup**   Many advanced Web editors (as discussed later in this chapter) add extra code to documents. If you know how to create and edit standard HTML, XHTML, CSS, and XML code, you can clean out extra code and reduce the size of your files. And remember—on the Web, size matters, and the smaller, the better. Furthermore, because Web editors are only designed by humans, at times, Web editors might miscode your page. In those instances, you can save yourself lots of time and aggravation by changing the code directly instead of hunting down the proper dialog box setting (if the setting even exists) in the Web editor.

- **Fine-tuning**   Another habit of advanced Web editors is that they sometimes use code that not all browsers support. You can use text editors to modify code so that it conforms to the capabilities of most browsers.

<aside>
**try this!**
Display www.creationguide.com/spacecamp (or any other Web page of your choice) in your browser, and then click **Source** on your browser's **View** menu. A Notepad document opens that displays a text version of the Web page's HTML code.
</aside>

Of course, learning HTML and XHTML (a stricter version of HTML based on XML principles) is a prerequisite to creating your pages in a text editor. In Chapter 8, "Demystifying Basic CSS and XHTML," we walk you through the process of hand-coding cascading style sheets and XHTML to give you an idea of how style sheets and XHTML work together to display Web sites. That chapter is just an introduction, however. You'll need to access additional resources if you really want to get serious about hand-coding Web sites.

The most popular text editors in use today include the following:

- **Notepad**   Notepad comes with the Microsoft Windows operating system and is about as bare-bones as it comes when you're talking about text editors.

- **TextWrangler** (www.barebones.com/products/textwrangler) TextWrangler is a basic text editor designed by Bare Bones Software for Macintosh computers.

- **WordPad**   WordPad is a step up from Notepad. It offers more word-processing features than Notepad, and it supports longer documents. Figure 5-5 shows an HTML document in WordPad.

**Figure 5-5**  *Using WordPad as a Web editor*

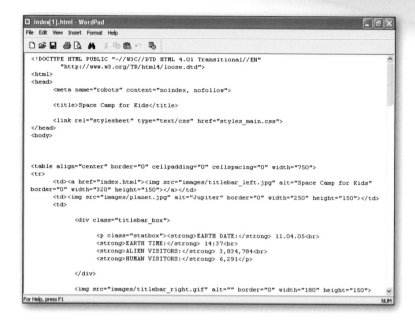

## Midrange Web editors

Midrange Web editors are one step up from basic text editors, and they include a number of time-saving and accuracy-assisting features. In this group, you'll often find applications that provide Web-coding-specific features, such as tag inspectors, tag generators, color coding, large file support, and more. Some of these editors start to enter the realm of WYSIWYG (such as Microsoft Word and Microsoft Publisher), but their main draw is that these programs include features designed to help you create HTML, CSS, XHTML, and related Web code. In this category, we recommend a few applications. You should test a couple to find which one feels most comfortable for you:

- **BBEdit** (www.barebones.com/products/bbedit)   This HTML editor from Bare Bones Software is popular among Macintosh Web developers. BBEdit enables you to edit, search, transform, and manipulate text.

- **HomeSite** (www.macromedia.com/software/homesite) Macromedia's HomeSite is a popular code-only Web design tool used by many professional Web developers. You can download a 30-day trial version to test the product.

- **NoteTab** (www.notetab.com)  The NoteTab editor by Fookes Software is Notepad on steroids (lots of them!). You can download NoteTab light for free, or purchase NoteTab Standard or NoteTab Pro to gain additional functionality.

- **sciTE** ( www.scintilla.org/SciTE.html)  The sciTE editor is a SCIntilla-based free text editor that provides a clean and easy-to-use interface for HTML, CSS, XML, and many other coding languages.

- **TextPad** (www.textpad.com)  TextPad, created by Helios Software Solutions, serves as another beefed-up text editor.

- **Word and Publisher** (www.microsoft.com)  Word and Publisher enable you to use a familiar interface to create Web documents via the Save As command. When you save an Office document as a Web page, the application automatically creates the HTML, CSS, XML, or other relevant source code. Chapter 9, "Diving into Design with Publisher Templates," shows you how to create a Web site using Microsoft Office Publisher, and Chapter 10, "Swimming Deeper Into Web Waters with Word and XML," shows you how to use Word to create an informational Web site. Figure 5-6 shows a Web page in Word's Page Layout view as well as in the HTML Source view.

**Figure 5-6**  *Web Layout and HTML Source views of a Web page created in Word (with a WordArt title)*

> **note**  Similar to Word and Publisher, other Microsoft Office programs—such as Excel and PowerPoint— enable you to save your files as Web pages or XML documents. In Chapter 9, you learn how to create a Web site and newsletter using Publisher, and in Chapter 10, you create a Web site using Word. One point you should keep in mind is that Office applications are useful for creating simple Web sites and editing simple Web pages that were created using a particular Office application. Office applications do not always work as well when you attempt to edit more advanced sites or Web sites created in applications other than those in Microsoft Office.

### Advanced Web editors

The third and final group of Web editors includes the advanced applications that enable you to create and edit Web pages by using graphical interfaces. In advanced editor applications, you can view and edit source code directly as well as work in the WYSIWYG interface. Further, most advanced editors provide a preview feature, which enables you to view how a Web page will be displayed online (sometimes in various browsers) before you view the page in your browser as well as other advanced tools, as you'll discover in the walkthrough project in Chapter 11, "Going All Out with FrontPage." Popular advanced Web editors are well documented online, so instead of wasting page space here summarizing online statistics, we've provided pertinent URLs for the Web sites that offer the applications appearing in our short list. Although other editors are readily available, the following applications are some of the most popular Web development programs around:

- Adobe GoLive (www.adobe.com/products/golive)
- CoffeeCup HTML Editor (www.coffeecup.com/html-editor)
- Macromedia Dreamweaver (www.macromedia.com/software/dreamweaver)
- Microsoft FrontPage (office.microsoft.com)
- NetObjects Fusion (www.netobjects.com/products/html/nof8.html)

Of the preceding applications, Dreamweaver is probably the most popular (yet most challenging to learn) Web editor among professionals for a number of reasons, including its support for the latest developments in Web technologies, advanced scripting and authoring, and integration with other Macromedia development tools. On the other hand, FrontPage (shown in Figure 5-7) is the easiest advanced HTML editor for beginners to learn and provides many of the advanced features offered by Dreamweaver. Further, FrontPage is also popular with the business community. As we mentioned, you'll get a feel for creating a Web site in FrontPage in Chapter 11.

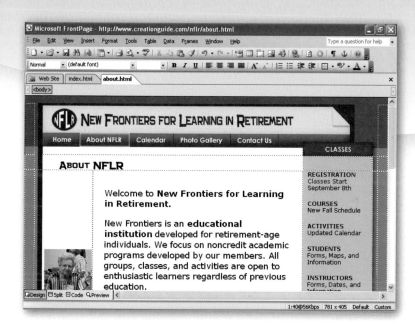

**Figure 5-7** *Microsoft FrontPage's WYSIWYG design view*

## Graphics Applications

When it comes to Web site development, graphics applications come in a strong second behind the all-important text or Web editor. After all, most sites use graphics, and you'll want to either create or tweak the graphics you use on your Web site. Therefore, you'll need to have a graphics package installed on your system. Our personal favorites are Corel Paint Shop Pro and Adobe Photoshop (or Photoshop Elements)—both appear in the graphics application list that you're about to run into after the next paragraph.

Regardless of your graphics package, the five main skills you'll need to acquire when using a graphics program are cropping, cutting, resizing, recoloring, and saving as a different file format. So check your application's help files to brush up on your technique. Now, here are some popular graphics programs along with their Web addresses:

● **Fireworks** (www.macromedia.com/software/fireworks)    This application is easy to use and especially convenient when you need to create buttons and other basic Web site graphics. Macromedia developed Fireworks specifically for creating Web graphics.

- **LView Pro** (www.lview.com)    LView Pro is a popular shareware graphics program that includes typical graphic features as well as Web page utilities

- **Paint**    Microsoft Paint is a graphics program that comes with Microsoft Windows. Paint is a scaled-down graphics package, but it serves as a handy graphics tool when you're in a pinch.

- **Paint Shop Pro** (www.corel.com)    Paint Shop Pro is an affordable, all-purpose graphics program used by many designers. Visit the Corel Web site to download a free trial demo. Figure 5-8 shows a Web site we created mocked up in Paint Shop Pro.

**Figure 5-8**  *Viewing a mocked-up version of a Web site in Paint Shop Pro before building the site*

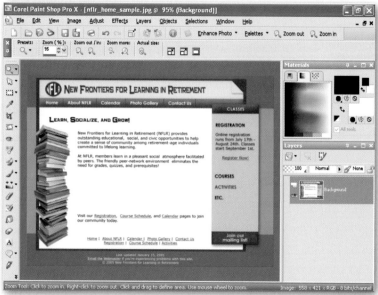

**note**    The newest kid on the Web graphics block is Microsoft's Expressions Suite. Be prepared to hear a lot more about this graphics package in relation to Web development. You can edit both vector-based and pixel images in the Acrylic program, which is part of the suite.

- **Photoshop** (www.adobe.com/products/photoshop)    Photoshop is probably the leading image-editing program. It can be a little tricky to use when you're first learning it, but once you get the commands mastered, you'll be highly satisfied with the application's flexibility.

- **Photoshop Elements** (www.adobe.com/products/photoshopelwin for Windows, or www.adobe.com/products/photoshopelmac for Macintosh)    Photoshop Elements is a photo editing software application for consumers. For Web developers, Photoshop Elements includes a Save For Web optimizing feature that you can use to resize and compress images for your Web sites.

In addition to the preceding graphics applications, you can also use illustration programs to create *vector-based graphics*. In a vector-based graphic, you can move, resize, and otherwise manipulate an image's elements (such as moving an entire shape around within an image). Vector-based illustration programs that frequently come in handy when creating Web pages include Adobe Illustrator (www.adobe.com/products/illustrator), Macromedia Freehand (www.macromedia.com/software/freehand/), and CorelDraw (www.corel.com).

> **lingo** *Vector-based graphics* are images made with lines and shapes instead of shaded computer pixels.

## FTP Utilities

Last but not least, you might need one of those mysterious FTP utilities. Actually, FTP utilities aren't at all mysterious, but whenever we mention "FTP" to people, the color drains from their faces. Basically, FTP utilities are programs that allow you to copy files and directories from your computer to another computer across the Internet. For example, whenever we complete a chapter of this book, we FTP the chapter's graphics to Microsoft Learning in Redmond, Washington, even though we're just down the hill a bit, in beautiful Portland, Oregon.

You can find numerous FTP programs online, many of which are shareware or freeware programs. Popular FTP programs include the following:

- BulletProof FTP (www.bpftp.com)

---

**try this!**
If you want to include an animated GIF on your Web site but you aren't itching to build one from scratch, you'll be glad to hear that Microsoft Office XP includes a number of small animations that you can use on Web pages. To insert an animated GIF:

1 Open Word (or other Office application), and on the **Insert** menu, click **Picture**, and then click **Clip Art**.

2 In the Clip Art task pane, search for a clip art item, and double-click an item that is displayed with a gold star in the lower-right corner.

3 To see the animation in action, on the **File** menu, click **Web Page Preview**.

As we've suggested before, insert animated components in moderation. Animation can quickly become overly distracting, which will detract from your page rather than add to its appeal.

- CoffeeCup Direct FTP (www.coffeecup.com/free-ftp)
- CuteFTP (www.globalscape.com/cuteftp)
- Fetch (www.fetchsoftworks.com)

Now that you know vaguely what FTP programs do and that you can download them from the Web, don't worry too much about them. At this point, knowing that they exist is enough—if you're really gung ho, you can download an FTP application so that you're ready to upload pages after you create them, but you don't need to do that now. We help you out with FTP programs and file management later in this book, in Part 3. But before we do that, we want to finish our discussion in Part 1 as well as tackle the fun stuff in Part 2, "The Walk—Creating Web Sites."

## A Bit About Browsers

> **tip**  No two browsers (or browser versions) process Web code in exactly the same way. Therefore, view the Web pages in as many browsers as possible before publishing your site.

We'd be completely remiss if we wrapped up this chapter without addressing the most obvious software application tool of all—a browser. You need to have a browser (or a few browsers) installed on your computer so that you can preview your pages before you publish them online. Remember that browsers are applications that interpret Web files. Unfortunately, not all browsers interpret Web files in exactly the same way. Therefore, a page you design and then view in Microsoft Internet Explorer could very easily be displayed as a shocking mess in another browser. Even well-designed pages appear slightly differently in various browsers.

Some of the ways Web pages can look different in various browsers include the following:

- Default bullet styles vary in size and fill. For example, the bullets on Internet Explorer and Safari are slightly bolder than the bullets in Firefox.

> **tip**   You probably won't need to use an FTP program if you're creating a blog or an online community Web page. Further, you can use the My Network Places feature in Windows to transfer files from your computer to your server space. Eventually, though, you might need to use an FTP utility to delete, copy, and otherwise manage online files. In Chapter 11, "Going All Out with FrontPage," and Chapter 12, "Sending Web Pages into the Real World," we fill you in on the details of online file management, where you'll see that being comfortable with FTP applications and My Network Places can come in handy.

- Margin spacing (or offset) around page perimeters varies. For example, Internet Explorer tends to leave more margin space at the top by default than other browsers.

- Default font size is smaller on Windows than on Macintosh, which means that text wraps differently on Macintosh systems than on Windows-based systems.

- Because text wraps differently in different browsers, varying amounts of information appears "above the fold."

- Browser window widths vary due to toolbar and scroll bar widths.

A number of browsers exist on the Web. You might or might not want to verify that your pages are displayed appropriately in all browsers out there. For most designers, ensuring that pages are displayed properly in the biggies—Internet Explorer and Firefox—is plenty; combined, these two browsers account for over 90 percent of all browsers accessing the Internet. Of course, you must always consider your audience. If you *know* your viewers will be using Safari browsers, you better ensure that your page looks good in Safari. For edification purposes, here's a short list of browsers you can find lurking on the Web:

- AOL Explorer (downloads.channel.aol.com/browser)
- Apple Safari (www.apple.com/macosx/features/safari)
- Microsoft Internet Explorer (www.microsoft.com/windows/ie)
- Mozilla Firefox (www.mozilla.org)
- Netscape (browser.netscape.com/ns8)
- Opera (www.opera.com)

Previewing your Web site simply entails displaying your Web documents in a browser window locally—so the process is quick and simple. Most important, though, you should ensure that you have access to at least one version (Windows or Macintosh) of Internet Explorer and Firefox for testing and previewing purposes. Don't worry—we'll remind you a few more times in Part Two about the importance of previewing your Web pages in more than one browser as well as in more than one version of each browser, if possible.

**note** Although cross-platform fonts—Arial, Comic Sans, Courier, Georgia, Times New Roman, Trebuchet (MS), and Verdana—are displayed on both Windows-based and Macintosh systems, their default sizes vary, with the fonts consistently displayed smaller on the Macintosh.

**tip** To see which browsers other readers are using, visit www.creationg.guide/2cents and view the results for the Web Browsers poll.

# Tracking Tools   While browser statistics are readily available online, you can gather your own browser and visitor statistics for the sites you build. To do this, you use tracking tools, which tell you how many people visit and how visitors view your site. Knowing these types of details can help you make informed design decisions.

Some common statistics gathered by tracking tools include time zones, languages, monitor resolutions, and color depths. Sometimes, you can see how many visitors' computers support JavaScript, style sheets, and other technologies. Often, you can see how long visitors stay on each page, which pages visitors view most, and which pages visitors view last before they leave your site (which sometimes indicates a design flaw).

Many hosting services provide some logging capabilities and tracking services. In addition, we recommend Site Meter (www.sitemeter.com), a free tracking tool that you can add to a Web site. To view Site Meter in action, click the rainbow-colored square located at the bottom of this book's companion Web site, at www.creationguide.com.

## Web Extras

In addition to the standard tools we introduce in this chapter, which are necessary to create Web sites, loads of other applications and tools are available to create added functionality. For instance:

- If you want to include multimedia elements such as movies, audio, and animations, you need special programs to develop those.

- If you want to include payment services, you need to find secure payment options and applications, such as PayPal (www.paypal. com) and VeriSign (www.verisign.com).

- If you want to dynamically display text from content services, you might need to work with custom interface utilities.

- If you want to supply information from databases, you need a database to handle the information.

The preceding list of Web tools is just the tip of the iceberg, and many of these topics are deserving of a book of their own. With that said, we're all for introducing you to as much as we can fit into this book.

You don't need to collect tools for advanced Web features yet. The goal here is to help you gather basic tools for getting a custom Web site online—Internet connectivity, server space, a Web editor, a graphics program, a file transfer application, and a browser or two.

# check it!

- You need Internet connectivity and server space to display a Web site online.
- You'll find that free Web space is readily available online, particularly on blogging and online group sites, or you can purchase a domain name and buy server space to have full control over your Web site and Web address.
- You can use templates and Web editors to create Web sites. Web editors range from all-text programs to midrange coding applications to advanced WYSIWYG interfaces.
- Graphics applications enable you to create Web graphics, edit pictures, and create mock-ups of future Web pages.
- You can find GIF animators, banner creation sites, button creators, and image map utilities online (in addition to lots of other freeware and shareware programs) and as part of graphics programs.
- FTP programs and the My Network Places feature enable you to copy files from your computer to a remote computer.
- Not all browsers are created equal—different browsers display the same Web files in various ways, so you should always view your Web pages in Internet Explorer and Firefox (at least) before publishing your Web site online.
- Tracking tools help you learn how visitors view your pages, which can help you make informed design decisions.
- Many tools are available that enable you to add functionality to your Web sites, including multimedia features, shopping utilities, databases, and so forth.

# planning
## your attack

# 6

Let's say you decide that you're more than ready for a relaxing beach vacation. Most likely, your first thoughts turn to money—so you set a budget and figure out how much you'll need to save or whether your vacation money stash can cover your expenses. Next you choose a destination and reserve a beach house. Then you purchase plane tickets, line up a rental car, and promise yourself that you'll exercise more regularly so that you'll look great on the beach. Finally, maybe a few months later, you pack your bags, including at least one new bathing suit, take care of minutiae so that your mailbox won't overflow and your pets won't starve, and as a result of your careful planning and preparation, take off to enjoy a most deserved ocean-side escape. Planning a Web site follows the same pattern (without the added exercise workouts, of course)—you start with the "big picture" goal and work down to the details.

# Building a Case for Planning

Now that you're overflowing with Web-centric knowledge from Chapters 1 through 5, we're going to walk you through a Web site planning process. You're aware of all the elements you need to consider; now it's just a matter of consolidating the information into some concrete review questions and checklists. As you've probably heard throughout your life, a little planning up front can save more than a few headaches down the road. Not surprisingly, this philosophy holds true with Web development as well—a little preparation and forethought go a long way toward smoothly achieving success on the Web.

You might have noticed that this is the final chapter in Part 1. We hope that you'll see this chapter as a bridge between Web theory and practice. In Part 1, we've covered a lot of Web design basics; in Part 2, you'll have a chance to apply what you've learned to hands-on exercises in which you'll be creating the overall structure of five Web sites (one per chapter).

In Part 2, you can either re-create the Web sites exactly as we describe or use the sample Web sites as templates for custom pages. For each Web site we present in Part 2, we summarize the planning process we completed before we created the actual site. We also tell you where the project is taking you in terms of your hands-on site development practice. If you're going to customize any of the Web sites we've included as samples, you'll need to do some custom planning as well. But here again, we help you get started by giving you customization tools, such as modified style sheets and templates. Eventually, after you've graduated beyond this book (and we have every confidence you will), you'll need to conduct your own planning sessions. Therefore, we designed this chapter to clearly outline each planning stage succinctly and in an easy-to-reference format. We even include a 10+1 list of tips from a successful professional creative director. In the future, if you're ever stumped about setting goals for your Web site, defining your audience, framing your Web site, or storyboarding your Web pages, grab this book off your shelf and turn to this chapter to help jump-start your thought processes.

To help illustrate the planning process, let's look at the evolution of the Curiosity Shoppe Web site. Figure 6-1 shows the final version of the shop's home page (www.creationguide.com/shoppe), a sample sub-page (the main Products page), and a sample product detail page (the Jen Wali ceremonial mask page). In the upcoming sections, we address some of the issues we considered when planning the Curiosity Shoppe Web site and explain what impact our decisions about those issues had on the final design. But first, take a look at the Top 10+1 List for Successful Web Site Planning. In this chapter, we show you how to put many of the list items into action.

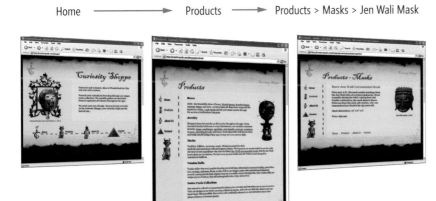

Home ⟶ Products ⟶ Products > Masks > Jen Wali Mask

**Figure 6-1** *The Curiosity Shoppe home page, sample Products page, and sample product detail page (also available online, at www. creationguide.com/shoppe)*

# Top 10+1 Tips for Successful Web Site Planning

Also available online, at www.creationguide.com/lists/webplanning.html

*Justin Garrity* is the creative director at PopArt, Inc., (www.popart.com) and past creative director of an educational online software development group. His portfolio overflows with Web development success, and there's a reason his job titles always seem to include words like *creative* and *director*. He's one of those multitalented types who is creative and technologically savvy—a great manager who naturally motivates and leads, always gets the job done, and genuinely cares.

Lucky for you, Justin tapped into his professional and educational background to pull together the following tips for successfully planning a Web site:

- **Content is everything**.   Think of a Web site like a book or a magazine. Without a story, the cover and layout do not add up to much.

- **Capture key use cases**.   Think of the types of visitors who will visit your Web site, and write down tasks that each type would probably try to accomplish. As you create your Web site, refer back to these use cases.

- **Create a site map**.   Organize the pages of your site like you organize files on your computer, by page type. Make sure you think about how your site will probably grow over time and organize for that growth.

- **Build a text-only version first**.   Before messing around with the design, imagery, animation, or font styles, build a simple plain-text-only version of the site first. This will help you focus on the content and how the site "reads." Don't get distracted with visual design until the text on the site is ready.

- **Simplify the language**.   Don't say things like, "Click here to read more about turtles," just give the subject matter of the link, "Turtles."

- **The menu should mirror the site map**.   The main menu of the site should reflect the highest level of folders/pages on the site map.

- **Embedded links should follow the use cases**.   While the menu follows the site structure, the embedded links within the content of each page should follow the use cases.

- **Tables are for tables, not for layout**.   Use cascading style sheets for layout. Stay away from using invisible tables to arrange the elements on the page. Using cascading style sheets reduces file size and centralizes all of the layout information about the Web site.

- **Each page is a table of contents**.   Each page is a way to get to another page. Prevent each page from becoming a dead end.

- **Unify the brand**.   If the Web site is for a business, align the site with the messaging and visual style of offline materials (*collateral*), like business cards and brochures.

- **Plus 1: Content is everything**.   Wait, did I already say that? It's true. Focus on the content, and everything else is just frosting.

# Defining Your Goals

Before you create a Web site, you must first step back, survey your concept, and isolate your intent. In other words, you need to clearly consider your goals and your site's purpose. To do this, you need to answer the following questions:

- Why do I want a Web site?
- What are my immediate goals for my Web site?
- What are my long-term goals for my site?
- What is my timeline?

By answering the preceding questions, you start the process of focusing on your content. For the Curiosity Shoppe site, the answers to these questions were fairly straightforward. First, the Curiosity Shoppe owners wanted to make their shop easily accessible to more customers through an online presence. The owners' immediate goals were to inform people about the store, provide a means of contact, and advertise their products and store location. Their long-term plans are to offer their entire line of products for sale online, update the home page daily with a featured item, and provide an online newsletter and mailing list. Finally, the owners' timeline can be summarized like this: static site online (*live*) within 2 months of the home page's inception, sales feature fully functional within 6 months after original site has gone live, and a full line of online products available within 12 months from the date the initial home page went live.

Most likely, your goals and timeline will be less complex than those of the Curiosity Shoppe. For example, your goals might simply be to create an online résumé and have your résumé go live by next month, with updates occasionally added as necessary.

# Getting to Know Your Audience

After you've outlined your goals for your site, you need to consider who's going to be visiting your site. In other words, you need to think about your audience. You must have at least some perception of the people you want to visit your Web space. You need to address this

**tip**   After you've interviewed and surveyed people, assimilated feed-back, and sum-marized your data, remember to specifically visualize a real-live audience person instead of a generic profile while you create and de-sign your Web site.

**try this!**   Look at Figure 6-1, and try to imagine how the Curiosity Shoppe's owners answered the "Analyzing Your Audience" questions.

planning step early in the process because, as mentioned in Chapter 4, "Mastering Web Design Basics," many design and content decisions are based on your audience.

The best way to get to know your audience is to talk to them, if possible. Consider interviewing or surveying the people who will view your pages. For example, if you're creating a school site, survey students, teachers, administrators, and families by taking advantage of established communication channels, such as e-mail lists, news-letters, flyers, parent-teacher organizations, announcement boards, school newspapers, and so forth.  Once you get the ball rolling, you'll often quickly collect plenty of ideas and suggestions regarding what your audience would like to see on the site. In addition, consider how users will be connecting to your page. Are they occasional Web surfers with dial-up connections? If so, keep your page sizes small and your layouts fairly simple. Are you designing a site for online gamers? Then take advantage of high-speed connections and cutting-edge technolo-gies. Designing for kids? Bright colors work well if they're younger; edgier X-Games-style graphics would be better for older kids. You get the idea. To help analyze your audience, answer the following ques-tions, which are also available online, at www.creationguide.com/lists/audience.html, in case you want to print them out and record your answers for your own site.

# Analyzing Your Audience

Also available online, at www.creationguide.com/lists/audience.html.

- **Who makes up the core of my target audience?**   Customers, students, employees, extended family members, snowboarders, bird watchers, hipsters, realtors, musicians, kindred spirits, activists, neighbors, marathon runners, wine collectors, club members, kayakers, artists, or…?

- **What does my audience want to find out from my site?**   Note that this is different from asking yourself what *you* want to tell your audience. Listen to prospective site users so that you can design accordingly and make your site relevant to them. (Remember to use the language of "you.")

- **How experienced with the Web are the members of my audience?**   Novices, casual Web surfers, cyberspace champions, or…? Experienced users can frequently figure out "what's going on" in complex or uniquely designed sites, but beginning users generally require more guidance. For example, if you're catering to beginning surfers, you should make it a point to clearly and consistently identify the site's navigation elements.

- **What types of Internet connections and bandwidth capabilities will audience members have?**   Dial-up, an internal corporate network (called an *intranet*), a high-speed connection such as DSL (digital subscriber line) or cable, or...? Bandwidth speeds affect how you design your Web site, including the types of elements you'll incorporate. (If you've ever viewed a cable company's home page for members, you'll see maximum design for high-speed Internet connections.) For example, if you're certain that your viewers will be accessing your Web site on high-speed connections, you'll be freer to include video clips and numerous graphics with a minimal risk of losing viewers. If you include video and numerous graphics on a Web site accessed by users with dial-up connections, however, you'll risk losing those viewers before your site is displayed because they'll understandably get tired of waiting for the large elements to be downloaded.

- **Where is my core audience located?**   At work, on campus, in home offices, in living rooms, at cybercafés, in your neighborhood, or...? This specification relates closely to the preceding question—if you know where your core audience is located, you'll most likely get a good feel for the types of connections they'll be using to access your site. Further, location can come into play if you're designing a regional site versus a national or an international site. For example, a Johnny Depp site might have an international audience, whereas your Annual Pirate Party site would probably cater mostly to your friends or neighborhood (or surrounding geographic area if your Pirate Party is especially notorious). This differentiation is similar to the variations of information found in a newspaper's front-page section, which would correspond to a nationally or internationally focused Web site, compared to the local section, which would correspond to a locally oriented Web site.

- **What's the typical age group among audience members?**   Appeal to the general age group you're targeting. This question is rooted in common sense—whether you like it or not, you can make some minor sweeping, albeit conservative, assumptions based on your audience's age, and these assumptions can help you throughout the Web page creation process. Knowing your audience's typical age (*typical* being the key word) helps you to make appropriate design decisions. For example, preteen bubblegum-pink backgrounds usually don't work well on sports sites that target 18-to-40-year-old males (although a case could be made for the swimsuit edition). Furthermore, age parameters help you to choose words—particularly slang and colloquialisms—wisely, such as whether to "dude" or not to "dude." In addition, age information enables you to create meaningful metaphors—for example, will retirees really know (or care) what it feels like to get kicked in the head in a mosh pit? Finally, age specifics can help you determine the types of information you'll include on your Web pages. For example, if you're creating a kids' site, you wouldn't feature AARP information, but you might seriously consider addressing the "Harry Potter vs. Eragon" debate.

- **How will audience members find out about my site?**   Word of mouth, online directories, hard-copy Web directories or phone books, links from a "parent" page, search engines, paid commercial advertisements on TV or radio, business collateral, or...?  Thinking about how visitors will find your site helps you to identify how to advertise and publicize your site.

# Audience Personalities   Even though you clearly define your
audience to yourself, you still need to cater to differences among your audience members' personalities. You can do this by providing a variety of ways visitors can read and navigate through your site. According to *Persuasive Online Copywriting*, by Bryan Eisenberg, Jeffrey Eisenberg, and Lisa T. Davis (Wizard Academy Press, 2005), the four main audience types and their approaches to information are:

- **Amiable**   An amiable audience member values authenticity, a personal touch, friendliness, and furthering a unique identity. This audience type appreciates Web sites that address values and provide assurances rather than a litany of plain cold-hard facts. Amiable types most often seek answers to the question, *Why?*

- **Analytical**   An analytical audience member values organization, task completion, facts, hard data, information, and documentation of proof. This audience type is very businesslike, wants to solve problems, and requires you to provide hard evidence and validation. Analytical types most often ask, *How?*

- **Expressive**   An expressive audience member wants to belong, feel useful, fulfill a responsibility, and care for others in creative and entertaining ways. This audience type appreciates testimonials, true tales, and incentives. Expressive types most often seek answers to the question, *Who?*

- **Assertive**  An assertive audience member wants to understand, control life, learn constantly, and face challenges. This audience type is goal oriented and appreciates options, probabilities, and challenges. Assertive types most often seeks answers to the question, *What?*

When you design your Web site, make sure your design and content speak to all of your audience's personality types. At a minimum, ensure that your site answers *Why?*, *How?*, *Who?*, and *What?* on every page in some way.

# Drawing the Blueprints for Your Site

After setting your goals and defining your audience, you're ready to frame your Web site. If possible, your first step should always be to collect your content before you design. As we asserted in Chapter 2, "Composing and Shaping Web Text," organizing your content—or at least its main concepts—helps you to organize your overall site in a logical manner. Beginning now, you should work toward piecing together the framework of your site by connecting pages and ideas logically through word-based associations. Figure 6-2, on the next page, shows a framework with a slightly more advanced setup using actual file names instead of just words and descriptive phrases.

After you gather the main types of information you want to include in your site (don't worry—your text and graphics don't have to be polished at this point), you need to figure out how best to present your information. For example, you can organize your site in any number of ways, including the following:

- Alphabetically
- Chronologically
- Graphically
- Hierarchically
- Numerically
- Randomly (not recommended—but it's out there)
- Topically

**Figure 6-2** *Framing the Curiosity Shoppe site, including directories and files used within the initial site*

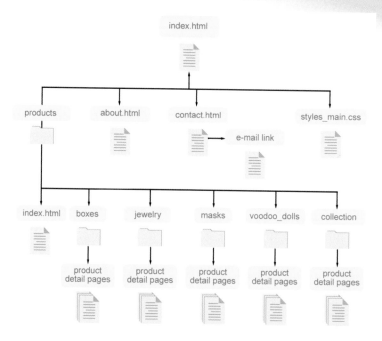

By far, most sites are organized hierarchically. A hierarchical site presents a home page that contains catchy introductory text and links to the site's main pages. This setup is widely used by designers and greatly appreciated by users who mostly just want to *use* Web sites—not figure out how they're organized.

Another critical (although certainly less exciting) aspect of organizing your site involves naming your files. After all, when you boil it all down, your site is entirely made up of files—so organizing your site must include systematizing your files. Before we get to the Site Planning Checklist, let's take a look at some file-naming practices that you can mull over now and implement later.

## Keeping Your Files in Line

As you now know, Web pages usually consist of a few files working together to create the appearance of a single page. Further, a Web site consists of multiple Web pages, which in turn consist of multiple files. Because of this multifile nature of Web pages and Web sites, you're going to have to come up with a plan for naming and organizing your Web site's files. (In Part Two, we explain how we've organized each project site's files, so you'll have lots of chances to get the hang of naming and organizing files before the end of this book.) For the most part, a standard Web site can consist of the following simple structure:

- **Main directory**   Contains Web files (.html, .htm, .xml, .css, .xsl, .pdf, .doc, and so forth), an images directory, and subdirectories (if any). You can provide any name for this directory when designing your pages on your local machine. When you upload your pages to a hosting service, you'll probably place the main directory folder's contents into your top-level online folder (named Web, or some other basic name provided by your hosting service) and copy the entire images folder (folder and all) into the folder.

- **Images directory**   Contains the .gif, .jpeg, .jpg, and .png image files used on your Web site. This directory is usually stored within the main directory.

Figure 6-3 illustrates a typical Web site's file and directory structure.

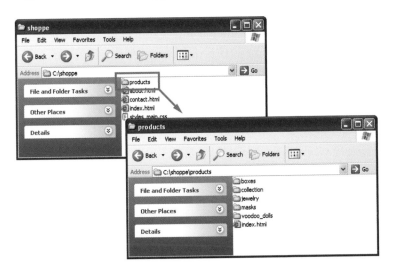

**Figure 6-3**  *Directories and files for the Curiosity Shoppe Web site stored in a local directory*

Notice in Figure 6-3 that the main directory currently holds one cascading style sheets file (styles_main.css), three HTML files (about. html, contact.html, and index.html—one file for each of the Web site's main pages), and a subdirectory (products), which contains index. html and subdirectories for each classification of products along with the files for the product detail pages (as shown earlier, when you viewed the framework of the site in Figure 6-2). Keep in mind that an HTML file's name is the name that appears in the Web page's URL address. For example, to visit the Curiosity Shoppe's About page, you would enter **www.creationguide.com/shoppe/about. html**. As you can see, the preceding URL consists of the domain name (*www.creationguide.com*), the directory or folder name (*shoppe*), and a file name (*about.html*).

For most home pages and many subpages, you might have noticed that you don't have to enter a file name. For example, when you visit Microsoft's home page, you simply type the Microsoft domain name, **www.microsoft.com**, or if you visit the Curiosity Shoppe's Products page, you type **www.creationguide.com/shoppe/products**. If no file name is indicated after a domain name or directory (folder), most servers will display a particularly named file by default—most likely index.html, although some servers also cater to index.htm, default. htm, default.html, main.html, main.htm, home.html, home.htm, or some other specific file name. Ask your hosting service which name you should use for your home page and main pages in each folder (or test each file name online to see which one works by default). Nine times out of ten (and probably more frequently than that), index.html or index.htm is the way to go when naming your home page and your safest bet when you're unsure.

Because your file names and directory names will appear within your Web pages' URLs, you should follow a few basic rules to keep life simple for you and your site's visitors:

> **tip**  Make sure that every HTML or XHTML file name has an .htm or .html extension and that every image file name has a .gif, .jpeg, .jpg, or .png extension.

- **Keep file names short, simple, and meaningful.**   Users might want to access a subpage directly, so make the URL easy for them to type and remember. For example, use a file named products. html instead of p1-2001m.html.

- **Avoid symbols and punctuation.**   Most people find typing symbols and adding punctuation slows their typing speeds considerably and dramatically decreases their typing accuracy. Further, symbols and punctuation can create new avenues for confusion. For example, if your page is named www.creation-guide.com, users could easily forget the hyphen and type www. creationguide.com (thereby missing your page altogether and visiting ours by mistake).

- **Use an underscore (_) to indicate a space (if you have to use a space).**   Some older servers don't recognize spaces, so use underscores instead to indicate blank spaces. But even when you use underscores, you run into the same problem as you do with any symbols and punctuation—underscores are easily forgotten and leave room for errors (lots of them).

- **Use all lowercase letters.**   Once again, think "ease of use" for your Web site visitors. While domain names aren't case sensitive, directory names and file names are case sensitive. Randomly uppercased letters can lose more than a few visitors. All-lowercase file names are easy to type and easy to remember.

## Naming Images

In addition to naming your Web page files, you'll need to name your image files. Generally, users don't access image files directly; instead, source code included in Web documents references image file names whenever an image needs to be displayed. Therefore, you have more leeway when it comes to labeling your images.

One handy image-naming trick we use to identify each image's purpose is to tag a simple prefix or suffix to the file's name. This helps us to quickly identify and find files when we need them. Specifically, we precede image names with $p\_$, $b\_$, or $t\_$. A $p\_$ image is a picture. For example, p_mask indicates that the image is a picture of a mask. A $b\_$ image is a button. For example, b_products indicates that the image is the navigation bar's Products button. And a $t\_$ image refers to a title bar. For example, t_contacts specifies that the image is the title bar graphic used on the Contacts page. We also use the suffix _th after image names to identify thumbnail images. For example, p_mask_th indicates that the image is a thumbnail of the p_mask picture. The reason we add the *th* to the end of the image name instead of the beginning is because we want the thumbnail and full-size image files to appear next to each other when we view the file names alphabetically.

By now, you should be realizing that organization plays an important part in Web site planning. You need to streamline your thoughts as well as start to consider how you'll systemize your files (which, again, are basically your Web site's Web pages and graphics). You can

> **tip**   Have you ever noticed *%20* in long URLs while browsing the Internet? That's how the Internet names a space. So if you name a file *walking the plank competition.html*, browsers will interpret that as *walking%20the%20plank%20competition.html*. Spaces add more clutter than clarity when naming Web files and directories, which is one of the reasons we recommend that you avoid them.

streamline the site organization phase by performing the tasks and addressing the issues in the upcoming Site Planning Checklist.

After (or while) you address the items on the Site Planning Checklist, you should frame your site's structure, as described in Chapter 4, "Mastering Web Design Basics." In other words, you should illustrate the relationships among your site's pages and information to ensure that you've created a clear site layout that includes all your information in an easily accessible format. Figure 6-2 (shown earlier in this chapter) represents one of the Curiosity Shoppe's initial framework. You can make frameworks even more detailed than the one shown in this chapter by including short descriptions of what's going to appear on each page or by showing cross-link connections. For example, in the framework shown in Figure 6-2, you could add margin notes such as *The contact.html page contains an e-mail link and a map showing the shop's location.* You can even create note pages for each page in the framework if you have quite a bit of information to organize.

## Site Planning Checklist

Also available online, at www.creationguide.com/lists/siteplanning.html.

The items in this checklist outline the basic tasks you should perform while planning your Web site. Address each listed task and issue, and sketch your site's informational relationships as you plan to create your framework:

❑ Visit similar sites to see what you like and don't like, and figure out how you can make your site unique.

❑ Be sure that your site specifies who you are and (if appropriate) your organization's identity.

❑ Pick colors that evoke an appropriate emotion for your site. (See the "Color Emotions" sidebar, later in this section.) Also ensure that your color scheme presents a clear contrast for easy reading, analyze whether the colors work to further your site's goals, and try to use colors from the 216-color Web-safe palette. For a quick refresher on Web-safe colors, see Chapter 3, "Creating and Using Art on the Web"; and the CreationGuide.com 216 Web-safe colors (www.creationguide.com/palettes), Web-safe color chart (www.creationguide.com/colorchart), and color wheel (www.creationguide.com/colorwheel).

❑ Verify that the main point of your site is clearly identified up front, not buried a page or two deep into your site or missing altogether, and that each page clearly identifies its purpose. You don't want readers to visit your home page and wonder what they're supposed to do now that they've found your Web site.

❑ Classify your site to yourself so that you don't lose your focus. For design purposes, label your site as commercial, informative, educational, entertainment, navigation, community, artistic, or personal or as some other type of site.

❑ Design the site to reflect how users will most likely navigate through your pages. (Refer to the "Audience Personalities" sidebar, earlier in this chapter.) You can get an idea of what users want during your audience-analysis stage. Make sure that you include umbrella topics (meaning main topics—not weather gear) on your home page, and then provide more specific links on each subpage. For example, provide a Contacts link on the home page, and provide departmental links on the Contacts page.

❑ Ensure that your site offers viewers a few ways in which they can contact you— physical address, e-mail address, phone number, carrier pigeon, and so forth.

❑ Name your files appropriately, as discussed earlier in this chapter.

❑ Create easy-to-understand button names that clearly reflect your site's structure. Cryptic buttons might look awesome, but they tend to confuse readers, especially when no explanatory text accompanies your esoteric creation.

❑ Divide your content into logical units. Don't divide one page into two just because it seems like the page is getting too long. On the other hand, if you see a logical break in a long page, by all means, divide the page—just ensure that you don't lose the newly created page by burying its link deep within your site.

❑ Analyze your information, and make your most important information the most accessible.

❑ Determine ways in which you can create a unifying look or theme throughout your site. Don't forget to include a logo and use consistent navigation links on every page. Keep in mind that the nitty-gritty design aspects of your site's look and theme are addressed more thoroughly in the next planning stage, when you design your home page and subpages.

❑ Include at least one element that will encourage users to return, such as a daily or weekly updated element or a chat room.

# Color Emotions

He was *green* with envy. She was feeling *blue*. What does color have to do with envy and sadness? Research has proven that colors have more to do with emotions than simply coloring clichés. Studies validate that colors elicit certain emotions in people. This sidebar offers a quick look at a few interpretations, but information about color and emotions abounds. You should look online and in your library for additional information about the relationships between color and emotions to complement the following descriptions:

- **Black**   Professionalism, career-oriented, dignity, aloofness, solitude, stability, earthiness, reliability, evil, stored energy, success, classy, serious
- **Blue**   Knowledge, wisdom, health, decisiveness, tranquility, calmness, relaxation, loyalty, security
- **Brown**   Coziness, grounded, stability, neutrality, common sense, naturalness, aged, eccentricity
- **Green**   Family-oriented, life, vigor, resurrection, youth, joy, love, abundance, balance, self-control, nature, renewal, wealth, prestige, mental concentration
- **Purple**   Wealth, helpfulness, spirituality, royalty, dignity, sophistication, richness, mysticism, power, intuition, inspiration, creativity
- **Red**   Fame, life, warmth, vitality, strength, alertness, aggression, sexuality, intensity, high energy, passion with a touch of danger, courage, self-confidence
- **White**   Pleasure, innocence, purity, truth, absence of life (such as ghosts, white light, and so forth), cleanliness, simplicity
- **Yellow**   Health, caution, information, stimulating, wisdom, clarity, happiness, attentiveness, brightness, energy in balance

Keep in mind that this list represents only a few of the traits associated with some colors. Furthermore, various shades of colors can elicit different emotions altogether. For example, while standard yellow communicates happiness and wisdom, intense yellow increases feelings of anxiety. After you identify the emotions you want to portray on your site, conduct some color research to see how to best communicate your message. When you create and use a color palette, understand each color's emotions so that you can use your palette most effectively.

# Laying Your Home Page's Foundation

After the site-planning dust settles, you're ready to design your home page and subpages. By now, you should have a very strong idea of what your home page should include—logo, title bar, links to your site's main pages, and so forth. For the most part, you should have taken care of the practical side of page design, such as determining a file-naming structure, analyzing your audience, and determining hardware limitations. Now your creative juices get to take over while your organizational synapses rest and rejuvenate. In this design phase, focus your attention on how you can creatively present all the necessary home page components in a way that reflects your site's goals, optimizes your site's theme, and elicits the proper "emotional" response from users. For example, the Curiosity Shoppe wanted to convey the feeling that the store sells artifacts and treasures that have been discovered throughout the world. Therefore, we came up with the ancient map theme and the compass rose logo for the Curiosity Shoppe's owners.

After you think of creative ways to present your ideas, sketch various layouts and ideas to kick off the storyboarding process. You'll start to see what works best, and some ideas will spawn others until you come up with a page design that does the trick. Figure 6-4 shows a storyboard of the Curiosity Shoppe's home page. Because we designed the home page to make a unique impression, its design is notably different from the layout of the site's subpages. Therefore, we also sketched a subpage to illustrate how title bars and navigation links will be displayed, as shown in Figure 6-5. While you're storyboarding your home page, refer to the Home Page Planning Checklist to ensure that you've covered all your bases.

**try this!**
Quick—think of three sites you've visited recently. Now analyze why those three sites made an impression on you. Are there any elements you can adopt and modify for your site? Were those sites easy to navigate? Does an element that you didn't like stand out in your mind? Use your personal experience to your benefit. After all, you know what you like when you're surfing the Web.

**tip**   Even though the Home Page Planning Checklist looks lengthy, your home page shouldn't. At all costs, avoid overloading your home page. You're better off adding a few links to your navigation menu instead of cramming information into every corner (and beyond) of your users' screens.

**Figure 6-4** *The Curiosity Shoppe home page sketch*

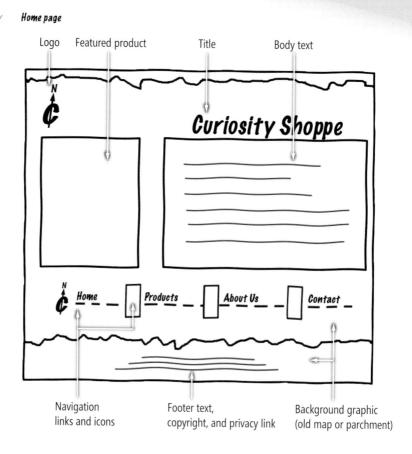

*Home page*

Logo   Featured product        Title            Body text

**Curiosity Shoppe**

Home    Products    About Us    Contact

Navigation              Footer text,                Background graphic
links and icons         copyright, and privacy link  (old map or parchment)

# Home Page Planning Checklist

Also available online, at www.creationguide.com/lists/homepage.

You need to verify that your home page includes the elements listed in the following checklist. If you purposely omit certain elements, ensure that you understand why. Keep in mind that the list doesn't weight the importance of elements by order—in fact, the list is alphabetized specifically to avoid promoting any elements over others. (We're tricky like that.) Make sure that one way or another, you address *all* the following elements in relation to your home page's design:

- ❏ Clear purpose
- ❏ Clear steps for visitors, beyond clicking the Back button, and appealing navigation for all potential audience personalities

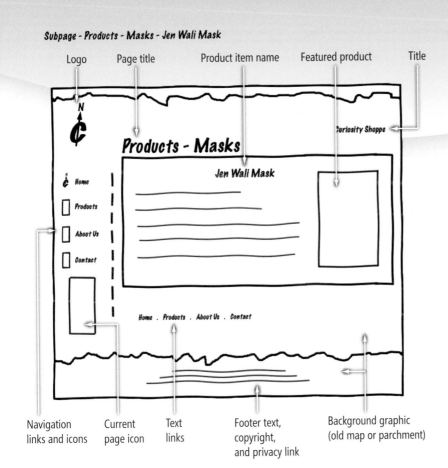

Subpage - Products - Masks - Jen Wali Mask

Logo    Page title    Product item name    Featured product    Title

**Figure 6-5**  *The Curiosity Shoppe subpage sketch*

**Products - Masks**

*Curiosity Shoppe*

*Home*

*Products*

*About Us*

*Contact*

*Jen Wali Mask*

*Home . Products . About Us . Contact*

Navigation links and icons    Current page icon    Text links    Footer text, copyright, and privacy link    Background graphic (old map or parchment)

- ❑ Copyright information
- ❑ Creation or revision date
- ❑ Easily identifiable and consistently displayed navigation links or buttons
- ❑ Important information displayed above the fold
- ❑ Informative page title in the body of the page
- ❑ Informative title bar text
- ❑ Intentional emotional effect or theme created via words, colors, layout, font, and so forth
- ❑ Logo, home page icon, or other identifying graphic, such as a family crest or departmental code, that can be shown on subpages and linked to the home page

❑ Opening page "hook" to catch viewer's interest (home pages generally varying at least slightly from subpages) and use of "you" text to draw visitors attention

❑ Privacy policy

❑ Quick loading approach (because gigantic images really do make extremely poor backgrounds, and you truly don't need to show 90 pictures on your home page)

❑ Subheads to break up long blocks of text (if necessary)

❑ Text links included along the bottom of the page

❑ Upper-left corner put to good use, preferably with your logo

❑ Your identity or your organization's identity

## Gathering Supplies and Preparing to Build

**tip**   Remember, if you decide to purchase a domain name, the name should be short, simple, and influenced by your Web site's purpose.

As you might remember from Chapter 5, "Considering Tools and Stockpiling the Goods," after you've specified your goals, met your audience, organized your site, and designed your home page's layout, one final planning component remains—rounding up your tools and supplies. This stage includes ensuring that you have well-written and well-edited text, appropriately sized graphics (which you might have to tweak a little when the actual page design process begins), scanned or otherwise digitized pictures, and the tools to arrange all the items on your Web pages. As you can see, the tasks at this stage are concrete and straightforward, but completing them generally takes a significant amount of time—so plan accordingly. Luckily, although this stage usually takes the longest, we can describe the process fairly succinctly. Basically, before you create your Web page, you need to gather the supplies listed in the following Supplies Checklist.

**note**   We're not trying to discourage you by stating that the supply-gathering stage of the Web site game can be time-consuming. It's just that gathering, creating, and modifying text and graphics almost always seems to take slightly longer than planned. (Or at least that's been our experience—and not just because we inherently tend to enjoy creating, modifying, and playing with graphics and text!) Fortunately, you don't need to worry about "gathering supplies" types of delays. The goal in this book is *easy* Web design. To that end, in each walkthrough project in Part Two, we've listed the supplies necessary to create the Web site. You can simply download the images and copy the text you'll need from the CreationGuide.com Web site. In other words, the hunting and gathering stages detailed in Part Two are brief and painless.

# Supplies Checklist

Also available online, at www.creationguide.com/lists/supplies.

Before you start to create your Web site, you should have the following elements on hand and easily accessible—or at least in the process of being finalized:

- ❑ Text—edited, spell checked, and proofread
- ❑ Photographs, graphics, and illustrations (including buttons, title bars, and a high-quality logo)
- ❑ Site framework, storyboard sketches, and templates
- ❑ Web editor or Web site creation tool, such as blog templates, an online community wizard, a desktop publishing program (for example, Microsoft Office Publisher), and so forth
- ❑ Graphics program
- ❑ Domain name (either purchased or assigned)
- ❑ Server space
- ❑ File transfer tool, such as an FTP application, a Web publishing wizard, My Network Places, and so on (as described in Chapter 12, "Sending Web Pages into the Real World")

Now that the theory and planning phases are fully covered, you're ready to get your hands dirty and tackle Part Two of this book. So roll up your sleeves—it's time to create!

# check it!

- Define your Web site's goals.
- Know your audience.
- Frame your Web site's hierarchy, organizational flow, and overall feel.
- Storyboard your home page and subpages.
- Gather your supplies and tools.
- Get ready to create a Web site and go live!

# the walk—
# creating web sites

# 2

When you learned to drive a car, you probably spent some time listening to an instructor, watching defensive-driving movies, memorizing street signs, and studying driving-related facts in the Department of Motor Vehicles handbook. Sure, those learning exercises were helpful, but most likely, the art of driving truly sank in only after you got behind the wheel as a student driver and took a few spins around town with your driving instructor. Experience counts quite a bit in the real world. This sentiment isn't exactly new—Einstein summed it up pretty well when he said, "One cannot learn anything so well as by experiencing it oneself." In Part Two, we put you in the driver's seat and let you put the theories you learned in Part One of this book into practice.

In this part, you'll find five project chapters designed to help you acquire some well-rounded, hands-on experience as you test-drive the Web site creation process. Throughout these chapters, we attempt to make the learning process as enjoyable, straightforward, and intuitive as possible. To that end, the chapters are arranged progressively, from simple blogging templates to advanced Web editors, so that you can ease your way toward using more advanced Web site creation tools. In addition, each Web site is created using an application that is either already on your computer or easy to access. That's the basic landscape of Part Two. Now all you have to do is buckle up your Web knowledge in the passenger seat as you cruise into the hands-on stretch of this book.

# posting a web site

## within an hour
## (or so)

You could walk into your nearest computer-geek store and buy all the components necessary to build yourself a new computer—you could buy a motherboard, some memory, a microprocessor, a tower case, a CD-DVD drive, and so forth; pack it all home; and then spend a few hours (probably more) assembling all the pieces into a working computer. Some people wouldn't upgrade their hardware in any other way. Another approach to acquiring a new computer would be to forgo leaving the comfort of your home. You could simply fire up your old computer, go online, and order a completely upgraded computer system directly from the manufacturer. For some, convenience is the way to go. In this chapter, we're going to show you the easiest—and fastest—way to create a basic presence online. Welcome to the world of blogging!

**lingo**  A *blog* is a personal Web site that's regularly updated, like a journal, and contains all sorts of information. Blogging services provide a cost-effective (usually *free*) way for people to publish information on the Web, regardless of their level of technical expertise.

To create the Web site, which is a Web log (more commonly known as a *blog*), described in this chapter, you need the following "supplies":

● An Internet connection.

● A browser (ideally Microsoft Internet Explorer version 6 or later).

● Figures (optional) downloaded from www.creationguide.com/ch07/images, including fable.jpg, myth.jpg, ninja.jpg, phattigercat.jpg, porkchop.jpg, romeo.jpg, and tiger_attack.jpg. To download these figures, connect to www.creationguide.com/ch07/images, right-click an image's file name, and save a copy of the file (referred to as the Target on Internet Explorer's shortcut menu, as shown in Figure 7-1) to a folder on your computer. Repeat the process for each image you want to save on your computer, or simply download the ZIP file of all the images used in this project.

**Figure 7-1**  *Downloading image files from the Internet*

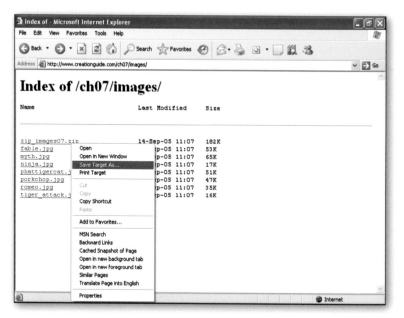

## Introducing MSN Spaces and Blogs

Here's some good news—by reading this chapter and following along with the walkthrough, you'll have an official Web presence by the time you reach the end of the chapter. Furthermore, you won't need to partake in any deep-breathing exercises, calisthenics, or caffeine-laden drinking binges to get your Web site up and running. In other words, building your first Web site is going to be a piece of cake.

For this chapter's purposes, let's imagine that your goal is to have some information online today. Let's also say that you'd prefer not to spend any money at this point for an online presence. Amazingly enough, this goal is realistic and easily achieved. You can quickly create a free Web site by taking advantage of the simplest and least-expensive Web publishing approach around—*blogging*.

To create your blog, all you need to invest are some graphics (if desired), text, possibly some links and opinions, and a little time. Our tool of choice for this chapter's project is MSN Spaces, which is located at spaces.msn.com. Figure 7-2 shows the MSN Spaces Sign In page. Figure 7-3 shows a sample MSN Space.

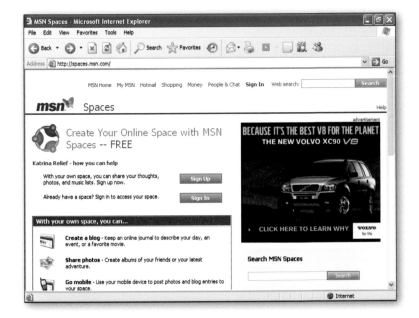

**Figure 7-2**   *The MSN Spaces home page*

As you can see on the MSN Spaces home page, you can sign up and sign in on this page. Furthermore, the page provides a search tool to find MSN Spaces and lists summaries of several MSN Spaces features. If you scroll down a bit, you'll find general information about MSN's newest features, such as the MSN Toolbar.

Looking at the sample MSN Space in Figure 7-3, you can get a feel for some of the features you can include on your blog. Juliana's blog (the blog shown in Figure 7-3) incorporates a number of standard

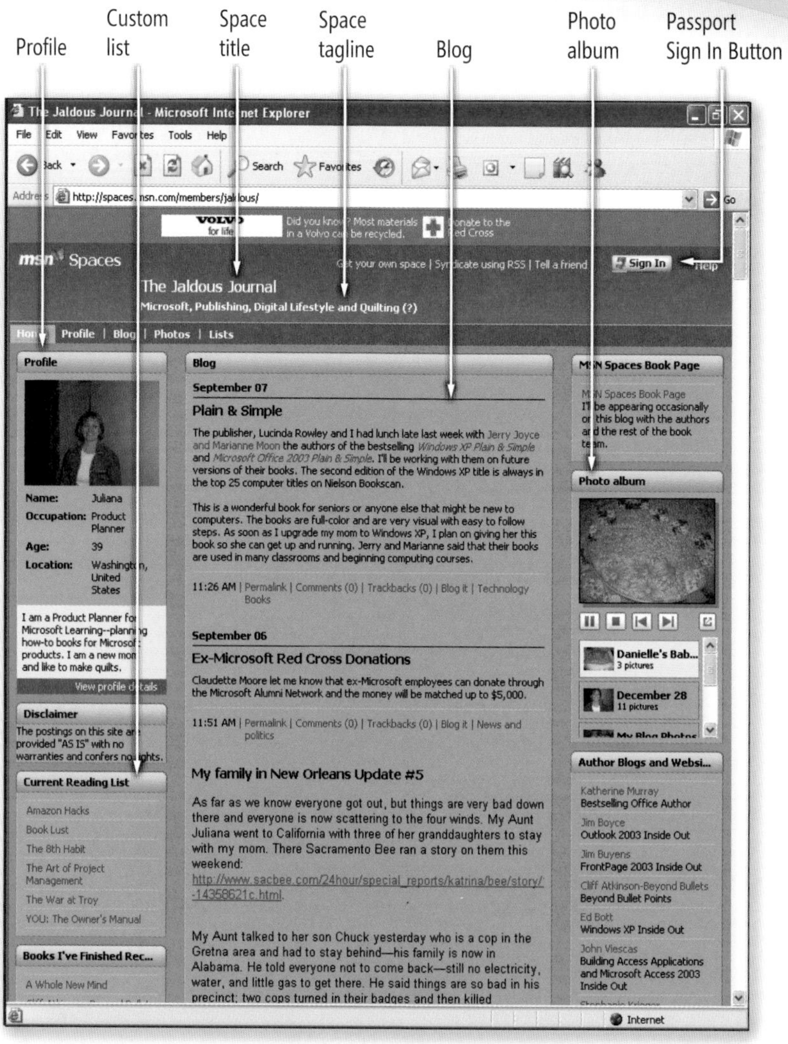

Custom
Profile    list

Space    Space
title    tagline    Blog

Photo    Passport
album    Sign In Button

**Figure 7-3**  *A successful and active MSN Space*

and custom features. When you first create a space, MSN Spaces automatically provides the following sections for you:

- **Home**    Your MSN Space home page is the first page visitors see when they visit your space. You control the content on this page by selecting and deselecting content modules. You'll learn more about content modules in the next section, "Planning an MSN Space."

- **Profile**    The Profile area introduces you to your visitors. You can show or hide this information, and you can include text and an image. Your profile information comes from your MSN Member Directory entry. When you make changes to your directory listing, your profile changes as well. We show you how to create an MSN Member Directory entry later in this chapter, in the section "Developing Your Profile."

- **Blog** The Blog area is where you post your "journal" entries. You can allow others to view and respond to your entries, and you can control how many entries appear in your MSN Space at a time.

- **Photos** The Photo Album area enables you to display photos and photo albums accompanied by short descriptions. You are limited to 30 MB to store all the photos used in your MSN Space. As long as you stay within that size restraint, you can create any number of albums and include any number of photos in a single album.

- **Lists** In your MSN Space, you can compile up to 11 lists, and each list can hold up to 100 entries (although each entry must have a unique name). Unfortunately, you cannot reorder items in a list, which means that you should enter the information in the order in which you want it to appear in the list. Common list topics include favorite books, recommended movies, helpful Web sites, personal goals, notable quotations, most-watched TV shows, important contacts, and so forth.

- **Music** You can create up to 25 music lists, and each list can hold up to 100 songs. Visitors can view and rate your lists, and they can purchase music from MSN Music with a click of a button. You can create music lists manually or upload a Microsoft Windows Media Player playlist.

After you create an MSN Space, you can add and remove any of the preceding elements to customize your site as well as add additional *content modules*, themes, and layout settings, as discussed throughout this chapter's walkthrough. Additionally, you can provide an opportunity for others to view and post responses on your blog.

Now that you have an idea of where you're headed with MSN Spaces, let's get started with your first Web site project. As with all Web sites, this project starts with a planning phase. In this walkthrough, we show you how to create an MSN Space for a fictional client.

**note** MSN Spaces is one of the newer blogging services in the *blogosphere*. (Now there's a term that's even too geeky for us!) MSN Spaces first appeared in test, or *beta*, form in December 2004. Since its introduction, over 4.5 million people have set up a personal space on MSN Spaces, and the number grows daily.

**lingo** A *content module*, or just *module*, is a unit that contains a particular type of information in your MSN Space. MSN Spaces modules include Archives, Blog, Profile, Lists (Custom, Music, Blog, and Book), Photo Album, and more.

# Completing the MSN Walkthrough

One of the beauties of the Web is its dynamic nature. Information can be updated at any time. This dynamic nature also adds a level of unpredictability. For instance, the steps required to plan and build an MSN Space could very well change between the time we write this text and the time you read it. Therefore, we've placed this walkthrough's steps for planning and building an MSN Space online. To access the steps, visit www.creationguide.com/msn. Figure 7-4 shows the sample MSN site that you can build by following the walkthrough's online steps.

**Figure 7-4**  *Viewing the sample walkthrough site*

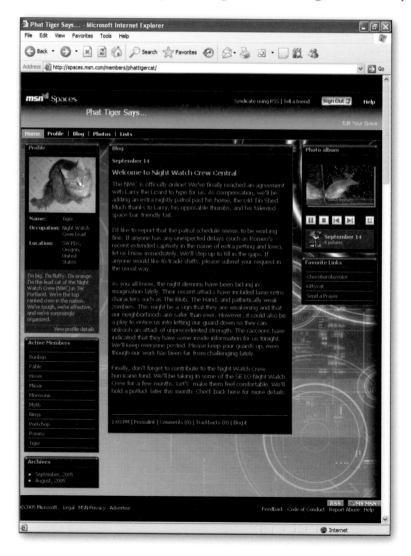

In addition to working through the walkthrough, we recommend that you check out *Share Your Story: Blogging with MSN Spaces* (Microsoft Press, 2005), by one of our favorite Microsoft authors, Katherine Murray, and her coauthor Mike Torres, an MSN Spaces Product Manager. To whet your appetite, we've included a Top 10+1 list for building and maintaining successful blogs, compiled by Katherine Murray.

# Top 10+1 Tips for Successful Blogging

Also available online, at www.creationguide.com/lists/blogging.html.

*Katherine Murray* is a long-time blogger; the author of many books on hardware, software, and the digital lifestyle; and the owner of reVisions Plus, Inc. (www.revisionsplus. com), a publishing services company. Katherine uses blogs for communicating with groups of all kinds (professional and personal) and believes that blogs give us an opportunity to share what we do, who we are, and what we care about. To help you get started (and get comfortable!) in the world of blogging, Katherine offers the following top 10+1 blogging tips:

- **Read your favorites.**   Before you begin blogging, read other bloggers. Notice the layout of blogs, the color, and the tone. Pay attention to how photos are used; make a note of what you do like—and what you don't.

- **Find a design that fits you.**   Choosing a template or designing a page that really says something about who you are can help your viewers identify with you more quickly. What are your favorite colors? Which fonts really communicate the tone you want to convey?

- **Write the way you speak.**   One of the great things about blogs is that they seem to give us an authentic sense of the person writing. We see into their ideas, their opinions, their loves, their concerns. Don't struggle to write perfectly formed sentences for your blog. Write the way you talk. If you're not sure whether your words sound stilted, read a post aloud, just to be sure.

- **Choose engaging photos.**   Blogs are as different as the bloggers who create them. Some people make photos the main focus of their page; others blog text and use photos sparingly. Whatever you choose to do with photos, be sure that the photos you post are engaging, edited, and compressed to as small a size as possible. You can use a simple photo editor like Microsoft Picture Manager to fix lighting issues, crop to the most fetching elements, and compress the image for the Web.

- **Use your own stuff.**   Copyright is an important issue whether you are posting to your own blog or writing for someone else. Use your own photos, music, video clips, and more on your blog. (Or if you want to use someone else's work, be sure to get their permission *and* give them credit on your site.)

- **Link liberally.**   The blogosphere is one big interrelated conversation. You don't have to go too far to find one blogger linking to another who links to another. Your posts will be more interesting to viewers (and most likely get more traffic) if you're generous in linking to others you refer to. That helps build the web of connections (and might increase your ability to be noticed and picked up on other large-traffic sites).

- **Use lists.**   Lists are a quick, fun way to share bits of information your viewers can connect with. Top 10 lists (or top 10+1, like this one!) provide a simple way for visitors to discover what you value or what you're interested in. Lists are also easy to create, so you can change them regularly and keep your content moving.

- **Update regularly.**   Readers who like your blog will likely check back regularly to see whether you've posted anything new, so be sure that once you start to blog, you update regularly (at least weekly is a good rule of thumb). Many bloggers start their blogs, are gung ho about it for a few weeks, and then abandon the site. You don't have to post everyday, but if building readership is important to you, post often enough that your visitors get used to checking your site for something new.

- **Use RSS.**   RSS (or Really Simple Syndication) is a simple way to get your content out to interested readers. This syndication method delivers content from your blog directly to their desktops; they can then click the link to go to your site and add comments or read additional items. Visitors need software known as an RSS reader to view the downloaded content (which includes text and images).

- **Invite feedback.**   Enabling comments on your site encourages others to participate in your conversation online. Creating a guestbook also encourages others to communicate with you and lets them know you're glad they came by.

- **Plus 1: Have fun with it!** Not everyone is a born blogger—some people are more reticent about sharing ideas, opinions, and experiences than others. And that's okay. Know your own comfort zone, and if you want to keep personal things private, that's cool. Just find something you're passionate about to share on your blog—cooking, art, nature, sports—whatever you spend time thinking about and doing is good material for your blog. Have fun with it! Share what gets you going in the morning, and blog the quirky or funny things that happen through your day. Ultimately, blogging is just about telling your stories your way—and connecting with others all over the world who are doing the same.

## check it!

- MSN Spaces enable you to create a Web presence quickly and easily.
- Planning an MSN Space entails selecting a theme, a layout, and a group of content modules.
- You can easily change theme, layout, and module selections, as well as drag modules on your page to reposition content.
- Generally, you must join a blogging service before you can create a blog. To join MSN Spaces, you must have a .NET Passport.
- Your MSN Space's Profile module displays the information you provided in your MSN Member Directory profile.
- The Blog module enables you to post blog entries.
- You can use the MSN Photo Upload Control window to store and label pictures in photo albums.
- Custom lists allow you to name and build lists to suit your needs.
- The Settings window contains tabs that offer a variety of site settings you can configure.
- You can delete content, delete selected content modules, or delete your entire MSN Space.
- MSN Spaces is a dynamic service. Keep an eye out for new and improved features as the service continues to expand.

# demystifying
## basic css and xhtml

Can you remember the intense and conscious effort it took to learn the sounds and shapes of the alphabet way back when? Eventually, after lots of practice, you got it. After you learned about letters, you slowly began to understand how to combine the letters into words, words into sentences, sentences into paragraphs, and so on. At this point, reading and writing probably seems natural to you. Most likely, you read the newspaper and write notes without thinking much about individual letter sounds and shapes. That's because over the years, you've developed your foundation in letters and words into a seemingly innate ability to read and write. Learning how to create Extensible Hypertext Markup Language (XHTML) and cascading style sheets (CSS) files from scratch—by using tags, classes, ids, and so forth, and understanding how XHTML and CSS work together—is a lot like learning to read and write. The process might take some patience and lots of practice at the beginning, but if you take the time to learn about XHTML and CSS now, you'll eventually be able to understand and hand-code Web pages almost as naturally as you read and write throughout the day.

# Gathering Project Supplies

To create the Web site described in this walkthrough, you'll need the following "supplies":

- A basic text editor, such as Microsoft Notepad or WordPad (applications that are included with Microsoft Windows) or TextEdit (which comes with Macintosh OS X).

- A browser and an Internet connection (necessary only to download the sample project's graphics from this book's companion Web site).

- The following figures, downloaded from www.creationguide.com/ch08/images. To download the image files used in this chapter's walkthrough, download the zip_images08.zip file that contains the necessary JPG and GIF files, or right-click each file name and save a copy of the file to a folder named C:\roadside\images on your computer (as shown in Figure 8-1).

  - b_submit.gif
  - banner.gif
  - logo.gif
  - p_az_dino.gif
  - p_mt_jackalop.gif
  - p_or_shark.gif
  - p_va_octopus.gif
  - pc_blockhenge.jpg
  - pc_blockhenge_th.jpg
  - pc_dino.jpg
  - pc_dino_th.jpg
  - pc_jackalope.jpg
  - pc_jackalope_th.jpg
  - pc_octopus.jpg
  - pc_octopus_th.jpg

**tip**   If you prefer, you can download just the zip_images08.zip file and extract the image files locally. If you take this route, make sure you save the images directly in the images directory (not in a folder within the images directory) after you extract them.

- pc_shark.jpg
- pc_shark_th_jpg
- t_arizona.gif
- t_contact.gif
- t_home.gif
- t_oregon.gif
- t_states.gif
- t_tips.gif
- t_virginia.gif

- The following optional CSS files, downloaded from www.creation-guide.com/ch08 and stored in C:\roadside on your computer:

  - styles_presentation_blue.css
  - styles_presentation_green.css

**see also** For detailed download-ing steps, see the section "Getting Your Folders and Graphics in Place," later in this chapter.

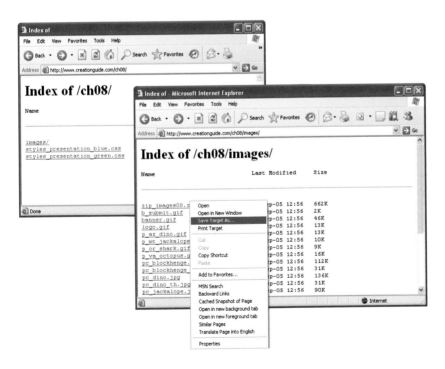

**Figure 8-1** *Downloading image files from the Internet*

# Why Hand-Code?

In Part 1, we briefly introduced you to cascading style sheets (CSS), Hypertext Markup Language (HTML), and Extensible Hypertext Markup Language (XHTML). Basically, you construct Web sites by including HTML or XHTML commands (also called *tags*) in a simple text document and creating style sheets to format and shape your Web content. Although other technologies (such as XML, or Extensible Markup Language) are beginning to emerge in Web development, HTML is the foundation of most Web pages today, and XHTML is currently the most up-to-date HTML coding standard. Therefore, if you're going to create Web pages, you need to know about XHTML.

Quite possibly, you might not feel ready to create a Web site from scratch using only a blank document and vaguely familiar-sounding technologies named CSS and XHTML. But believe it or not, you're ready—so for now, just go for it. We're having you use CSS and XHTML in the first major Web page project in this book because you'll find that understanding these basics will come in extremely handy whenever you create Web sites in the future—no matter how

**HTML vs. XHTML**    HTML is currently the most widely used markup language on the Web, so you might be wondering why we're teaching you to use XHTML. Our reasoning is sound. XHTML is the next formulation of HTML. XHTML combines HTML and XML, which makes XHTML backward compatible with older browsers and forward compatible with XML-enabled browsers and devices. In other words, XHTML is designed to be readable by the highest number of old and new browsers, devices, and software. By using XHTML to build your Web pages, your pages will have the greatest chance of being properly understood on the greatest number of platforms.

The differences between HTML and XHTML are few but important. Most notably, XHTML has more strict and specific rules. While that might sound bad, it's actually good. Having strict and specific rules to abide by makes coding easier, because you aren't faced with ambiguities. While you (and many others) can still get away with using HTML to create your Web sites, we think you should start using XHTML now. That way, you'll be set for today *and* tomorrow.

you create those pages. This baptism-by-fire approach means that you'll be hand-coding Web documents in the very near future.

In some ways, you might find that this chapter's walkthrough is the most important project in all of Part 2. If you're going to create Web sites, knowing at least some XHTML and CSS will enable you to modify and tweak pages to suit your preferences, even if the pages you're modifying have been generated by a Web editor. Further, knowing how to code XHTML and CSS means that you'll be able to remove unnecessary (and sometimes proprietary) code that some Web editors tend to add to Web documents. Removing unnecessary code can make your Web documents smaller, which in turn means that your pages will load faster. Finally, as you become more proficient at hand-coding Web documents, you'll probably find that you can make changes more quickly and precisely by adding, deleting, or modifying code instead of modifying a Web page in a Web editor.

We're now ready to get started. The first order of business, before we commence creating a Web site, is to briefly (very briefly) go over some basic XHTML and CSS theory. By the way, when we say *theory*, we're talking clear, helpful information—not complex rhetoric. Think of the upcoming theory discussion as spreading a blanket before picnicking—you might as well kick back, get comfortable, and discourage at least a few of the pests up front.

> **note** Although you use XHTML coding practices in your source code, XHTML documents are still text documents saved with an .html or .htm file extension.

## Web Standards—They're Good For You!

All of the XHTML and CSS code you create in this walkthrough adheres to current Web standards. You'll be happy to hear that the phrase *Web standards* doesn't just refer to some vague notions of popular usage. Instead, Web standards are rules and specifications designed for the Web and developed by the World Wide Web Consortium (W3C). W3C was founded by the same person who invented the Web—Tim Berners-Lee. The consortium consists of an international group of member organizations, staff members, and public developers who work together to develop standards and guidelines to ensure the long-term growth of the Web. You can access the standards online, at www.w3.org. In this walkthrough, you'll use the official XHTML standards to provide structure in your Web pages and the official CSS standards to style your Web pages and content.

Keep in mind that following standards isn't anything new. Contractors follow standard measurements (such as for doorways and appliance openings), mechanics use standard-size tools, cooks use standard measuring devices, and on and on. Standards enable people to build reliable products consistently without having to invent special tools before every job. Web standards serve the same purpose. By using accepted Web standards, you can ensure that your creations will be accessible to the greatest possible number of browsers and devices. Not only that, but you'll be well positioned for future compatibility. Now let's get down to some markup language basics.

# XHTML and CSS Basics

Fundamentally, XHTML commands serve as instructions that tell a browser how to display a Web page's content. In other words, XHTML commands provide information that controls the structure of your Web page's text and graphics. Keep the purpose of XHTML commands in mind. You'll see later how XHTML commands structure page divisions and weave their way in and around your Web page's content in an XHTML document, but basically, an XHTML document contains two types of information:

- Content, including headings, body text, references to graphics, and so forth, displayed on visitors' browsers
- XHTML tags, which control the structure of the Web page's content and are not displayed in visitors' browsers

In this chapter, we show you how to enter XHTML tags and content into plain-text documents to create Web pages. Further, you'll link the pages you create so that they can work together to create a Web site. To accomplish this feat, you'll need to use Notepad or WordPad (if you're running Microsoft Windows) or TextEdit (if you're using a Macintosh). Figure 8-2 shows how fully coded XHTML documents appear in TextEdit, Notepad, and WordPad. When you start this chapter's walkthrough, you'll begin with a blank page. To open Notepad, click Start, point to All Programs, point to Accessories, and then click Notepad. To open WordPad, click Start, point to All Programs, point to Accessories, and then click WordPad. To use TextEdit, double-click the TextEdit icon on your hard drive, and then on the TextEdit menu, click Preferences. In the Preferences dialog box, select the Ignore Rich Text Commands In HTML Files check box.

**Figure 8-2** *Viewing an XHTML document in WordPad, Notepad, and TextEdit*

**note** Don't be put off by the seemingly in-comprehensible conglomeration of XHTML commands shown in Figure 8-2. XHTML can look complex, but it really consists only of combinations of letters, numbers, and symbols with a little organization thrown in. You're obviously familiar with letters, num-bers, and symbols, so rest assured that learning to use XHTML commands is well within your skill set.

To reiterate in the name of clarity, *XHTML tags* take care of defining and structuring content on the Web page, and *content* is the actual information that is displayed on the Web page (such as text, graphics, headings, and so forth). You might notice that we haven't mentioned any formatting or style issues. That's because, for the most part, CSS takes care of how information appears (boldface, italic, left-aligned, and so forth). We'll get to CSS a little later, in the section "Using CSS." First let's look at how to use XHTML tags to define content and create page structure.

## Using XHTML Tags

In this section, we introduce the basic rules of XHTML along with a few common tags. Keep in mind that this section does not define every XHTML tag out there; quite a few tags exist, and plenty of books devoted to XHTML provide comprehensive lists of commands. (If you want to find out more about XHTML than what we cover here, check out any of our favorite XHTML references, which are listed in the section "Additional Resources," near the end of this chapter.) Our philosophy is that if you learn the basic rules of using XHTML tags, you'll be able to use any of the tags you discover online or in XHTML books.

Let's start our discussion of XHTML tags with a simple rule:

> *XHTML tags consist of commands that appear within angle brackets (<>).*

**lingo**  *Source code* refers to the text, numbers, and symbols included in the XHTML document that creates a Web page. Most browsers enable you to view a Web page's source code. For example, to display a Web page's source code in Microsoft Internet Explorer, display a Web page, and on the View menu, click Source.

For example, a Web page's source code typically includes <body>. This tag tells a browser where the main content in an .html document begins. When a browser interprets an .html file, it knows that any text inside angle brackets is a command to be processed and any text outside angle brackets is content to be displayed.

Here's the second rule you need to remember:

> *XHTML tags must be lowercase.*

This means that <body> is correct, but <BODY> and <Body> are unacceptable. If you're familiar with using HTML, you might know that most browsers don't care whether HTML tags are lowercase, uppercase, or mixed-case. In this book, we're showing you how to use XHTML, which has stricter rules than HTML. One of the stricter rules is that all XHTML tags must be lowercase (except the <!DOCTYPE...> tag—but we'll talk about that later) .

Here's rule number three:

> *XHTML tags must always be closed.*

Because most XHTML tags are used primarily for structuring and presenting content, XHTML tags often come in pairs, consisting of a *start tag* and an *end tag* (also referred to as an *opening tag* and a *closing tag*). This pairing enables you to tell browsers where a particular type of content or structure (such as a navigation bar) starts and ends. It's like when you go to the movies with a few friends and two friends save seats while the rest of the group goes to the concessions counter. The two people saving the seats sit separately to mark a span of seats that will contain the friends. If the seat-savers were XHTML tags, they'd tell the browser that all the seats between them should be formatted as their friends' seats.

Start tags and end tags have slightly different purposes—namely, a start tag indicates when an action should start, and an end tag indicates when an action should stop. (See, we're not talking rocket science here.) While start and end tags appear very similar, they have a minor yet critical difference. End tags are differentiated from start tags by the inclusion of a forward slash (/) just after the left bracket, like this: </body>. As you might suspect, the </body> tag indicates the end of a Web page's body content. Going back to the movie theater example, let's say that one seat-saver is sitting in an aisle seat and the other seat-saver is sitting in the middle of the row. The seat-saver sitting in the middle of the row is wearing a red shirt. Suddenly, a new arrival asks the seat-saver sitting in the aisle seat whether the seats are taken. The seat-saver would say something like, "Yes—all the seats down to the person in the red shirt are taken." That's the role of a start tag; the red-shirted seat-saver serves as an end tag. For example, a <strong> tag tells a browser, "Please format all the text starting after me with a strong format, like boldface, until you run into that </strong> tag over there."

For further illustration, let's look at an example of text that uses XHTML tag pairs. The following sentence includes XHTML start and end tags that format the sentence as a paragraph (<p></p>); display the phrase *butter flavoring* with mild emphasis, usually italic (<em></em>); and format the word *popcorn* with strong emphasis, usually boldface (<strong></strong>):

```
<p>Do you want <em>butter flavoring</em> on your <strong>
popcorn</strong> or do you like it plain?</p>
```

Figure 8-3 shows the formatted text (also available online, at www. creationguide.com/popcorn).

**Figure 8-3** *Viewing the popcorn question in a browser (also available online, at www.creation-guide.com/popcorn)*

The popcorn sentence also illustrates an interesting concept called *nesting*. In XHTML, nesting has nothing to do with twigs and feathers and everything to do with the order in which XHTML tags appear. In the popcorn sentence, the emphasis tag pair (<em></em>) and the strong tag pair (<strong></strong>) are nested within the paragraph tag pair (<p></p>). Here's a key rule that you should follow when you're nesting XHTML tags:

> *Nested XHTML tag pairs must be closed in the reverse order in which they are opened.*

That rule might seem a little confusing, so let's look at an example. Basically, start and end XHTML tags shouldn't get their lines crossed. Here's a correct pattern:

```
<body>  <p>  <strong>  </strong>  </p>  </body>
```

# Closing Unpaired Tags
Some tags don't work in pairs, because there's no need for marking the start and end of an element. For example, it takes only one command to tell a browser that you want a line break or a horizontal rule. In HTML, single tags didn't present a problem. If you wanted to include a line break, you typed **<br>**; if you wanted to generate a horizontal rule, you typed **<hr>**. But XHTML requires *all tags* to be closed. Therefore, the XHTML specification includes a way to close single tags. To close a single tag, you simply add the closing forward slash inside the tag, like this: <hr /> and <br />. You must include a space before the forward slash to ensure that older browsers read the tag properly. Adding the forward slash in XHTML is a small detail yet another step toward conforming to Web standards.

In this example, the <strong> tags are nested within the <p> (paragraph) tags, which are nested within the <body> tags. In most browsers, this setup would result in bold text within a paragraph within the body of a Web document. The following setup would also work:

```
<body>  <p>  <em>  </em>  <strong>  </strong>  </p>  </body>
```

Notice that this nesting example uses the same pattern as the popcorn sentence. In this example, the emphasis tag pair and the strong tag pair aren't nested inside each other, but both tag pairs are independent and nested within the paragraph tag pair.

Now let's lighten up the discussion a bit and look at a more clear-cut rule:

> *By default, XHTML documents display a single space between text elements.*

This rule might seem odd to mention, but spacing issues are a great concern on the Web for a number of reasons (mostly because designers have had to deal with content that resizes and reflows—issues that are nonexistent in printed documents). In an XHTML document, adding any number of spaces within your code by using the SPACEBAR, the TAB key, or the ENTER key results in a single space. Therefore, typing

```
<em>Music Instruction</em>
```

in a Web page, displays the same content as

```
<em>Music                    Instruction</em>
```

which displays the same content as

```
<em>            Music Instruction                </em>
```

which displays the same content as

```
<em>
Music Instruction
</em>
```

When the four preceding examples are used as separate paragraphs in an XHTML page, the text appears as shown in Figure 8-4 (also available online, at www.creationguide.com/spacing).

Now you're ready for the next rule, which adds some spice to XHTML tags:

> *Some XHTML start tags can contain properties (also called attributes), which further refine an XHTML tag's instructions. Attributes must always include quoted values.*

In other words, you can frequently customize the instructions related to an XHTML command. For example, you can add a **class** or an **id** attribute to a <p> tag to style text in a specific way, like this:

```
<p class="footer">copyright 2006</p>
```

If you inserted the preceding sentence into an XHTML document, the *copyright 2006* text would be formatted according to the formatting styles defined for the **footer** class in your style sheet. We'll explain style sheets and classes in a bit—for now, we merely want to show you how attributes and values can be included in XHTML tags. In this example, the **class** attribute contains the **"footer"** value.

The preceding rules are designed to provide you with a starting place. You'll get more of a feel for XHTML as you build the Web site in this chapter's walkthrough. There's nothing like hands-on experience to gain knowledge. Additional XHTML tags and concepts are introduced in the project as we go. For added assistance, you might want to keep Table 8-1 handy while you work.

## Table 8-1   XHTML tags used in the hand-coding walkthrough

| Tags | Description |
|---|---|
| <a href="*xxx.xxx*"></a> | Marks the *anchor,* or clickable, portion of a hyperlink. The **href** attribute points to the information that should be displayed after the anchor's content is clicked. Anchor content is specified between the anchor tags (<a></a>) and can include text and images. |
| <blockquote></blockquote> | Offsets a paragraph from the regular body text, usually by indenting the paragraph's left and right margins. |
| <body></body> (required) | Marks the start and end of a Web page's displayable content. |
| <br /> | Inserts a line break. The <br /> tag doesn't have an end tag, and this tag is frequently used consecutively to create white space on a Web page. |
| <div></div> | Defines a division on a Web page, such as the navigation bar area, a column, or footer section. |
| <!DOCTYPE html PUBLIC...> (required) | Tells the browser what markup language the document uses so browsers can display the page accordingly. Note that although usually XHTML tags must be all lowercase, parts of the <!DOCTYPE> tag must be typed in all uppercase, as per the official Web standard. |
| <em></em> | Indicates to apply emphasis, usually italics, to the text appearing between the <em> and </em> tags. Preferred over the <i></i> (italics) tag pair. |
| <form></form> | Indicates the start and end of a form. Forms cannot be nested inside other forms. |
| <h1></h1><br><h2></h2><br><h3></h3> | Specifies heading text. Heading levels range from h1 through h6, with h1 being the largest heading size. |

**tip**   In Table 8-1, ellipses indicate areas where pre-defined browser instructions should be inserted in the XHTML tag. In contrast, *xxx* text serves as placeholder text in areas where values should be inserted, such as an image file name.

| Tags | Description |
|------|-------------|
| <head></head> (required) | Provides an area in which you can display your Web page's title, include search engine information, add advanced formatting information, embed CSS code or link to a style sheet, and write scripts. Other than the text within the embedded <title></title> tags, visitors viewing your Web page online won't see most of the head information, because most of the head information consists of browser instructions. |
| <html ...></html> (required) | Delineates the start and end of an XHTML document. No content should be placed before the <html...> tag or after the </html> tag, although the <!DOCTYPE> tag (which is a command—not content) should appear before the <html ...> tag. |
| <img src="*xxx.xxx*" alt="*xxx*" /> | Displays an image on a Web page. The **src** attribute points to the particular image that should be displayed. The **alt** attribute is required in XHTML, and it specifies the text that is displayed when the image is not displayed, when a mouse pointer is positioned on the image, or when a text reader (an application that provides audio assistance for low-vision users) encounters the element. |
| <input... /> | Defines a form input field, such as a Go button next to a drop-down list used to select an option. |
| <li></li> | Identifies a list item within an unnumbered (bulleted) list <ul> or an ordered (numbered) list <ol>. |
| <link... /> | Defines the relationship between two documents. For example, the <link /> tag can be used to link an XHTML document to a style sheet. |
| <meta ... /> | Contains information about the document, such as keywords, descriptions, and the document's character set. This tag must by nested between the <head></head> tags in an XHTML document. |
| <ol></ol> | Defines the start and end of an ordered (numbered) list. |

| Tags | Description |
|------|-------------|
| <option></option> | Specifies an item in a drop-down list. The option tag pair is nested within the <select></select> tags. |
| <p></p> | Indicates the start and end of a paragraph. By default, paragraphs are left-aligned. The </p> end tag is *not* optional in XHTML. Browsers typically insert a blank line (plus a little extra space) before starting a paragraph. |
| <select></select> | Creates a drop-down menu or scrolling list. The select tag pair contains option tags, which identify each item in the menu or list. |
| <span...></span> | Marks an area within another area (such as some text within a paragraph) that receives special formatting. |
| <strong></strong> | Indicates to apply strong emphasis, usually bold-face, to the text appearing between the <strong> and </strong> tags. Preferred over the <b></b> (bold) tag pair. |
| <title></title> (required) | Enables you to insert a Web document's title text, which browsers' display in the title bar. |
| <ul></ul> | Defines the start and end of an unnumbered (bulleted) list. |

## Using CSS

CSS is the paint and fabric in your XHTML room. An XHTML document builds the areas and walls of your Web document, while CSS provides the color, texture, and design. In fact, that's why *style* is part of the technology's name—cascading style sheets.

### Style sheets—here, there, everywhere

Style sheets can be embedded in an XHTML document, or they can be created as separate documents and linked to XHTML documents. Linking style sheets is the optimal approach as well as the

**lingo** *Style sheets* can be likened to templates that you use in desktop publishing applications. Like a template, a style sheet contains a collection of format settings and design rules that can be applied to all elements in a single Web page, multiple Web pages, or an entire site.

most common. When you create an external style sheet, you can link it to multiple XHTML files, thereby instantly providing consistent formatting to all the linked documents.

## Style sheets are good

The theory behind style sheets is that you can define a style for any type of element (such as a heading) in one place and the formatting will be applied to all instances of the element in an entire Web page, group of Web pages, or Web site. For example, let's say that you want all your headings in your Web site to be green. In the olden days, before style sheets, you would have to change every heading tag on every page in your site to include a **color** attribute that specifies to make the heading green. In a style sheet, you can simply state once that any text marked as a heading should be green. Fundamentally, CSS is that simple, although you'll see that there are a few details and rules you need to follow to ensure that your style sheets work properly and comply with current CSS Web standards.

## Parts and pieces of styles

In this walkthrough, you'll create two style sheets—styles_main.css and styles_presentation.css. The styles_main document links to the XHTML file. The styles contained in the styles_presentation style sheet are imported into the styles_main style sheet (which is in turn linked to the XHTML file). This setup enables you to easily change your Web site's colors, themes, and formatting by simply modifying or changing the styles_presentation style sheet. Figure 8-5 shows the relationship between the three documents you'll create in this project.

**tip** For organizational purposes, the file names of this project's style sheets all start with *style_*. By using this prefix, we ensure that all the style sheets will be grouped together in any folder that's organized by file name (which makes finding the file you need much easier).

**Figure 8-5** *Cascading style sheets in action*

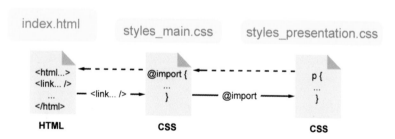

Each style in a cascading style sheet consists of a selector, an opening brace, a declaration, and a closing brace. The *selector* is the name of the style, and the *declaration* supplies the formatting specifics. For example, here's a style that instructs browsers to show all level 1 headings in blue:

```
h1 { color: blue; }
```

> **lingo** In CSS, a *selector* specifies the name of the style, and the *declaration* supplies the style's formatting specifics.

In the preceding example, **h1** is the selector, and **color: blue;** is the declaration. Let's take a closer look at selectors and declarations. Selectors come in a few varieties. In this walkthrough, you'll use the three main kinds of selectors–**type**, **class**, and **id**. Here's a quick rundown of each:

- **type selector**   A **type** selector applies styles to XTHML tag elements. For example, the **p** selector specifies styles for the <p> (paragraph) tag. Declarations associated with **type** selectors are applied to an XHTML document automatically.

- **class selector**   A **class** selector name is preceded with a period, like **.footer**. A **class** style can be applied within multiple XHTML tags on the same page (unless its purposefully restricted to a specific **type** selector). For example, in an XHTML document, the **footer class** style could be applied to paragraph text <p class="footer"> and an unordered list's text <ul class="footer"> on the same Web page.

- **id selector**   An **id** selector name is preceded with a number sign, also called an *octothorpe*, like **#banner**. An **id** style can be applied with *one* type of XHTML tag per page. For example, in an XHTML document, the **#banner** style could be applied to a page division <div id="banner">, but it could not later be used in a paragraph or heading tag on the same Web page.

Regardless of whether you're creating a style using a **type**, a **class**, or an **id** selector, each style must have at least one declaration that defines the style. (Remember–the declaration is the information between the curly braces.) Each declaration consists of two parts–property and value–formatted as *property: value;* (and notice the space after the colon and the trailing semicolon after the value–both constructs *must* be entered properly). In short, the *property* defines *what* you want to customize, and the *value* tells *how* you want to customize it. For example, let's expand our blue level 1 heading example from earlier to the following:

```
h1 {
    color: blue;
    font-weight: bold;
    font-variant: small-caps;
    }
```

**lingo**  In a style sheet, a *declaration block* is the name given to a group of declarations applied to a single selector. Keep in mind that we don't just make up the properties and values as we go. CSS has a set group of properties and values that you can use. You can find the properties and values on the W3C Web site (www.w3c.org) as well as in the resources listed at the end of this chapter.

In this example, **h1** is the **type** selector, and it's followed by a *declaration block*. The first declaration in this example calls the **color** property and assigns **blue** as the value, the second declaration calls the **font-weight** property and assigns the **bold** value, and the third declaration calls the **font-variant** property and assigns the **small-caps** value. This style indicates that all content appearing between an <h1> and </h1> tag pair in the linked XHTML document will be displayed as blue, bold, small-capped heading text.

To help you acclimate to the upcoming walkthrough, Tables 8-2 and 8-3 introduce you to the styles you'll create in this chapter. These tables include the **type**, **class**, and **id** selector names, along with brief descriptions of their functions. Keep in mind that these style names are specific to this walkthrough. When you create your own style sheets, you can create your own **class** and **id** names for your styles, although you'll have to define your custom styles using approved CSS properties and value settings.

Just as a last note in this section before we move on, we want to make a minor disclaimer. While we're confident that you can create XHTML and CSS documents from scratch, please keep in mind that this chapter serves only as an introduction to hand-coding Web sites. Covering all the available XHTML tags and attributes and CSS properties and values in a single chapter is unrealistic, but this chapter is packed with helpful coding tips, and you'll find some leads on good XHTML and CSS references in the "Additional Resources" section near the end of this chapter. The goal here is to introduce you to the big-picture

**Table 8-2   types, classes, and ids in styles_main.css**

| type, class, or id | Description |
| --- | --- |
| body | Sets the top, left, and right margins for page content |
| p, h1, h2, h3 | Sets the top, right, bottom, and left margins for paragraph and heading text |
| .banner_link | Positions a link in the banner area |
| .logo | Left-aligns the logo, with some space on the left and top |
| .page_title | Adds space (or *padding*) along the top and left edges of the page title image |
| .photo | Right-aligns photos, with some padding on all sides |
| .postcard | Adds a 2-pixel margin along bottom of each postcard image |
| .searchbar | Positions the drop-down list in a fixed point from the top and right edges |
| #banner | Sets the height of the banner, indicates which graphic to display, and repeats, or *tiles*, the graphic horizontally |
| #centercolumn | Positions the center column between the left and right columns and 165 pixels from the top |
| #leftcolumn | Positions the page layout's 150-pixel-wide left column at 25 pixels from the left edge and 180 pixels from top |
| #rightcolumn | Positions the page layout's 150-pixel-wide right column at 25 pixels from the right edge and 180 pixels from the top |

concepts. If you create the Web site described in this chapter's walk-through, you'll gain a strong foundation in XHTML and CSS theory as well as have templates that you can customize to create unique Web sites. (We even tell you how to use the walkthrough site's XHTML document and style sheets as templates later in this chapter.)

**Table 8-3**    **types, classes, and ids in styles_presentation.css**

| type, class, or id | Description |
| --- | --- |
| body | Sets the background color of the page, the default font family, and the default font size |
| h1, h2, h3 | Defines the default font, color, and font variant for all h1, h2 and h3 tags |
| a.link_on | Defines the display of the navigation link in the navigation bar for the current page a user is viewing |
| a.nav | Adds margins to the left and right of each link in the main navigation bar |
| a.nav:active | Defines the active (mouse down) style for the main navigation links when visitors are actively clicking the link |
| a.nav:hover | Defines the hover (mouse over) style for the main navigation links when visitors position the mouse pointer over the link |
| a.nav:link | Defines the default style for the main navigation links |
| a.nav:visited | Defines the default style for the visited main navigation links |
| .dropcap | Defines a drop-cap styled element |
| .footer | Describes how to display footer information |
| .footer_links | Describes how to display the text navigation links inserted at the bottom of the page |
| .leftbar_title | Defines the title text in the boxes in the left column |
| .mainnav | Defines how to display the text in the main navigation bar |
| #leftbar_box | Specifies custom formatting for boxes in the left column |
| #leftbar_box li | Formats the list items included in a left column box |
| #linkbar | Defines the background color of the main navigation bar |
| #shell | Encloses all the content on the page and adds a solid color background behind the page |

# Style Sheet Precedence

Styles can be defined inline within page content (such as a special style applied to a sentence in a paragraph), in a <style> area within an XHTML document's code, in an external style sheet linked to the XHTML document, or in all three areas. When you have inline, internal, and external styles defined, the browser must decide which styles to apply when multiple styles exist for the same element—in other words, the browser needs to know which styles carry the most weight. Basically, the rule of thumb is that the closer the style is to a Web document's actual content, the more weight it will carry. In other words, a style defined directly within content (inline) is considered *very* close to content, so the style earns top precedence. If no inline style is defined, the browser applies internal styles stored in the current document's <style> area in the source code. If no internal styles apply, the browser refers to styles defined in an external style sheet that's linked to the XHTML document. This flow of style precedence and application provides some of the cascading nature of cascading style sheets.

## Handling XHTML Documents and Web Graphics

By now, you should be comfortable with the concept that when you create a Web site, you usually work with multiple files. Often, you'll have your home page (an .html file generally named index.html or index.htm), possibly at least one .css style sheet, an image file for each graphical element on your page, and additional .html files for linked pages. Before you start creating a Web site, you need to devise an organizational scheme so that you don't drive yourself crazy later. We highly recommend that you create a folder to contain all the files used in your Web site, and within the main folder, create a subfolder named images. You can then store all your .html and .css documents in the main folder and place your graphics in the images folder. To illustrate, see Figure 8-6, which shows the online folders containing the documents and images necessary to create the completed Roadside Attractions project site.

**Figure 8-6** *Organizing a Web site's files and folders*

**see also**
Chapter 11,
"Going All Out
with FrontPage,"
describes how
you can upload
the Web pages
you create to the
Internet.

Keeping your files organized is imperative when you're adding graphics and creating hyperlinks, because you must include instructions in your Web documents regarding where the browser should look for a particular graphic or linked page. Further, being organized can greatly simplify the file uploading process when you're ready to go "live" by transferring your local files to a Web server. Your best bet is to create a folder that you can use consistently throughout the Web site creation process.

Along with being organized, you should rigorously save and preview your Web pages throughout the development process.

## Saving and Previewing XHTML Documents

**tip**  "Save, save, save!" should be one of your mantras when you're working with computers.

When you create Web documents—especially when you're hand-coding XHTML and CSS—you should save and preview with abandon. Speaking from firsthand "we can't believe we just lost all that data" experiences, we can recommend without reservation saving your work frequently—that pretty much goes without saying whenever you're working on any file on any computer. If monitors grew grass, our mice would create a well-worn diagonal path to the Save button—not to mention that we both knowingly contribute to the steady erosion of our CTRL and S keys by pressing CTRL+S so frequently.

In addition to frequently saving your files, you should preview the Web pages you build numerous times throughout the creation process. Previewing an XHTML page simply means looking at your

XHTML document in a browser (or a few browsers) as opposed to staring at the text and XHTML code version of the document in a text editor. Performing this exercise, you can see how your XHTML and CSS is working together (or not!) to format your content, and you can troubleshoot display problems early. We'll often alter a site's layout simply because what looks good on paper doesn't transpose well to an online page.

To preview a Web page in your browser, use any of the following procedures after you've created an .html file:

- Open the folder containing the .html document, and double-click the document's icon.

- Right-click your .html file, click **Open With** on the shortcut menu, and then click your browser application's name.

- Open your browser application (such as Internet Explorer), and type the .html file's location in the Address bar

- Open your browser application, open the folder containing the .html document, and drag the file's icon to the browser's Address bar.

We've covered a good bit of theory; now it's the witching hour. If you've read the previous few pages, you're ready to tackle this Web site walkthrough. You should have a workable knowledge of basic XHTML tags and CSS styles, realize that you should organize your XHTML documents and images in designated folders, and recognize the importance of frequently saving and previewing your Web site throughout the creation process. We're satisfied that you're ready, so let's get the project rolling.

## Planning an XHTML Site

For the XHTML walkthrough, we decided to create a Web site for an American studies professor at a well-known university. The Web site tells visitors about quirky-yet-significant roadside attractions in the United States. Our first planning step involved meeting with the professor and finding out what types of information she wanted to include on her Web site. In our initial consultation, we found that the professor had quite a bit of general travel information that she wanted

**note** We'll suggest specific points at which you should save and preview the project Web site in the next section. Feel free to save and preview your files more frequently than we suggest, however—especially if you take a break while creating.

to impart on the Web site, as well as information sorted by state. Based on this information, we initially attempted to design a two-tier navigation bar, but the design started to look too cluttered. We determined that we could make a cleaner site by using four specifically named buttons (which allows room to add another link or two in the future) and providing a search drop-down list so that visitors could quickly find information about each state. The final design resulted in a clean, flexible, user-friendly layout.

After you create the Roadside Attractions Web site, you can use your XHTML and CSS documents as templates to create a similar Web site that has a completely different look and feel (as we describe in the section "Using the Roadside Attractions Site as a Template," later in this chapter). Figure 8-7 shows the framework we came up with to illustrate the pages we wanted to include in the Roadside Attractions site using three state pages as sample state pages. Figure 8-8 shows a storyboard sketch of the Roadside Attractions site's home page.

**Figure 8-7** *Illustrating the Roadside Attractions site's framework*

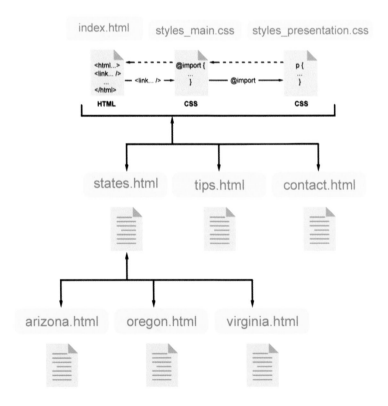

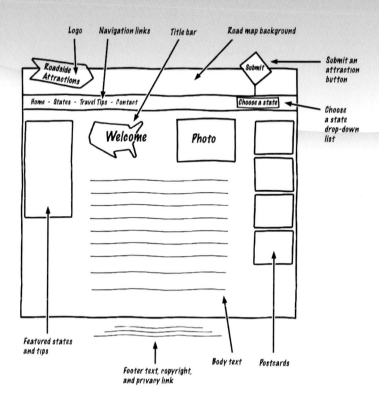

**Figure 8-8** *Sketching the Roadside Attractions site's home page design*

> **note** Notice in Figure 8-8 that we initially planned to insert the footer information below the site's bounding box. Later, during the design process, we realized that placing the footer information inside the site's bounding box makes more sense because the information is part of the Web site.

# Getting Your Folders and Files in Place

As we mentioned earlier in this chapter, your first task is to create a folder for your Web files and organize your graphics. Here's the process we suggest you follow (but feel free to change the folder location and name to suit your preferences):

1 Create a folder on your C drive, and name the folder **roadside**.

2 Open your browser, and display **www.creationguide.com/ch08**.

3 If desired, right-click and save the sample style sheets (**styles_presentation_blue.css** and **styles_presentation_green. css**) in the **C:\roadside** folder for experimentation purposes at the end of the walkthrough.

4 After you download the CSS documents, create a subfolder named **images** in the **C:\roadside** folder.

5 In your browser, display **www.creationguide.com/ch08/images**.

> **tip** When you've finished experimenting with the Roadside Attractions Web site, you can delete the C:\roadside folder if you want. Creating the roadside folder on your C drive without burying it in other folders will make it easy to find and delete later.

6 Right-click the **b_submit.gif** image (or right-click the **zip_images08.zip** file, if you're familiar with ZIP files and your system can extract them), and click **Save Target As** (if you're using Internet Explorer) to display the **Save As** dialog box.

7 In the **Save As** dialog box, navigate to the C:\roadside\images folder, and click **Save**.

8 Extract the ZIP files, or right-click the next graphic in www.creationguide.com/ch08/images and save the file to the images folder. .

9 If you are downloading the graphics one at a time, repeat step 8 until you've saved all the graphics files to your computer.

Your final file structure should look like the structure shown in Figure 8-9.

**Figure 8-9** *Exercise files properly arranged*

As you download the graphics for the roadside site, notice the naming scheme we've used to label the images:

- **b_xxx**   Specifies that the image is a button. In this project, we show you how to create text navigation links, so you'll only insert one button—a graphical button in the banner area that visitors can click to send an e-mail message to the site's owner.

- **banner.gif**   Identifies the background graphic for the banner area at the top of the page.

- **logo.gif**   Identifies the logo graphic. The roadside site uses the same logo graphic throughout the site, but you might have a few versions of a logo graphic (especially if you're using a smaller or modified version of the logo on subpages). Figure 8-10 shows the banner.gif, logo.gif, and b_submit.gif buttons that combine to complete the top portion of the Roadside Attractions Web site.

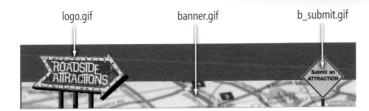

**Figure 8-10**   *Viewing the three graphic files used together to create the banner area at the top of each page*

- **p_xxx**   Specifies that the graphic is a photograph. The roadside site has one photograph in the body content area per page.

- **pc_xxx**   Indicates that the graphic is a full-size version of the postcard element. The roadside site includes a column of thumbnail postcards that show roadside attractions. Visitors can click a thumbnail postcard to view the full-size postcard in a separate window.

- **pc_xxx_th**   Indicates that the graphic is a thumbnail image of a postcard.

- **t_xxx**   Specifies that the image is a title bar banner graphic. For example, t_arizona.gif is the title bar banner graphic for the Arizona page.

When you create your own Web pages and Web graphics, you'll probably devise your own naming scheme. We've shown you the method we used to name our graphics to give you an idea of how helpful a naming system can be. By naming related types of pictures with a prefix, we can easily group elements. You'll see the benefit of a well-planned graphics-naming scheme as you start to code XHTML and CSS documents.

# Preparing Your Home Page Files

After you have your folders and files in place, you're ready to begin creating your site's home page. As we mentioned earlier, you'll be hand-coding three documents—index.html, styles_main.css, and styles_presentation.css. To begin the creation process, you first need to create index.html, the home page document that contains the standard tags that appear in all XHTML documents. Table 8-4 lists the standard tags that are required in every XHTML document.

**Table 8-4    Standard XHTML tags**

| Tags | Description |
|---|---|
| <!DOCTYPE html PUBLIC ...> | Specifies to browsers what markup the page uses so that the page can be displayed accurately (or as accurately as possible). An XHTML page's document type definition (DTD) can be *strict* (extremely sensitive to rules), *transitional* (the most Web-developer friendly declaration), or *frameset* (if your site uses frames, which we don't recommend). In this project, you'll use the transitional DOCTYPE declaration. |
| <html xmlns=...> </html> | Delineates the start and end of the XHTML document. In addition, this tag defines the *namespace* and *language declaration* in XHTML documents. The namespace ensures that browsers interpret the document as an XHTML document, and the language declaration identifies the page's language, such as English. |
| <head></head> | Provides an area in which you can display your Web page's title and meta tags, include search engine information, add advanced formatting information, and write scripts. Other than the text within the embedded <title> </title> tags, most head information provides instructions to browsers and is not displayed as content on a Web page. |

| Tags | Description |
|---|---|
| \<meta ... /\> | Provides information about the page, such as key-words, page descriptions, and the set of characters (such as English, Dutch, Russian, Polish, Arabic, and so forth) that should be used to render the page. Meta tags do not have a separate end tag, and they are nested in the \<head\> \</head\> area. |
| \<title\>\</title\> | Enables you to insert a Web page's title text, which browsers display in the title bar. |
| \<body\>\</body\> | Marks the start and end of the Web page's displayable content. |

**note**  Remember that XHTML Web standards require tags to be all lower-case. For instance, you must type **\<body\>** in your code; you cannot type **\<BODY\>**, **\<Body\>**, **\<BoDy\>**, or any other combination of uppercase and lowercase letters. Only the \<!DOCTYPE...\> tag contains uppercase and lowercase letters.

Figure 8-11 shows the proper way to nest the standard XHTML tags in an XHTML document and how to insert title text. (In Figure 8-12, shown later in this section, you'll see how the HTML tags with  title text added would appear in a browser.) After you type the standard XHTML tags in a text document, you need to save the text document as an .html document, as described in the following procedure.

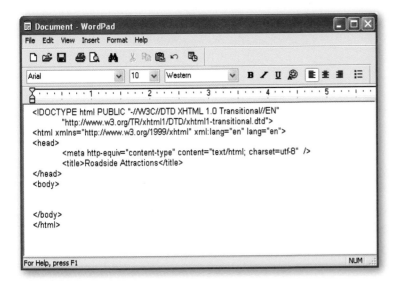

**Figure 8-11**  *Viewing XHTML standard tags with title text inserted between the \<title\> tags*

To begin creating the roadside site's home page, follow these steps:

1  Open Notepad, WordPad, TextEdit, or another text editor. We used WordPad throughout this project.

2  In a new document, type the following DOCTYPE declaration, and then press ENTER:

```
<!DOCTYPE html PUBLIC "-//W3C//DTD XHTML 1.0 Transitional//EN"
          "http://www.w3.org/TR/xhtml1/DTD/xhtml1-transitional.dtd">
```

> **note**  When you use a Web editor, such as FrontPage, the !DOCTYPE statement is added automatically.

3  Type the following HTML start tag text, required for XHTML documents, and then press ENTER:

```
<html xmlns="http://www.w3.org/1999/xhtml" xml:lang="en" lang="en">
```

4  Type **<head>**, and then press ENTER.

5  Type the following *metadata* to define the *UTF-8* (the most universal) character set:

```
<meta http-equiv="content-type" content="text/html; charset=utf-8" />
```

> **note**  Notice that the <meta /> tag includes a forward slash before the closing angle bracket. This is because the meta tag is a stand-alone tag, without a start and end tag pair, and in XHTML, all tags must be closed.

6  Press ENTER, type **<title>Roadside Attractions</title>**, and then press ENTER again.

7  Type **</head>**, and then press ENTER.

8  Type **<body>**, press ENTER a few times (to give you some breathing room when you enter the content information in the body of your Web page), type **</body>**, and then press ENTER again.

9  Type **</html>** to complete the standard XHTML tag setup.

You're now ready to name and save the file to your **C:\roadside** folder.

> **lingo**  In source code, *metadata* is descriptive text inserted in a <meta /> tag that provides information about the Web document.

10  On the **File** menu, click **Save**. The **Save As** dialog box opens.

11  In the **Save In** drop-down list, navigate to the **C:\roadside** folder.

12  Type **index.html** in the **File Name** box, and ensure that **Text Document** is selected in the **Save As Type** list. (If necessary, click the down arrow to select the **Text Document** option.)

13  Click **Save**.

14  Close WordPad.

Your C:\roadside folder should now contain an index.html file, and the file icon should indicate that the file is an .html document. At this point, you can already view your file in your browser. To view your newly created XHTML file, double-click index.html. The file should open in your Web browser, as shown in Figure 8-12. Notice that the only content is the Web page's title text, which your browser displays in title bar.

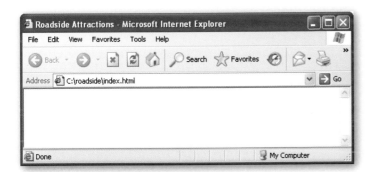

**Figure 8-12** *Viewing an XHTML document that contains only standard XHTML tags and title text*

Now that the Web page's title and standard XHTML tags are in place, let's create the CSS files so that you can set up the page layout and format the **type** selector styles.

## Page Layout and Formatting Type Selectors

Now that you have your index.html document set up, you need to set up your style sheets. Like HTML documents, CSS documents are text documents saved with .css extensions. Each style sheet is simply a list of styles. Each style tells a browser how to display certain elements. This will make much more sense as you work with the technology, so let's get started. In this section, you will work with all three of the files you're creating in this walkthrough—index.html, styles_main.css, and styles_presentation.css.

**lingo** *UTF* stands for Unicode Transformation Format, and different UTF encoding schemes can represent different character sets to accommodate specific languages. Specifically, UTF-8 can represent many of the world's alphabets, so it's one of the most widely used encoding schemes.

**note** Content text—text between and outside XHTML tags—appears in browser windows in the same case as it is entered in the text document. Thus, if you type **ROADSIDE ATTRACTIONS** instead of **Roadside Attractions** in step 6, the page's title will appear in all uppercase letters. Also, remember that you don't have to worry about putting too many spaces (including blank lines) between content text and XHTML tags. When a browser displays the document, it ignores the extra spaces.

## Creating CSS Documents

The first order of business is to create and name your style sheets:

1  **Open WordPad or another text editor.**

    You're going to save two blank text documents as your .css files.

2  **On the File menu, click Save. In the Save As dialog box, navigate to C:\roadside, type styles_main.css in the File Name box, click Text Document in the Save As Type list, click Save, and then click Yes.**

3  **On the File menu, click Save As (*not* Save). In the Save As dialog box, type styles_presentation.css in the File Name box, click Text Document in the Save As Type list, click Save, and then click Yes.**

4  **Close WordPad, and view the contents of C:\roadside. Your folder should now look like Figure 8-13. The files you created are index.html, styles_main.css, and styles_presentation.css.**

**Figure 8-13**  *Verifying file creation*

## Linking XHTML and CSS Documents

Even though your documents are blank, you can link them so that their relationships are set for later. For this walkthrough, you'll use the <link... /> tag in the XHTML document to link to the styles_main. css document. Then, in the styles_main.css document, you'll use the

@**import** method to include the styles defined in styles_presentation. css. Here are the steps:

**tip** You can also open HTML and CSS documents in WordPad by displaying C:\road-side, right-clicking the document you want to open, clicking Open With on the shortcut menu, and then selecting WordPad.

1 Open WordPad or another text editor, and then click **Open** on the **File** menu.

2 In the **Open** dialog box, click **All Documents** in the **Files of Type** list.

3 Double-click **index.html**. The XHTML document you created earlier is displayed.

4 Click after **</title>**, press ENTER, and type the following text to link to your styles_main.css document. (Notice that the CSS document's name is the value for the **href** attribute.)

```
<link rel="stylesheet" type="text/css" href="styles_main.css" />
```

5 Click **Save**.

6 Click **Open** on the **File** menu, and then double-click **styles_main.css**.

7 To attach the styles_presentation.css style sheet to the styles_main.css style sheet, type the following:

```
@import url(styles_presentation.css);
```

8 Save the document, but don't close it. Now that your documents are linked, you're ready to define some page layout styles

## Defining Page Layout and Type Selector Styles

The Web site you're building in this walkthrough consists of a banner area above three columns—the left and right columns are set to 150 pixels wide, and the center column is designed to expand relative to the visitor's window size. The entire site is built with 25 pixels of space (or padding) around the page. You'll define the page setup by creating type selector and **id** styles in your CSS documents. Then you'll code page divisions in your XHTML file that reference the styles in your CSS files. That might sound a tad complicated, but if you follow along carefully and compare your code to the samples shown along the way, you'll do fine.

In this section, you create the necessary styles; in the next section, you add tags to your XHTML document. Your first task is to define the margins for the Web page's <body> XHTML element in the styles_main.css document:

1 Press ENTER twice, and then type the following **type** selector and declaration block, pressing TAB to indent each *property: value* pair and following each value with a semicolon:

```
body {
    margin-top: 0px;
    margin-left: 25px;
    margin-right: 25px;
    }
```

2 Press ENTER twice, and then type the following top, right, bottom, and left margin settings (in that order) for the paragraph (<p>) and heading (<h1>, <h2>, <h3>) elements used in the walkthrough, making sure to separate each **type** selector with a comma and a space:

```
p, h1, h2, h3 { margin: 10px 20px 20px 20px; }
```

Next you'll define the left, center, and right columns by assigning position placement and margins. In this page setup, the left and right columns are assigned absolute positions so that they are always displayed a set distance from the left and right edges of the browser window. The center column's width is not defined so that it can expand and contract depending on the size of the browser window. The following three steps create **id** styles (identified by the leading number signs) named **leftcolumn**, **centercolumn**, and **rightcolumn**:

**tip**   Later, when you're contemplating customizing the layout, you can experiment with changing the width settings in the **leftcolumn** and **rightcolumn** styles to modify the page layout.

3 To specify the structure of the fixed, 150-pixel-wide left column, press ENTER twice, and then type the following **id** selector and declaration block:

```
#leftcolumn {
position: absolute;
top: 180px;
left: 25px;
width: 150px;
}
```

**4** **To specify the structure of the center expandable column, press ENTER twice, and then type the following id selector and declaration block:**

```
#centercolumn {
   top: 165px;
   margin-left: 157px;
   margin-right: 157px;
   }
```

**5** **To specify the structure of the fixed right column, press ENTER twice, and then type the following id selector and declaration block:**

```
#rightcolumn {
   position: absolute;
   top: 180px;
   right: 25px;
   width: 150px;
   }
```

**6** **Save your work. Your styles_main.css document should look like the one shown in Figure 8-14.**

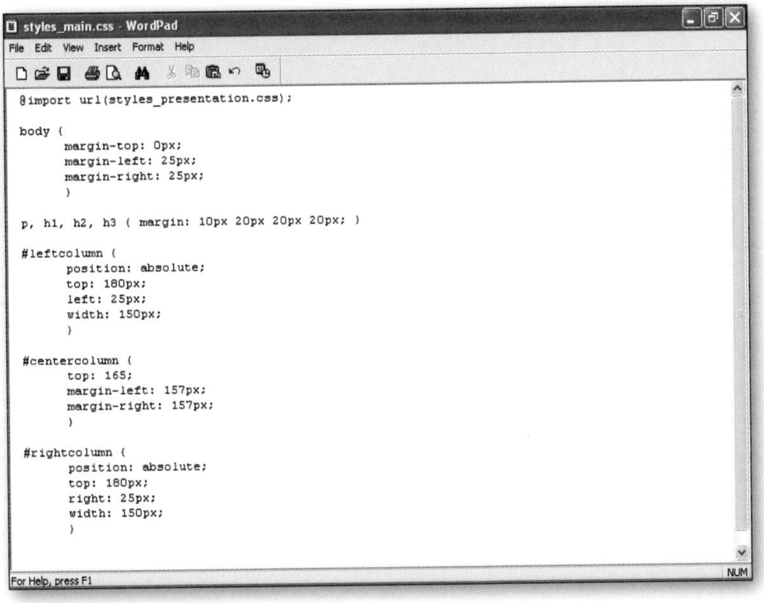


```
@import url(styles_presentation.css);

body {
      margin-top: 0px;
      margin-left: 25px;
      margin-right: 25px;
      }

p, h1, h2, h3 { margin: 10px 20px 20px 20px; }

#leftcolumn {
      position: absolute;
      top: 180px;
      left: 25px;
      width: 150px;
      }

#centercolumn {
      top: 165;
      margin-left: 157px;
      margin-right: 157px;
      }

#rightcolumn {
      position: absolute;
      top: 180px;
      right: 25px;
      width: 150px;
      }
```

**Figure 8-14** *Page structure styles in styles_main.css*

The styles_main.css document handles the page layout spacing issues, and the styles_presentation.css style sheet handles the formatting issues, including background colors, font sizes, and other formatting settings. The rationale for putting formatting styles in their own document is based on the idea that it will be easy for you to modify your Web site's formatting later. This type of accessibility can make updating your site with seasonal color schemes or making other aesthetic changes easy to implement.

At this point, you'll create default formatting for the Web site's body, headings, and background *shell* color. (The shell area contains the main content of the Web page.)

7 **On the File menu, click Open, and then double-click styles_presentation.css.**

8 **Type the following style selector and declaration block to set the Web page's background-color to dark gray; the font-family to Verdana as a first choice, Arial as a second choice, and sans-serif as a third choice (each browser will use the first font in the font-family list that's installed on the computer); and the font-size to small:**

```
body {
    background-color: #696969;
    font-family: Verdana, Arial, sans-serif;
    font-size: small;
    }
```

9 **Press ENTER twice, and then type the following formatting properties and values for the headings used in the Web site. (On the roadside Web site, headings are rust color and in small caps.)**

# Hexadecimal Color Values
Many times, color properties in XHTML and CSS source code are defined using hexadecimal color values, such as #FFFFCC. Hexadecimal (a base-16 numbering system) values are notated with a number sign (#) followed by six number or letter values (three pairs of two). Each set of two letters or numbers defines the Red, Green, or Blue (RGB) value of the color. The first two letters define Red, the next two define Green, and the last two define Blue. For example, #000000 is black (no colors), #FFFFFF is white (all colors), and #FFCC00 (a mix of red and green) is gold. You can find a number of free tools on the Web that help you create and define hexadecimal color values. To help you get started, we show you the Web-safe colors in hexadecimal values at www.creationguide.com/colorchart.

```
h1, h2, h3 {
   color: #952C29;
   font-variant: small-caps;
   }
```

**10** Press ENTER twice, and then type the following **id** style to set the background shell on the Web page to light gray:

```
#shell { background-color: #D1D1D1; }
```

**11** Save styles_presentation.css without closing your text editor. Your presentation style sheet should look similar to the style sheet shown in Figure 8-15.

**Figure 8-15** *Page layout formatting styles in styles_presentation.css.*

## Setting Up a Page Structure in XHTML

At this point, you have basic page structure styles defined in your CSS documents but nothing in your XHTML document defining the Web page's structure or formatting. Therefore, you now need to apply the styles from the CSS document to areas in your XHTML document. To do this, you define divisions in your Web document using <div...> </div> tags and specify which style applies to each division, as follows:

> **tip** For added assistance, you can refer to Figure 8-16 while you add page divisions and style references to your XHTML document.

**1** In WordPad or your text editor, open index.html.

**2** Click after <body>, and then press ENTER twice.

**3** To set up the banner area in your Web page, type **<div id= "banner">**, press ENTER, type **</div>**, and then press ENTER twice.

**tip**   Whenever you enter XHTML code, always verify that you've included all angle brackets (<>) and quotation marks ("") in your XHTML code as well as spelled commands, property names, and values properly. Missing small elements or misspelling commands can cause your Web page to be displayed incorrectly or not at all. We've included figures showing the code you're creating throughout this chapter so that you can easily check your work.

4   To begin the shell formatting, type **<div id="shell">**, and then press ENTER twice. (Note that this tag will be closed later in the document, after the rest of the page's content.)

5   To specify an area for the link bar (the color background that contains the navigation bar's links), type **<div id="linkbar">**, press ENTER, type **</div>**, and then press ENTER twice.

6   To specify an area for the center column, type **<div id="centercolumn">**, press ENTER, type **</div>**, and then press ENTER twice.

7   To specify an area for the left column, type **<div id="leftcolumn">**, press ENTER, type **</div>**, and press ENTER twice.

8   To specify an area for the right column, type **<div id="rightcolumn">**, press ENTER, type **</div>**, and then press ENTER twice.

9   To end the shell division started earlier (and to define the bottom of the light gray page background), type **</div>**.

10  Save index.html. Your XHTML code should look like the code shown in Figure 8-16. The newly added code in the figure is shown in red for easy reference.

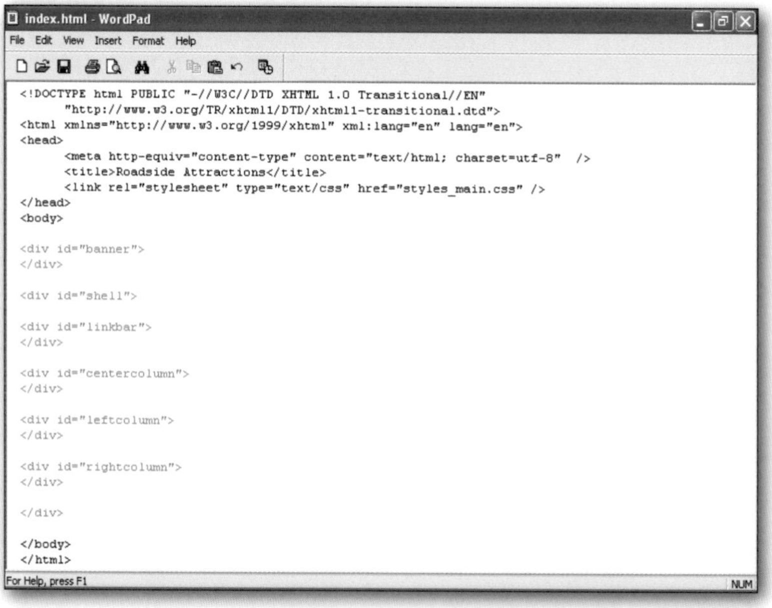

**Figure 8-16**   *Marking and applying styles to page divisions.*

```
index.html - WordPad
File  Edit  View  Insert  Format  Help

<!DOCTYPE html PUBLIC "-//W3C//DTD XHTML 1.0 Transitional//EN"
     "http://www.w3.org/TR/xhtml11/DTD/xhtml11-transitional.dtd">
<html xmlns="http://www.w3.org/1999/xhtml" xml:lang="en" lang="en">
<head>
        <meta http-equiv="content-type" content="text/html; charset=utf-8"  />
        <title>Roadside Attractions</title>
        <link rel="stylesheet" type="text/css" href="styles_main.css" />
</head>
<body>

<div id="banner">
</div>

<div id="shell">

<div id="linkbar">
</div>

<div id="centercolumn">
</div>

<div id="leftcolumn">
</div>

<div id="rightcolumn">
</div>

</div>

</body>
</html>
For Help, press F1                                                              NUM
```

# Building the Banner Area

With the basic page layout taken care of, you can now start to add content. As you add content, you'll be able to watch your page take shape visually as well as in the source code. The banner area, which appears at the top of your Web page, provides a logical starting point. To create the roadside site's banner, you will position and insert three graphics. Two of the graphics will serve as links, and the back-ground graphic will *tile*, or repeat, to accommodate variously sized browser windows. You might have caught a glimpse of the banner setup earlier in this chapter, in Figure 8-10.

**lingo** *Tiling* refers to repeating an image across a window's area or down (or both) until the entire space or window is filled with the repeating image.

## Creating Banner Styles

To set the banner styles, you define the banner **id** (which you've already referenced in the XHTML document earlier) and two classes in styles_main.css. Then you insert some XHTML commands in index.html. The first step is to set up your styles:

1 Open **styles_main.css** in your text editor, click below the **#rightcolumn** declaration block (refer to Figure 8-17 if necessary), and then press ENTER.

   The banner **id** style names the graphic that will be displayed in the banner area's background (which means you can customize the background by changing the graphical image reference). The banner **id** also specifies to repeat the image horizontally (along the x-axis) to fill the banner area and sets its height to 135 pixels.

2 To create the banner **id**, type the following **id** selector and declaration block. (Notice that the **background-image** value includes the folder and file name for the image reference.)

```
#banner {
    background-image: url(images/banner.gif);
    background-repeat: repeat-x;
    height: 135px;
    }
```

Next you'll create two classes to position two graphics that appear in front of the background graphics. These classes position the logo graphic and the Submit button graphic.

**3** To position the logo graphic, create the following class:

```
.logo {
   float: left;
   position: relative;
   margin-left: 20px;
   top: 14px;
   }
```

**4** To position the banner_link graphic, create the following class:

```
.banner_link {
   float: right;
   position: relative;
   margin-right: 25px;
   top: 15px;
   }
```

**5** Save your changes. Your styles_main.css document should look like the style sheet shown in Figure 8-17.

**Figure 8-17** *Adding styles for the banner area*

## Inserting Graphics

The styles you defined for the banner area make coding your XHTML document quick and easy. In fact, you've already added a graphic to your XHTML document because you've defined the banner graphic for the banner **id**, which you've already referenced in a <div> tag. At this point, you need to add, position, and link the logo and Submit button graphics.

The roadside design uses a standard page design, so we opted to insert the logo in the top-left (prime real estate) corner. You'll use the home page as a template for your subpages, so we show you how to link the logo to the home page. That way, when you use the home page as a template, all subpages will automatically include a logo that links to the site's index.html home page.

When you insert a logo, you're basically inserting an image. To insert an image in an HTML document, you use the <img> tag with the **src** attribute, which points to a particular graphic, and the **alt** attribute, which describes the image. For example, to specify the roadside site's logo, you'd type **<img src="images/logo.gif" alt="roadside attractions">**. Similarly, when you insert your logo and format it as a hyperlink, you use the same XHTML tags that you would use to link any graphic or text. So pay attention to the following steps—you'll find yourself using these commands quite a bit. First let's insert the logo graphic. (We'll take care of linking the graphic in just a bit.)

> **tip**  Adding spaces and returns in your XHTML code won't affect your Web page's appearance, so you don't need to add returns in your XHTML document to match the examples in the text. In some cases, our text examples had to be shortened to fit properly within the book's page design. Your code can be entered as shown in the project's XHTML reference figures included throughout this chapter.

The <img> tag's attributes used in the roadside site are defined as follows:

- **src**   Specifies the file name and location of the image (the source of the image) to be displayed. (Required attribute.)

- **alt**   Enables you to provide descriptive text that shows when the mouse pointer is positioned over the image area and is spoken by automated text readers. (Required attribute.)

- **width, height**   Specify the image's width and height. You should specify the sizes of your images to help browsers display your Web page's layout faster. Keep in mind that any actual image resizing (as in making an image larger or smaller) should be done in your image editing program and not by using **width** and **height** attributes in your XHTML document—ideally, you want each image to be sized as closely as possible to the size your Web page will display it.

- **border**   Specifies the thickness of the border around the image. By default, a 1-pixel border appears around graphics that are formatted as hyperlinks. Generally, designers change the default by setting the **border** attribute to **0**, since most people realize that when the mouse pointer changes over an image, the image is clickable.

- **class, id**   Points to the **class** or **id** style that has been defined in a style sheet.

To insert the logo and Submit button graphics, follow these steps:

1 **Open index.html in your text editor. Notice that you've already created a page division for the banner and referenced the banner id you defined in your styles_main.css document. This means your banner area already has a background image. Click after the <div id= "banner"> tag, and then press ENTER.**

2 **To insert and position the logo image, press TAB, and type the following image tag:**

```
<img src="images/logo.gif" alt="Roadside Attractions" width="218"
height="121" border="0" class="logo" />
```

3 **Press ENTER.**

4 **To insert and position the Submit image, press TAB, and type the following image tag:**

```
<img src="images/b_submit.gif" alt="Submit an Attraction"
width="95" height="120" border="0" class="banner_link" />
```

5 **Click Save.**

Next you'll format the logo.gif image to serve as a hyperlink to the home page, and you'll format the b_sumit.gif image to serve as a hyperlink to a blank e-mail message form.

## Linking Graphics

Creating a hyperlink entails embedding some text or a graphic to serve as an *anchor* by nesting it inside the <a></a> tag pair and then specifying to the browser what should be displayed after the anchor

> **lingo**  An *anchor* is either the clickable text or graphical component of a hyperlink or a specified target area within a document. Anchor text is surrounded by the <a></a> tag pair in XHTML documents.

element is clicked. To make the logo a hyperlink to the home page and the Submit graphic a hyperlink to a blank e-mail message form, follow these steps:

1 Click before the **logo.gif <img... />** tag, and then type **<a href= "index.html">** to specify that when users click the logo, they will be taken to the home page. (As mentioned earlier, this linking information will come in handy when we copy the home page to create subpages.)

2 Click after the closing **/>** of the **<img... />** tag, and then type **</a>** to specify the end of the anchor's contents.

3 To change the b_submit.gif graphic to a hyperlink, click before the **b_submit.gif <img... />** tag, and then type **<a href= "mailto:mm@creationguide.com">** to specify that when users click the Submit button graphic, an empty e-mail message form will open, addressed to the specified e-mail address.

4 Click after the closing **/>** of the <img... /> tag, and type **</a>** to specify the end of the anchor's contents.

5 Save index.html. Your XHMTL code should look similar to the code shown in Figure 8-18.

> **tip** In step 3, you should enter your own e-mail address in place of mm@ creationguide.com. That way, you can test your hyperlink to see if you entered the XHTML code properly.

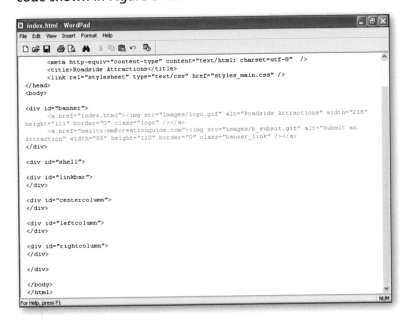

**Figure 8-18** *Viewing the banner code in index.html*

6 Close or minimize your text editor, and then open index.html in your browser window to preview your Web site's progress. Your site's banner should look similar to the one shown in Figure 8-19. Click each link in your page to verify that you don't encounter any errors.

**Figure 8-19** *Previewing the completed banner area*

> **tip**   You must save your XHTML document before you can view the document's changes in a browser window. If your most recent changes aren't displayed in your browser, verify that you've saved your XHTML document. If you still aren't seeing the changes, click the **Refresh** button in your browser to ensure that you're viewing the most up-to-date version of your page.

## Building the Navigation Bar

Some navigation bars use graphical buttons. For this walkthrough's navigation bar, we chose to use text links instead of buttons so you can see how to set custom link colors in place of default hyperlink colors. As an added bonus, we include a drop-down search list feature that you can easily customize and use in other Web pages. As with other procedures in this walkthrough, we'll start by defining some styles, and then we'll add the XHTML code to index.html.

# Adding Navigation Bar Styles

In this section, you'll define the styles used in the navigation bar. First you'll create the **searchbar** class to specify that the search drop-down list is positioned on the navigation bar, 25 pixels from the right edge:

**1** In your text editor, open styles_main.css, click below the banner_link declaration box, press ENTER, and then type the following style code to position the search box:

```
.searchbar {
    position: absolute;
    top: 139px;
    right: 0px;
    width: 175px;
    }
```

**2** Save styles_main.css, and then open styles_presentation.css in your text editor.

**3** Click below the shell **id** declaration, press ENTER, and then type the following link bar **id**, which specifies the link bar's background color (rust), height (28 pixels), border size (1 pixel), style (solid line), and color (orange):

```
#linkbar {
    background-color: #952C29;
    height: 28px;
    border: 1px solid #CC9966;
    }
```

**4** Press ENTER twice.

Next you'll define the font styles and padding (space around all the navigation text) for the links in the navigation bar by creating the **mainnav** class. Then you'll format each button state by creating a series of related classes, including the following:

- **a.nav**   Sets the left and right margins of each link.

- **a.nav:link**   Formats the link in a rest state.

- **a.nav:visited**   Specifies how the link should appear after the associated page has been visited.

- **a.nav:hover**   Specifies how the link should appear when the mouse pointer is over the link.

- **a.nav:active**   Specifies how the link should appear when it is clicked.

- **a.link_on**   Specifies how the link should appear when the visitor is on the link's destination page.

**5** To create the **mainnav** class, type the following:

```
.mainnav {
    color: white;
    font-size: 11px;
    font-weight: bold;
    padding: 6px 0 0 10px;
    }
```

**6** Save your work.

**7** Press ENTER twice, and then type the following style definitions for the navigation bar's link states (as shown in Figure 8-20):

```
a.nav { margin-left: 10px; margin-right: 10px; }
a.nav:link { color: white; text-decoration: none; }
a.nav:visited { color: white; text-decoration: none; }
a.nav:hover { color: #FFFFCC; border-bottom: 1px dotted #FFFFCC; }
a.nav:active { color: #FFFFCC; border-bottom: 1px dotted #FFFFCC; }

a.link_on {
    color: #FFCC00;
    text-decoration: none;
    margin-left: 10px;
    margin-right: 10px;
    }
```

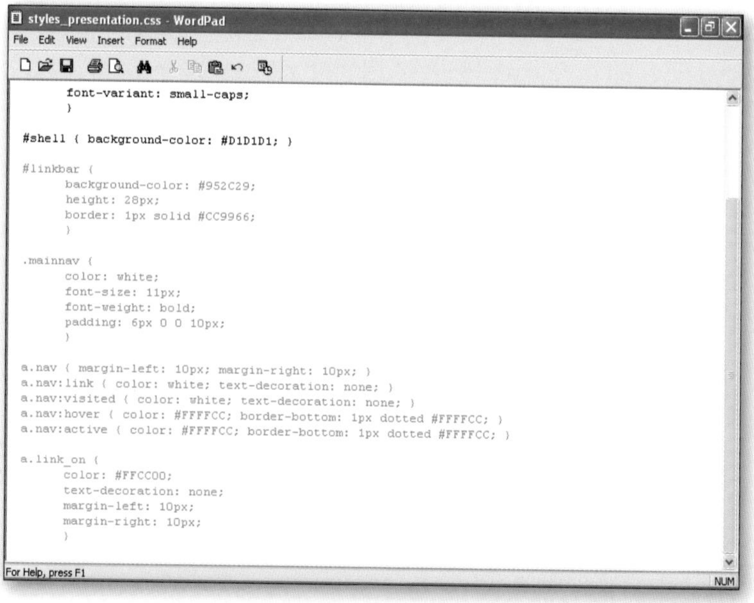

**Figure 8-20**  *Styles defined to format the navigation bar's text links*

**8** Save your work, and then verify that it matches the style sheet shown in Figure 8-20.

# Adding Navigation Bar Text and Hyperlink Properties

After you define navigation bar styles, you need to enter the text links and hyperlink properties in your .html document. Earlier, you set up a division on the page for the link bar, so you can enter the navigation bar code inside that page division's tags, as described in the following steps:

**1** Open index.html in your text editor, click after **<div id="linkbar">**, and then press ENTER.

**2** Press TAB, type **<div class="mainnav">** to add the **mainnav** style to the inside of the link bar area, and then press ENTER.

For each link on the navigation bar, you must specify the anchor reference and the class style. In addition, each link is separated by a long dash called an *em dash* (—). To include symbols in XHTML documents, you need to enter *character entity references*. (To see a list of character entity references that you can use in XHTML documents, visit www.creationguide.com/characters.) The character entity reference for the em dash is *&mdash;*, as you can see in step 3.

> **lingo**   A *character entity reference* is a special key combination that includes an ampersand (&) and enables you to display nonstandard characters— such as accent marks, registered trademarks, and so forth—in Web pages. For a printable list of common character entity references, see www.creationguide.com/characters.

**3** Press TAB twice, and then type the following navigation bar link information:

```
<a href="index.html" class="link_on">HOME</a> &mdash;
<a href="states.html" class="nav">STATES</a> &mdash;
<a href="tips.html" class="nav">TRAVEL TIPS</a> &mdash;
<a href="contact.html" class="nav">CONTACT</a>
```

In the preceding code, note that the text in all uppercase will be displayed on the navigation bar in all uppercase letters—this is a style preference, not a requirement. Further, you might have noticed that your navigation bar links to documents that don't exist. No worries—we show you how to create those pages later in this walkthrough. Finally, you might have noticed that the HOME link uses a different class. That's because the current page is the home page, so the HOME link is displayed as if it's turned "on" (with a bright yellow color). When you create the other pages, you'll change the HOME link's class to **nav** and the current page's class to **link_on**.

4 **Press ENTER, press TAB, type </div>, and then save your work.**

Before we wrap up the navigation bar code, you need to create the Search drop-down list, as described next.

## Inserting the Search List Box

> **lingo** *JavaScript* is a programming language that is commonly used to enhance Web pages.

The Search list box uses some JavaScript code. You can freely access JavaScript code and code generators online. We give you a few more JavaScript treats in Chapter 13, "Updating, Archiving, Moving On," but we wanted to show you how to insert a simple JavaScript drop-down list when you're hand-coding.

The main parts of the code sample that you're interested in at this point are the form name, which gives the list a name in your code; the option values, which identify where Web page users will go to when they select an option (such as arizona.html); and the option names, which is the text displayed in the drop-down list (such as *Arizona*) and between the <option></option> tag pair in your code. To help you test creating a Search list box, we've provided the arizona.html, oregon.html, and virginia.html files with the other project files that you downloaded at the beginning of this chapter.

Here are the steps to create the Search drop-down list used in this project's navigation bar:

1 **Press ENTER twice, press TAB, and type the following <form...> start tag. (You can give your form any name—in this sample, the form name is state_search.)**

```
<form class="searchbar" name="state_search">
```

2 **Press ENTER, press TAB, and then type the following code to create the code that will automatically take visitors to the selected page:**

```
<select name="menu" onChange="location=document.state_search.menu.
options

[document.state_search.menu.selectedIndex].value;" value="GO">
```

**3** Press ENTER, press TAB twice, and then type the following code to create the list of search options. (You'll create the arizona.html, oregon.html, and virginia.html pages referenced in your drop-down list later in this walkthrough.)

```
<option>Choose a State</option>
<option value="arizona.html">Arizona</option>
<option value="oregon.html">Oregon</option>
<option value="virginia.html">Virginia</option>
```

**4** Press ENTER, press TAB, and then type **</select>** to complete the list.

**5** Press ENTER, press TAB, and then type **</form>** to complete the form.

**6** Save your work. Your XHTML code, including the Search drop-down list JavaScript, should look like the code shown in Figure 8-21.

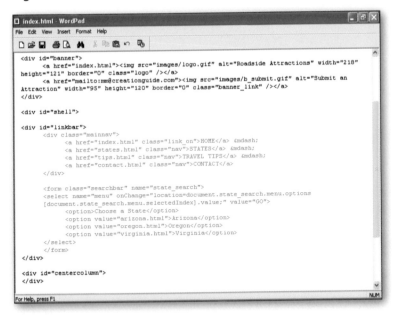

**Figure 8-21** *XHTML code to build the navigation bar*

> **lingo** *ActiveX* is a set of technologies developed by Microsoft that enable information sharing among applications. Web developers can use ActiveX controls to add advanced features to Web sites.

> **note** After you add the JavaScript drop-down list to your site, you might get an ActiveX message in your browser window when you preview your site locally in your browser. To proceed, simply tell your browser to show the content. The content is safe—after all, you created it! When you upload your page to the Web, the message won't be displayed, as you can see on the online version of the sample site, at www.creationguide.com/roadside.

**7** To see your Web page's progress, open index.html in your browser window. Your page should look similar to the page shown in Figure 8-22. Hover the mouse pointer over the navigation bar links to see the text effects. Keep in mind that if you click a navigation bar link, you'll get an error message, because you haven't created your site's subpages yet.

**Figure 8-22** *The navigation bar, with text links and a Search drop-down list*

## Adding Content to the Left Column

Up to now, you've done quite a bit of work setting up the page layout and getting the details in order. Next you'll fill your page with content, which often is the most rewarding part of the process, because your page will start to reveal the framework you've built. We'll start by filling the left column with text. In this section, you'll learn how to create a linked unnumbered list and a numbered list. Figure 8-23 shows the left column content that you'll create.

**Figure 8-23** *Creating linked and numbered lists*

## Creating a Linked Unnumbered List

An unnumbered list appears as a bulleted list on a Web page. In this section, you'll create a bulleted list in which each state name is linked to its state page. As you might imagine, you should first define the styles for the left column. The main areas you want to format are the title boxes, the white background area, and the spacing around the text.

1 Open styles_presentation.css in your text editor, click after the **a.link_on** declaration block, and then press ENTER twice.

2 To define the **leftbar_box id** (the white background box), the **leftbar_box li id** (for list items), and the **leftbar_title class** (to format the box titles), type the following code:

```
#leftbar_box {
    background-color: white;
    border: 1px solid #CC9966;
    }

#leftbar_box li { padding: 0 10px 0 0; }

leftbar_title {
    color: white;
    font-weight: bold;
    text-align: center;
    background-color: #952C29;
    border: 1px solid #CC9966;
    padding: 5px 0 5px 0;
    }
```

3 Save your work, and then open index.html in your text editor.

4 Click after the **<div id="leftcolumn">** tag, and then press ENTER.

5 Create the formatted box in the left column by pressing TAB and then typing **<div id="leftbar_box">**.

6 To add the title Featured States, press ENTER, press TAB twice, and then type the following:

```
<div class="leftbar_title">Featured States</div>
```

7 Press ENTER, press TAB twice, and then type **<ul>** to start the unnumbered list.

8 To create the first list item, press ENTER, press TAB three times, and then type **<li>**.

9 To add the linked text as the list item, type **<a href="arizona.html">Arizona</a>**.

10 Complete the list item by typing **</li>**.

11 Press ENTER, press TAB three times, and add the following two linked list items:

```
<li><a href="oregon.html">Oregon</a></li>
<li><a href="virginia.html">Virginia</a></li>
```

12 Press ENTER, press TAB twice, and then type **</ul>** to complete the unnumbered list.

13 Save your work.

## Creating a Numbered List

You're now ready to create a numbered list below the unnumbered linked list in the left column. When you code a numbered list, you don't have to enter the numbers—the XHTML tags take care of that detail for you. To create a numbered list, follow these steps:

1 To create a title for the numbered list in the left column, make sure that the insertion point is positioned after **</ul>**, press ENTER, press TAB twice, and then type the following code:

```
<div class="leftbar_title">Plan a Roadtrip</div>
```

2 Press ENTER, press TAB twice, and then type **<ol>** to start the ordered (numbered) list.

3 To create the first list item, press ENTER, press TAB three times, and then type **<li>Choose a state.</li>**.

4 Press ENTER, press TAB three times, and then add the following two list items:

```
<li>Select attractions.</li>
<li>Go!</li>
```

5 Press ENTER, press TAB twice, and then type **</ol>** to complete the numbered list.

6 Press ENTER, press TAB, and then type **</div>** to close the **leftbar_box id** page division.

**7** Save your work. Your code should look like the code shown in Figure 8-24, and your Web page should look like the page shown in Figure 8-25.

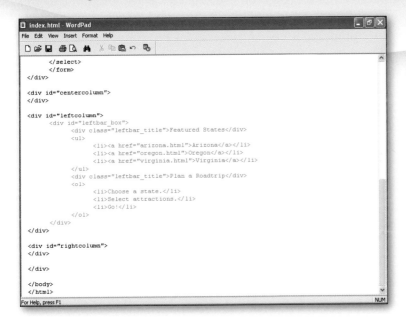

**Figure 8-24**  *Entering list code with styles*

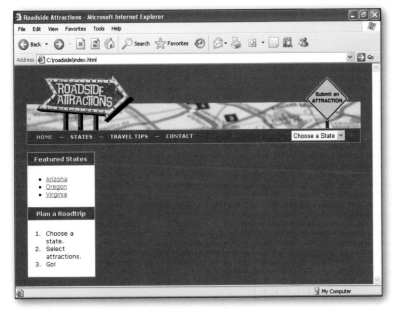

**Figure 8-25**  *Viewing lists entered into the left column*

# Adding Content to the Right Column

By now, you should be fairly comfortable with inserting and linking graphics. (You had a lot of practice just a little while ago when you were creating the banner bar.) For the right column on the roadside page, we opted to display thumbnails of postcard images. Visitors can click the thumbnails to view larger versions of the postcards if they want. The only style we created for this column was a style in the styles_main.css document that adds 2 pixels of space below each photograph to create space between the postcards. Other than creating that style, your main task will be adding and linking the graphic files in the XHTML document. Let's start by creating the **postcard** class:

1  Open styles_main.css in your text editor, click below the **.searchbar** declaration block, press ENTER, and then type the following **class** selector and declaration:

```
.postcard { margin-bottom: 2px; }
```

2  Save your work, and then open index.html in your text editor.

3  In index.html, click after the **<div id="rightcolumn">** tag, press ENTER, press TAB, and enter the following image tag:

```
<img src="images/pc_blockhenge_th.jpg" alt="Greetings from
Blockhenge postcard" width="150" height="105" border="0"
class="postcard" />
```

**tip**  To quickly add the four thumbnail elements, copy the entire Blockhenge code from <a href...><img..../> </a>, paste the code four times, and then change the image names and **alt** text for each reference.

4  To link the Blockhenge postcard to its full-size image and display the image in a separate window, click before the **<img... />** tag, type **<a href="images/pc_blockhenge.jpg" target="_blank">**, click after **<img... />**, and then type **</a>**.

5  If you want, you can practice adding and linking thumbnail images using four sample pictures. The code is shown here:

```
<a href= "images/pc_dino.jpg" target= "_blank"><img src="images/
pc_dino_th.jpg" alt="Prehistoric Times postcard" width="150"
height="105" border="0" class="postcard" /></a>
```

```
<a href= "images/pc_shark.jpg" target= "_blank"><img src="images/
pc_shark_th.jpg" alt="World's Largest Fossil postcard" width="150"
height="105" border="0" class="postcard" /></a>

<a href= "images/pc_jackalope.jpg" target= "_blank"><img
src="images/pc_jackalope_th.jpg" alt="When Rabbits Ruled postcard"
width="150" height="105" border="0" class="postcard" /></a>

<a href= "images/pc_octopus.jpg" target= "_blank"><img src="images/
pc_octopus_th.jpg" alt="Tale of the Giant Octopi postcard"
width="150" height="105" border="0" class="postcard" /></a>
```

6 Save your work. Your HTML code should look like the code
shown in Figure 8-26.

**Figure 8-26** *Linking thumbnail images to full-size photographs.*

7 Open index.html in your browser. You Web page should now
look like the page shown in Figure 8-27. Click each thumbnail
to make sure that your link text is entered properly. Clicking a
thumbnail image should open a larger image in a new window.

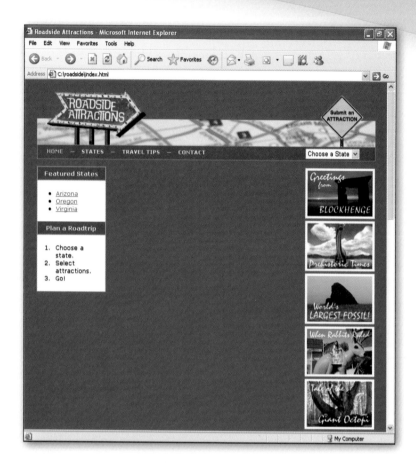

# Inserting Standard Content: Title Graphic, Photograph, and Heading

Your next task is to add a photograph, the page title graphic, and a level 1 heading to the center column. All subpages will have a photograph and title graphic in the main area (the heading is optional), so the elements you add in this section can serve as placeholders on subpages. The photograph has a style that positions the photograph to the right in the center column, and the title graphic has a style in the main style sheet that adds padding around the image. The heading style was defined earlier when you defined the Web document's type selectors. To add a photograph, the page title graphic, and a level 1 heading to the center column, follow these steps:

1 Open styles_main.css in your text editor, click below the **.postcard** declaration block, press ENTER, and add the following two **class** selectors and declaration blocks:

```
.page_title { padding: 10px 0 0 10px; }

.photo {
   float: right;
   position: relative;
   padding: 10px 10px 10px 15px;
   }
```

2 Save your work, and then display index.html in your text editor.

3 To add a photograph in the center column, click after the **<div id="centercolumn">** tag, press ENTER, press TAB, and enter the following image tag:

```
<img src="images/p_or_shark.gif" alt="a roadside attraction
photograph" class="photo" />
```

4 To enter the home page title graphic, press ENTER, press TAB, and enter the following image tag:

```
<img src="images/t_home.gif" alt="Welcome" class="page_title" />
```

5 To add a level 1 heading, press ENTER twice, press TAB, type **<h1>Offline and On the Road</h1>**, and then save your work.

In Figures 8-28 and 8-29, you can view the code, title graphic, and photograph additions along with the footer information and copyright information that you'll be inserting next.

**Figure 8-28** *Adding content information to the center column, including a title graphic, a photograph, a heading, bottom-of-the-page navigation links, and copyright information*

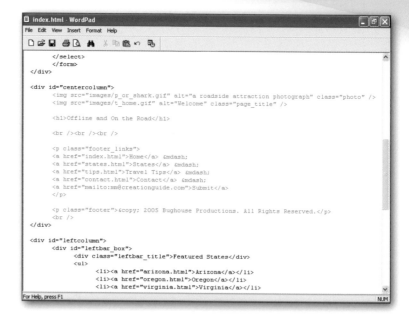

**Figure 8-29** *Viewing content in the center column*

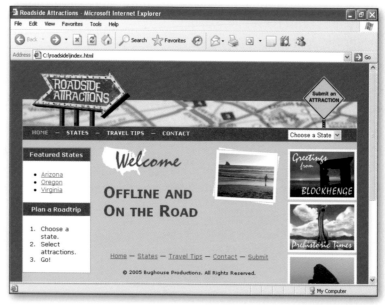

# Inserting Footer Information

Another element that should appear on all your Web pages is the footer. In this section, you add basic footer information to the center column. You'll add other content to the center column later, but by adding footer information first, you can use the index.html page without main body content as a template for your site's subpages. The roadside site uses two footer-related classes in the presentation style sheet along with the XHTML coding and text. Here's how to create the site's footer information:

1 Open **styles_presentation.css** in your text editor, click below the **.leftbar_title** declaration block, and then press ENTER.

2 To create the **footer** class that centers the footer text and sizes it very small, enter the following style:

```
.footer {
    font-size: x-small;
    text-align: center;
    }
```

3 To create the **footer** class that formats the text link navigation bar as centered at the bottom of the page and in a small font size, press ENTER twice, and create the following style:

```
.footer_links {
    font-size: small;
    text-align: center;
    }
```

4 Save your work, and then open index.html in your text editor.

5 The footer text is part of the center column's content, so begin by clicking after the **</h1>** tag that you created in the previous section, and then press ENTER twice.

6 To add three blank line spaces before the bottom-of-the-page text navigation links, press TAB, and then type **<br /><br /> <br />**.

7 Press ENTER twice, press TAB, and then type **<p class= "footer_links">** to start a paragraph to contain the text links.

8 Press ENTER, press TAB, and then type the following code to add text links that use the browser defaults for the text colors.

**note**   Notice that the last link in the bottom-of-the-page navigation bar contains a Mailto link and no em dash character entity. You should enter your own e-mail address in the Mailto link.

(Notice that our friend the em dash makes an appearance as a character entity again in the form *&mdash;*.)

```
<a href="index.html">Home</a> &mdash;
<a href="states.html">States</a> &mdash;
<a href="tips.html">Travel Tips</a> &mdash;
<a href="contact.html">Contact</a> &mdash;
<a href="mailto:mm@creationguide.com">Submit</a>
```

9  Press ENTER, press TAB, type **</p>** to close the paragraph, and then save your work.

The final component of the footer is the copyright information. In this procedure, you create a paragraph styled with the footer class and enter the copyright information. One interesting twist here is that you can use a special character entity reference to create a copyright symbol.

10  Press ENTER twice, press TAB, and then type the following:

```
<p class="footer">&copy; 2006 Your Name. All Rights Reserved.</p>
```

**note**   You might also provide a link to your privacy policy in your footer text.

11  Press ENTER, press TAB, type **<br />** to add a blank line after the copyright text, and save your work. Your footer text should look like the code shown earlier in Figure 8-28.

You might have noticed that we've designed everything on the home page except the main content. As we mentioned earlier, there's a method to our madness. Now that you've created the basic structure of the home page and added some placeholder items (such as the title graphic, photograph, heading, and footer), and because the site mimics the home page structure on the subpages, you can use the index.html file to quickly create the foundation pages for the subpages, as described in the next section.

## Copying the Home Page Framework to Subpages

By now, you've probably realized that you need to make some destination pages for the navigation bar, Search drop-down list, and text links to link to. Namely, the roadside site calls for the following pages:

- index.html (which we're already in the process of creating)
- states.html

- tips.html
- contact.html
- arizona.html
- oregon.html
- virginia.html

In this section, you're going to create the six additional .html pages that make up the remaining sample pages of the Roadside Attractions site. Ideally, the site also requires a page for every U.S. state (not just the three you'll create in this section), but describing that process would be overly redundant (as you might imagine!). To create subpages, you could copy all the code from index.html, paste it into a blank text document, and then save the text document as an .html file, but we're much lazier than that! Here's how we went about creating most of the code for the subpages:

1  Open the C:\roadside folder.

2  Right-click the **index.html** file, and then click **Copy** on the shortcut menu.

3  Paste six copies of the **index.html** file into the **roadside** folder.

4  Right-click the first copy of **index.html**, click **Rename** on the shortcut menu, type **states.html**, and then press ENTER.

5  Using the procedure described in step 4, rename the other five copies of the index.html file as **tips.html**, **contact.html**, **arizona. html**, **oregon.html**, and **virginia.html**.

6  To modify the states page to display the appropriate title bar text and title graphic, open states.html in your text editor, and then perform the following changes:

   a. In the <title></title> tag pair, change the title text to **States - Roadside Attractions**.

   b. In the link bar area, change the **class** for the HOME button to **nav** and the **class** for the STATES button to **link_on**.

   c. In the **centercolumn** page division, change **t_home.gif** to **t_states.gif**, and change the **alt** text **"Welcome"** to **"Choose a State"**.

7  Save states.html.

> **tip**   If you were building the roadside site as a real site, you would also want to replace the heading text and photographs on each subpage.

**note**   Using a completed foundation page to create subpages is fast and promotes consistency throughout your site.

You've just completed the foundation document for the states.html page. Pretty easy! You now have to repeat this short customization process in the tips.html, contact.html, arizona.html, oregon.html, and virgina.html pages. We've provided title bar graphics for all six sample pages. Note that for the state pages, the **nav** value should be shown for *all* link bar links because none of the link bar links serve as the actual current page when a state page is displayed. Also, the light gray background expands with text; therefore, it will not fill the page if you don't include any content. To "grow" the gray areas without entering visible content (since this is a sample site), simply add a few <br /> tags in the **centercolumn** area as a temporary display trick.

## Adding Content

In this section, you're going to insert some body text into the roadside site's home page. What this endeavor actually boils down to is practice in formatting text. The main content of the home page consists of a *drop cap* (a large letter at the start of a paragraph), some paragraph text with italic and bold formatting, a block quote, a heading, and a bulleted list. Some of these elements you've already created, so we've provided online steps for adding this site's content at www.creation-guide.com/ch08/extras. In those steps, we show you how to create styles and insert a drop cap as well as apply italic, bold, and block quote formatting to text.

## Checking Your Work

Finally, you need to check your work. At this point, checking your work entails clicking around your site and checking your links, graphics, **alt** text, and other page elements:

1  Open your browser, and display index.html (or if the document is already open in your browser, click **Refresh**).

2  Click every link to verify that the links work properly and your pages are displayed correctly. If any links don't respond as expected, open the proper Web document in your text editor and check the code carefully. Check your title graphics and title bar text to ensure that you've included the proper graphics and title text on each page.

If you'd like to visit an online version of the roadside site, display www.creationguide.com/roadside. You can use the Source command on the View menu in your browser to display the online Web site's source code. The source code might come in handy if you want to check your own code or if you need some assistance.

## Using the Roadside Attractions Site as a Template

After all your hard work creating the roadside site, you now have a very useful template that you can use to build a custom site. You can of course modify the site's contents by adding, removing, and replacing elements (such as the banner.gif graphic or the heading text). But even better than that, you can take advantage of CSS's powerful formatting capabilities to create Web sites with an entirely different look with very little effort. This is where planning pays off. Because you've carefully set up your Web site to use external style sheets, you can now make visual changes very easily by modifying style sheet property values. Furthermore, because you created a presentation style sheet (styles_presentation.css), you can quickly change formatting elements and apply the style sheet to your site by changing **@import url** in the styles_mains.css document.

To apply a couple of modified presentation style sheets to your Web site, we provided two sample style sheets that you downloaded at the beginning of this chapter—styles_presentation_blue.css and styles_presentation_green.css. Both style sheets were created by copying the styles_presentation.css style sheet and changing some of the formatting property values. To test the modified style sheets on your Web site, follow these steps:

1 **Open styles_main.css in your text editor.**

2 **At the top of the style sheet, locate the @import url (styles_presentation.css); text, and change styles_presentation.css to styles_presentation_blue.css so that the line appears as follows:**

```
@import url(styles_presentation_blue.css);
```

3 **Save your work, and then open index.html in your browser window.**

**Figure 8-31** *Same site with different presentation style sheets applied*

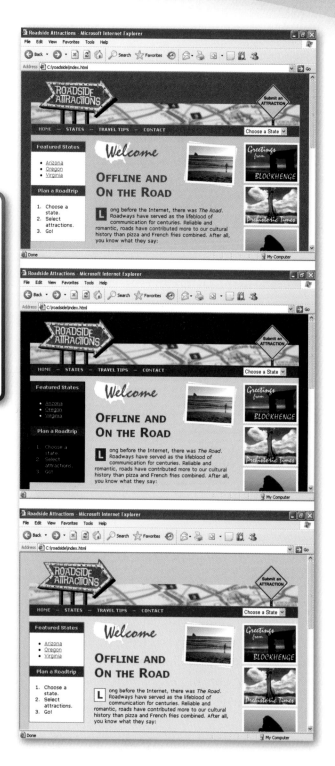

**tip**    Many of the graphics on the sample Web site were purchased from www.istock-photo.com for a few bucks each. We highly recommend that you visit the iStockphoto site whenever you're searching for images to use on your Web pages.

4 To try the other sample style sheet, change the **@import** reference in the main style sheet to point to **styles_presentation_green.css**, save your work, and then reopen or refresh your view of index.html. Figure 8-31 shows three views of the roadside site, each view using a different presentation style sheet.

## Additional Resources

As we mentioned, XHTML books and Web pages abound. Here are a few of our favorite CSS and XHTML resources:

- *Web Designer's Reference: An Integrated Approach to Web Design with XHTML and CSS*, by Craig Grannell (Friends of Ed/Apress, 2004).

- *Professional CSS: Cascading Styles Sheets for Web Design*, by Christopher Schmitt, Mark Trammell, Ethan Marcotte, Dunstan Orchard, and Todd Dominey (Wrox/Wiley Publishing, 2005).

- *Web Standards Solutions: The Markup and Style Handbook*, by Dan Cederholm (Friends of Ed/Apress, 2005).

- www.w3.org/TR/xhmtl1.   The W3C (World Wide Web Consortium) XHTML page.

## check it!

- XHTML commands serve as instructions that tell a browser how to structure a Web page's content.

- XHTML commands appear between angle brackets (< >), usually come in pairs, and must be lowercase.

- Styles can be used to format page layouts and content elements.

- A style consists of a selector (**type**, **class**, or **id**) and a declaration, which is made up of property names and values.

- When creating Web pages, save your XHTML documents and preview your pages in a browser frequently.

- Always verify that you've included all angle brackets (<>), quotation marks (""), braces ({}), colons (:), and semicolons (;) in your code. Missing small elements or misspelling XHTML commands can cause your page to render incorrectly (or not at all) in a browser.

# diving into design

## with publisher templates

# 9

Think about the last time you headed out to buy a quality pair of shoes. Before you arrived at the store, you probably decided on the type of shoe you needed based on where you were going to wear them (such as a seminar, camping trip, construction site, concert, track meet, hot date, or whatever). Then, after you arrived at the store, you probably gravitated toward a particular shoe style and picked out a color that worked well with your personal tastes and wardrobe. Next you most likely tried on the shoes and made sure they flexed and adjusted properly in all the most comfortable and expected ways. You probably didn't care too much about how the shoemaker (or factory) cut each piece of the shoes, what types of thread were used to bind the soles, and so forth. You just wanted shoes that looked good, felt good, and worked well. In this Microsoft Office Publisher walkthrough, you'll build the Web site equivalent of a good pair of shoes. You'll create a nice-looking Web site that feels comfortable to visitors and works well. And you'll do all this while paying very little attention to behind-the-scenes source-code specifics.

## Gathering Project Supplies

To create the Web pages described in this chapter, you'll need the following "supplies":

- Microsoft Publisher 2003 or later.

- A browser and an Internet connection. (An Internet connection is necessary only to download the sample project's two files from the CreationGuide Web site and to access the bonus content-creation steps, at www.creationguide.com/ch09/extras.)

- The welcome.doc text file and p_koury.jpg image file, which you can download from www.creationguide.com/ch09.

To obtain the files, create a folder named koury on your computer's hard drive. For convenience, we'll refer to your hard drive as the C drive throughout this chapter. Connect to the Internet, open your browser, display www.creationguide.com/ch09, right-click the welcome.doc file name, and save a copy of the file in the C:\koury folder on your computer. Repeat the process to save the p_koury.jpg file in the C:\koury folder, as shown in Figure 9-1.

**Figure 9-1**  *Download-ing the welcome.doc text file from the Internet*

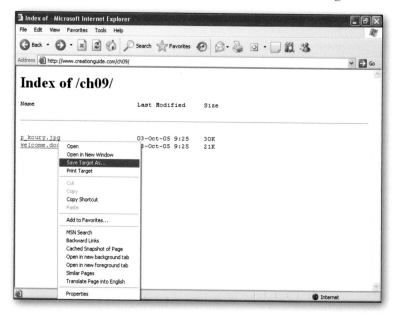

# Introducing Publisher as a Web Design Tool

Publisher built its reputation as the Microsoft application to turn to when you want to print formatted materials like brochures, newsletters, award certificates, business cards, calendars, and so forth. Nowadays, Publisher also provides a number of handy Web publishing tools. In fact, Publisher's Web capabilities have grown fairly significantly over the past few years to provide a nice selection of Web design tools. As you work your way through this walkthrough, you'll meet up with a few of those tools.

The main reason we're introducing Publisher to you as a Web development platform is because with it, you can use Web site templates and design schemes to create functional and appealing Web sites with nary a glance at source code. By building a site in Publisher, you'll spend some time addressing basic design decisions, such as choosing a color palette and properly aligning objects. In this way, Publisher is more advanced than most online Web publishing wizards and blogging sites, yet it's easier than hand-coding or using more advanced Web editors to create Web publications. Therefore, after you've learned quite a bit about Extensible Hypertext Markup Language (XHTML) and cascading style sheets (CSS) in the preceding chapter, this chapter focuses on design considerations. In the next chapter, the Microsoft Office Word walkthrough mixes design and coding to help you begin to blend your Web development skills.

## Approaches to Building Web Sites in Publisher

When you work on a Web publication in Publisher, you work in Web mode. While that seems like a fairly obvious statement, *Web mode* is more than just a fancy label for an application view. In Web mode, every available option is specifically tailored to creating Web sites and Web pages. Any print features offered by Publisher that aren't supported by the Web aren't available to you when you're working in Web mode. This is a useful arrangement, because you won't be able to use print design techniques that can't be rendered properly online. For example, browsers don't support font effects such as Outline, Shadow, Emboss, and Engrave, so those formatting options are not available in the Font dialog box when you're working in Web mode.

One of the first feature sets you'll encounter in Web mode is a selection of ways in which you can begin setting up your Web site. In Publisher, you can create Web sites and Web pages in a number of ways. You can:

- Save an existing Publisher print document as a Web publication (but be prepared for some shifts in your design and page layout).
- Import a text file or document, such as a Word document, and save it as a Web page.
- Open an existing HTML document and modify it.
- Create a blank Web page and add content.
- Select the Easy Web Site Builder or a Web site template in the New Publications task pane.

To take advantage of Publisher's many design features, you'll work with the Easy Web Site Builder and various design schemes in this chapter's walkthrough. Figure 9-2 shows the New Publication task pane with the Web Sites options list expanded.

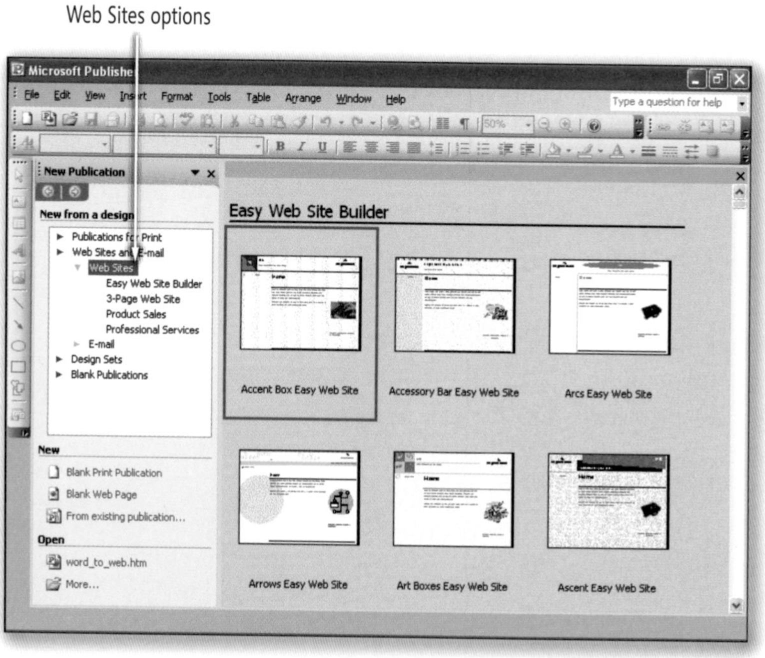

**Figure 9-2** *Publisher's Web Sites options*

Each available Web Sites option allows you to first select a design. After you select a design, the Web site setup process proceeds to set up page templates based on criteria you specify. The Web Sites options list offers the following site-building tools:

- **Easy Web Site Builder**   Allows you to use a checklist to specify the page templates you want to include in your site.

- **3-Page Web Site**   Generates a site that includes a Home page, an About Us page, and a Contact Us page.

- **Product Sales**   Generates a site that includes a Home page, an About Us page, a Contact Us page, a Product List page, and six Product Detail pages.

- **Professional Services**   Generates a site that includes a Home page, an About Us page, a Contact Us page, a Service List page, four Service Detail pages, and a Project List page.

Regardless of the initial setup of your Web site, you can add and remove Web pages and templates as you develop your site. In fact, you can even change the entire design of your site at any time.

After you set up your Web site's templates, you're ready to choose among various preconfigured settings, including navigation bar options, color schemes, and font schemes. When you're happy with your design choices, you can then add your custom content into the template's text boxes and picture frames. Figure 9-3, on the next page, shows the Publisher window containing a Product Sales site created using the Even Break publication design template.

# Planning Your Publisher Web Site

Now that you have the "big picture" view of Web development in Publisher, let's turn to the walkthrough to address the specifics. For this walkthrough, we think that jumping right into the action will prove more informative and effective for you than listening to us ramble on about all the ins and outs of the application up front. So let's start by briefly reviewing this walkthrough site's planning process.

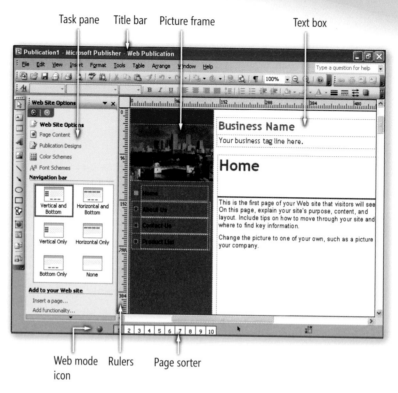

**Figure 9-3** *Building a Web site from templates*

The site you'll build in this walkthrough was designed for Ms. Koury, a fifth-grade teacher. Each year, students select a name for their class. This year, they've selected "Koury's Kids." The theme for the fifth-grade class is "discovery," so the site should make that clear. After talking to Ms. Koury, we found that she had only a few main goals for her class's Web site. Namely, she wanted to hit the following points:

- Display the class's chosen name to promote unity.
- Outline the year's main theme: discovery.
- Provide a simple monthly calendar.
- Display contact information.
- Link to an online version of the printed quarterly newsletter.

Ms. Koury also wanted to be sure that she could easily modify her Web site. She anticipated applying new color schemes throughout the school year, updating the calendar each month, and changing information on her home page as needed.

Based on Ms. Koury's needs, we created the simple framework shown in Figure 9-4. Notice that the newsletter page is linked to the home page, but it isn't part of the site's framework. That's because the site links to the printable newsletter, which is a quarterly publication designed to be sent home with the kids. Unfortunately, papers don't always make it home, so Ms. Koury likes to offer a link to the backup newsletter online. Technically, the newsletter is an external document. Because we're working with Publisher templates for this Web site, we didn't need to storyboard the home page. We're happy to create a site for Ms. Koury using Publisher templates and design schemes. By using a template, Ms. Koury will be able to quickly and easily modify the site's design, color scheme, and layout in the future.

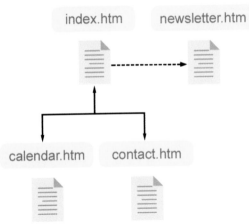

**Figure 9-4** *The framework for Ms. Koury's Web site*

Finally, we should mention that in many ways, Publisher provides a perfect interface for creating Ms. Koury's Web site. As a teacher, she's familiar with working with Microsoft Office applications, including Publisher, because she has used desktop publishing and word processing tools to create simple newsletters and award certificates for her students. Therefore, learning how to work in Publisher's Web mode won't be a huge stretch. Furthermore, the application includes a number of specific Web site creation tools and design features that Ms. Koury can use to easily create and modify her Web site. All in all, Publisher's familiar Office interface combined with its numerous Web-specific features provides just the right tool set for a busy teacher. In fact, Publisher provides just the right tool set for many busy people from all walks of life.

# Setting Up a Web Site

Setting up a Web site in Publisher entails choosing whether you want to use the Easy Web Site Builder, a Web site template (3-Page Web Site, Product Sales, or Professional Services), a blank slate, or an existing document. When you use the site builder or a template, you'll also be able to specify the following settings:

- Publication design
- Navigation bar(s) location
- Color scheme palette
- Font scheme

The following sections walk you through the process of setting up a basic Web site for Ms. Koury's fifth-grade class by starting with the Easy Web Site Builder.

## Choosing a Web Site Design

**tip**   If the task pane doesn't open automatically when you start Publisher, click Task Pane on the View menu or press CTRL+F1. You can control whether the New Publication task pane appears automatically when you start Publisher by clicking Options on the Tools menu and then selecting or clearing the Use New Publication Task Pane At Startup check box.

The first step in this walkthrough is to choose a process and then select a design. In this walkthrough, you'll use the Easy Web Site Builder so that you can view the types of design templates available in Publisher. You'll start by creating a Web site that contains a home page and a contact page. Later in this walkthrough, you'll add calendar page components to both the site and navigation bar. To begin building Ms. Koury's Web site, follow these steps:

1 Click **Start**, click **All Programs**, click **Microsoft Office**, and then click **Microsoft Office Publisher**. Publisher starts and displays the **New Publication** task pane by default.

2 In the New Publication task pane, click the Web Sites And E-mail link, click Web Sites, and then click Easy Web Site Builder.

3 In the design selection area, click the **Bubbles Easy Web Site** design. You might have to scroll down to see the Bubbles design. The home page template opens in the Publisher window, and the **Easy Web Site Builder** dialog box is displayed, in which you can specify the page templates you want to add to your Web site. By default, you can add any of the following page templates (in addition to adding a blank page at any time).

When you add a page template using the Easy Web Site Builder, Publisher also automatically adds an associated navigation button or link (shown in parentheses in the list below) to your navigation bar:

- Tell customers about my business (About Us)
- Tell customers how to contact us (Contact Us)
- Sell products (Product Catalog)
- Describe services (Services)
- Display a calendar or schedule (Calendar)
- Display a list of projects or activities (Projects)
- Display employee information (Employees)
- Provide links to other Web pages (Related Links)

4 In the **Easy Web Site Builder** dialog box, click **Tell Customers How To Contact Us**. Notice that a **Contact Us** button is inserted below the **Home** button, as shown in Figure 9-5.

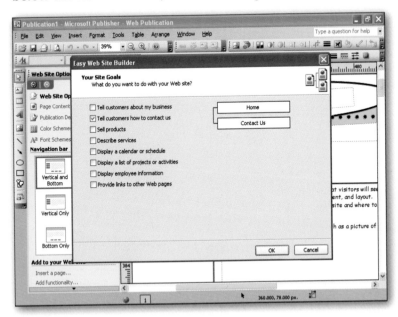

**Figure 9-5** *Selecting page templates using the Easy Web Site Builder*

5 Click **OK**.

**tip** Don't worry about choosing the perfect publication design the first time around. You can easily change your publication design later by using the Publication Designs task pane. In fact, you should sample a few of the designs before moving on to applying a color scheme in the next section so that you can get a feel for some of the design options Publisher provides.

**note** You can add and remove pages and navigation links at any time. The Easy Web Site Builder and other page-building tools help you to set up the main structure of your site up front in a quick, organized manner. Later in this project, we show you how to add a page template and modify the navigation bar.

**note**   You can manually move your navigation bar by dragging it around the page. The drawback of dragging your navigation bar is that only the navigation bar on the current page is repositioned. You will need to reposition the navigation bar on all other pages to keep your site consistent, as described in this project.

After you close the Easy Web Site Builder dialog box, notice that the Page Sorter at the bottom of the Publisher window shows two page icons. In addition, your navigation bar includes a Home link and a Contact Us link. The next order of business is to tell Publisher where to place your navigation bar.

## Choosing the Navigation Bar Orientation

Upon completing the Easy Web Site Builder, the first option you see in the task pane is the navigation bar orientation setting. By default, the selected design uses vertical and bottom navigation bars. For this site, we'll keep the default setting. You can also choose the options shown in Figure 9-6. Notice that not all orientation settings include bottom links. We recommend that you include bottom-of-the-page links in all your Web sites, so if you choose an orientation that doesn't include bottom-of-the-page links, we suggest that you manually add them later. To view the various orientation settings in action, click an option in the Navigation Bar section in the Web Site Options task pane. You can test out each orientation to see how Publisher repositions or removes the navigation bar buttons. Return to the Vertical And Bottom setting before proceeding to the next section.

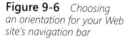

**Figure 9-6**   *Choosing an orientation for your Web site's navigation bar*

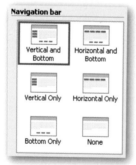

## Applying a Color Scheme

Publisher includes a sizable collection of color schemes. Each color scheme consists of five colors. To apply a color scheme to your site, click Color Schemes in the Web Site Options task pane. Then click a few color schemes to see how they affect the current design's colors. By default, the Bubble template uses the Tropics color scheme. For this project, we chose to use the Bluebird color scheme, as shown in Figure 9-7.

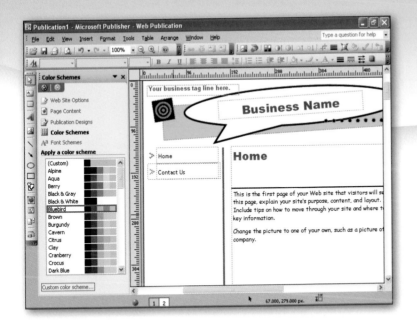

Figure 9-7 *Choosing a color scheme for your Web site*

# Recoloring Page Elements and Backgrounds

After you select a color scheme, you can reassign which color is used for which element. To help you stay within your selected scheme, the scheme's colors are shown in the top row in Publisher's color palettes, as shown here for the Bluebird color scheme.

Bluebird color scheme colors

To change any element's color on your Web page, simply recolor the element using a color from the selected color scheme. For example:

- To change an AutoShape's color, right-click the shape, click **Format AutoShape**, and then change the **Fill** color.

- To change the background color, click **Background** on the **Format** menu or click **Background** in the drop-down list of task panes, and select a scheme-approved background color. Usually, background colors are lighter shades of scheme colors to avoid overpowering content.

# Customizing Color Schemes

In some instances, you might want to customize an existing color scheme or create your own scheme. To do this, click the Custom Color Scheme link located at the bottom of the Color Schemes task pane. The image shows the Custom tab for the Fjord color scheme in the Color Schemes dialog box.

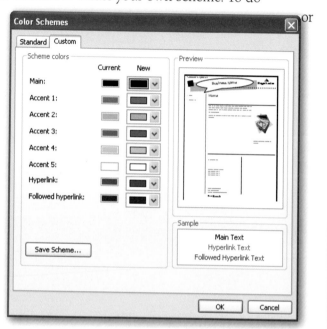

Notice in the image that the default Hyperlink and Followed Hyperlink colors in the Fjord color scheme are assigned to the colors purple and blue, respectively. This color scheme is the exact opposite of standard default hyperlink colors. Usually, unvisited hyperlinks appear blue and visited hyperlinks appear purple. We think the Fjord color scheme might confuse people. Therefore, if you ever use this theme, we recommend that you customize it by changing the Hyperlink and Followed Hyperlink colors to more expected (or at least less confusing) colors.

## Selecting a Font Scheme

At this point in the project, you've selected a design, specified navigation bar orientation, and applied a color scheme. Next on your to-do list is to select a Web-friendly font scheme. As you might recall from Part 1, only a few fonts are considered Web-friendly for both PC and Macintosh computers on the Web. Nicely enough, Publisher provides some font schemes that can help you limit your design to universal Web fonts. You can access the font schemes by displaying the Font Schemes task pane. (We bet you didn't see that one coming!) To apply a font scheme, simply select the scheme in the Font Schemes task pane. For this project, we chose the Online scheme, which uses Verdana Bold and Verdana fonts, as shown in Figure 9-8.

**Figure 9-8**  *Selecting a font scheme*

## Previewing Your Web Site

As you design a Web site, you'll want to frequently preview and save your site. Previewing helps you to see whether your design ideas live up to your expectations when you view them online. To preview your site, click Web Page Preview on the File menu. Your Web page is displayed in your browser window, and you can even click the navigation bar buttons to view each page in your site. Figure 9-9 shows the current state of the project after the Web Page Preview option is selected. When you preview your site, click your navigation links to make sure they work, and then close your browser window.

**Figure 9-9** *Previewing a Web publication*

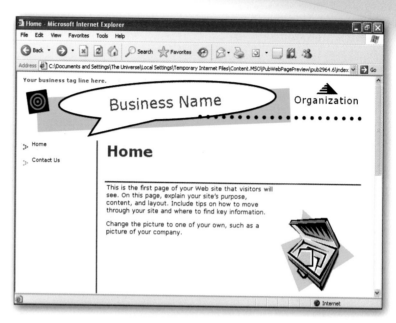

## Saving Your Web Site

To save your Web site for this project, follow these steps:

1 Click **Save** on the **File** menu, and then navigate to **C:\koury** in the **Save As** dialog box.

2 Click **Web Page (\*.htm;\*.html)** in the **Save as type** box, type **index.htm** in the **File name** box, and then click **Save**.

If you open your C:\koury folder after you save your Web publication, the folder's contents should look similar to the folder contents shown in Figure 9-10. Notice that Publisher automatically creates a folder named index_files to accompany your index.htm document. The folder contains the subpages and image files used in the Web site. When you upload your index.htm file to a server, you must upload the index_files folder to the server as well.

**Figure 9-10** *A saved Web publication consists of an .htm file and an associated folder*

# Opening an Existing Web Publication

After you save your Publisher-created Web publication as a Web page (.htm) file, you won't be able to double-click the file's icon to open the document in Publisher. If you double-click an .htm file's icon—even one created by Publisher—the file will open in your browser. Therefore, to open a Web publication in Publisher, perform either of the following procedures:

● Start Publisher, and then click **Open** on the **File** menu, press CTRL+O, or click the **Open** button on the **Standard** toolbar. In the **Open Publication** dialog box, open the index.htm file associated with your Web publication.

● Right-click the **index.htm** file, click **Open With**, and then click **Microsoft Office Publisher**. If the menu doesn't display Publisher, click **Choose Program**, and then browse to find the Publisher application in the **Open With** dialog box.

After you publish your Web site on the Web, you'll need to open your pages from your network place or download the most current pages from your server before you make changes. For this project, you're working with local files, so you don't need to be concerned with downloading and uploading files. Chapter 12, "Sending Web Pages into the Real World," discusses uploading and downloading files in more detail.

# Adding a Web Page

**tip**   You can also open the Insert Web Page dialog box by clicking Page on the Insert menu or by pressing CTRL+SHIFT+N.

Earlier in the planning stages, you saw that Ms. Koury wants to include a Calendar page in her Web site. We didn't have you add the page earlier, because we want to show you how easy it is to add a page and an associated navigation link in Publisher to an existing Web publication. To add the Calendar page to the Web site, follow these steps:

1 Display the Home page in Publisher, and then click the **Insert A Page** link located in the lower portion of the **Web Site Options** task pane. The **Insert Web Page** dialog box displays the types of pages you can add.

2 Click **Calendar** in the **Select A Page Type** list, and then click **Calendar**, as shown in Figure 9-11.

**Figure 9-11**   *Inserting a new page and associated hyperlink*

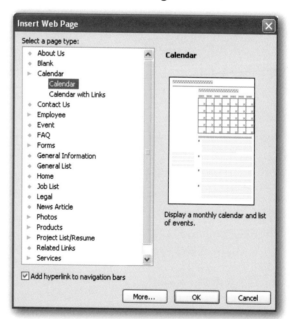

3 Ensure that the Add Hyperlink To Navigation Bars check box is selected, and then click **OK**.

When you insert a page in Publisher, the page is inserted after the currently selected page. For example, because the Ms. Koury Web site consisted of two pages and the Home page was selected, the Calendar page was inserted as the second page in the Web site.

Unfortunately, the link in the navigation bar is added to the end of the bar regardless of where you insert the page. We show you how to reorganize the navigation bar later in this walkthrough, in the section "Tweaking the Navigation Bar."

# Controlling Rulers and Ruler Guides

The three pages for Ms. Koury's site are now in place. For the remainder of this project, you'll work on customizing the templates and adding content. The presentation of your content plays a large role in people's perception of your site. Publisher offers rulers and guides to help you place elements on your Web pages consistently throughout a site. Consistency gives your site a professional look as well as aids visitors in navigating through your site, because elements appear where visitors expect to see them from page to page.

## Configuring Measurement Units

You can show or hide rulers—we recommend that you show them—and you can decide which measurement system you want to use. By default, rulers are shown in the Publisher window. You can toggle rulers off and on by clicking Rulers on the View menu. As for measurement settings, Publisher 2003 enables you work in any of the following measurement units:

- Inches
- Centimeters
- Picas
- Points
- Pixels

To specify measurement units, click Options on the Tools menu, and then select a unit of measurement on the General tab, as shown in Figure 9-12. For this project, we provide design instructions using pixels, because pixels are the measurement unit used in most Web design endeavors.

**tip**  You can reorder pages in your Web site by dragging the pages in the Page Sorter toolbar. Simply click the icon that represents the page you want to move and drag it to the proper location.

**tip**  In addition to controlling measurement units, you can also reposition the horizontal and vertical rulers anywhere on your page. To reposition a ruler, hold down SHIFT and drag the ruler to the desired position. Movable rulers are especially handy when you're manually aligning elements.

**Figure 9-12**  *Specifying the rulers' measurement units*

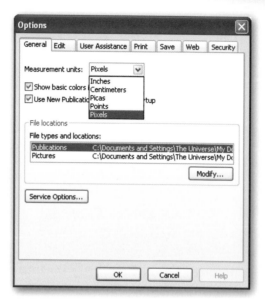

## Placing Ruler Guides

After your rulers are in place, you're ready to put ruler guides into action. *Ruler guides* are nonprinting lines that you can use while you design. Instead of guesstimating where objects go, you can use ruler guides to align objects to precise positions. The quickest way to add a ruler guide to a page is to click on a ruler and drag the mouse pointer to the desired location. You create horizontal ruler guides from the horizontal ruler and create vertical ruler guides from the vertical ruler. You can add as many guides as you need (within reason) and drag guides around the page at any time. Ruler guides are displayed as dotted green lines. You can either drag your rulers to the specified measurement, or you can enter the ruler location in the Ruler Guides dialog box, as described here:

1 Click **Rulers Guides** on the **Arrange** menu, and then click **Format Ruler Guides**.

2 In the **Ruler Guides** dialog box, shown in Figure 9-13, click either the **Horizontal** or the **Vertical** tab, type a **Ruler Guide** position, and then click **Set**.

**Figure 9-13** *Specifying the ruler position*

Now that we know that you've heard about ruler guides, be prepared. The upcoming section "Moving the Navigation Bar" kicks off your new habit of using ruler guides (and that's what we call giving you fair warning!).

## Tweaking the Navigation Bar

Navigation bars—you might call them the unifying pieces of all great Web sites. Visitors rely on navigation bars to help them get around your site. You rely on navigation bars to tie your site together. If your navigation bar is flawed, missing, or too difficult to use, both you and your visitors will quickly deduce that your site is useless. Nicely enough, Publisher helps you to control your navigation bar in a number of ways. As you saw earlier in this walkthrough, when you insert a new page, Publisher gives you the option of inserting a new hyperlink on your navigation bar. After the hyperlink is added to your navigation bar, Publisher leaves the tasks of renaming and positioning the hyperlink to you.

**tip** To remove a ruler guide, drag it back to the ruler, or right-click it and then click Delete Guide. To clear all ruler guides at once, click Ruler Guides on the Arrange menu, and then click Clear All Ruler Guides.

### Controlling Navigation Links

Publisher templates create navigation bars for you, but that doesn't mean you're completely free from navigation bar responsibilities *or* that you lack control over them. Far from it. In Publisher, you can exercise your Web development powers in many ways. For instance, when you work with navigation links, you can change their style, position, and display text. You do this by using the Navigation Bar Properties dialog box, which is shown in Figure 9-14.

**Figure 9-14**  *Controlling navigation bar properties*

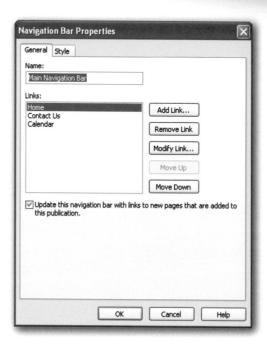

The following steps introduce you to a few of the ways you can customize navigation bars:

1 In the **Page Sorter**, click **page 1** to display the home page in the design pane.

2 Click the navigation bar. Selection handles appear around the navigation bar. By default, the parts of the navigation bar are grouped into a unified object.

3 Click **Navigation Bar Properties** on the **Format** menu to open the **Navigation Bar Properties** dialog box.

The first change you'll make is to move the **Calendar** link above the **Contact Us** link. Then you'll change the text *Contact Us* to **Contact** for both the navigation bar and the Contact Web page title bar.

4 Click the **General** tab, if necessary, and then click **Calendar** in the **Links** area and click the **Move Up** button once.

5 Click **Contact Us** in the **Links** area, and then click the **Modify Link** button. The **Modify Link** dialog box provides options you can use to change a link's display text and page title, as shown in Figure 9-15.

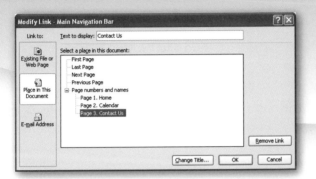

**Figure 9-15**  *Modifying navigation bar and title bar text*

6  In the Text To Display box, replace Contact Us with Contact.

7  Click the Change Title button, replace *Contact Us* with Contact in the Enter Text dialog box, click OK, and then click OK to close the Modify Link dialog box.

At this point, the links in the Navigation Bar Properties dialog box should be listed as **Home**, **Calendar**, **Contact** (in that order).

Now you're going to change the navigation bar's style.

8  On the **Style** tab, scroll down through the button style options, and then click **Offset**, as shown in Figure 9-16.

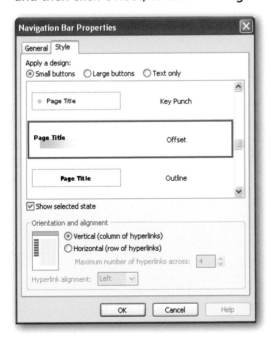

**Figure 9-16**  *Choosing a navigation bar button style*

9 Click **OK** to close the **Navigation Bar Properties** dialog box.

Finally, because this site has side and bottom navigation bars, you must repeat the general changes you made to the bottom-of-the-page links, as described next.

**note**   You don't have to change the Contact page's title bar text in step 12 when you modify the bottom-of-the-page links because you already changed the Contact page's title bar text in step 7.

10 Scroll to the bottom of the page, click near the bottom-of-the-page links, and then click **Navigation Bar Properties** on the **Format** menu.

11 Click **Calendar** in the **Links** area, and then click **Move Up**.

12 Click **Contact Us**, click **Modify link**, type **Contact** in the **Text To Display** box, and then click **OK** three times to close the open dialog boxes.

13 Click **Save** on the **Standard** toolbar to save your changes.

To check your work, use the Page Sorter to view your side and bottom navigation bars on each page. When you modify the navigation bar properties, Publisher automatically applies those changes to all pages in the Web site.

## Moving the Navigation Bar

Another way to modify your navigation bar is to reposition it on the page. If you do this, keep in mind that you'll have to reposition the object on each page in your site. Using ruler guides, the positioning should be fairly straightforward. Keeping an object aligned consistently from page to page—especially a navigation bar—avoids the appearance of objects "jumping" around. For this site, you're just going to move the navigation bar down a little so that you can insert a picture above the navigation bar later. To move the navigation bar, follow these steps:

1 Drag a horizontal ruler guide down to 308 pixels. You can see the pixel location in the status bar at the bottom of the window (displayed as vertical, horizontal), or you can manually set the ruler guide by using the **Ruler Guides** dialog box (click **Ruler Guides** on the **Arrange** menu, and then click **Format Ruler Guides**).

**2** Place a vertical ruler guide at 8 px.

**3** Position the mouse pointer over the navigation bar to display cross arrows, and then drag the navigation bar down so that the top of the navigation bar is aligned with the 308 px horizontal ruler and the left edge of the navigation bar is aligned with the 8 px vertical ruler guide, as shown in Figure 9-17.

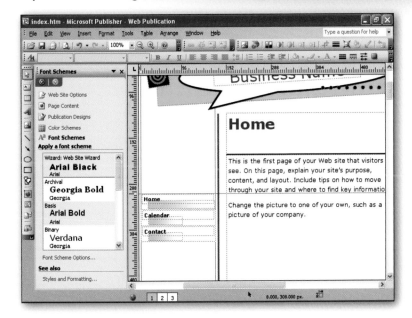

**Figure 9-17** *Using ruler guides to reposition a navigation bar*

**4** Save your changes, and then use the **Page Sorter** to display page 2. Notice that the navigation bar isn't repositioned and your ruler guides aren't inserted. You'll need to move the navigation bar down on pages 2 and 3 to keep your site consistent.

**5** Repeat steps 1 through 3 for pages 2 and 3 to place ruler guides and position the navigation bar throughout the site at 308 pixels down from the top of the page and 8 pixels from the left edge.

**6** Save your changes when you've finished repositioning the navigation bar.

**tip** You can see if you've positioned the navigation bar precisely by clicking through the Page Sorter icons (or previewing your Web site) and watching your navigation bar. If the buttons don't seem to "jump" when you change pages, you've done a great job.

# Working with Images

Some templates include clip art and pictures in the design, but most likely, you'll want to insert your own pictures and clip art on your Web sites. In fact, we highly encourage this practice. The more you customize a template, the less your site will look like a cookie-cutter site. Further, you'll find that inserting pictures and clip art in Publisher requires you to take the same steps you take to insert pictures and clip art in other Microsoft Office applications. You're most likely familiar with this process, so we'll whip through this section fairly quickly while you add a picture and a clip art item to Ms. Koury's Web site.

## Adding a Picture from a File

For this project, you'll insert a picture of Ms. Koury and her dog, Marley (p_koury.jpg). Marley often accompanies the class on volunteer days and Saturday cross-country hikes, so he's considered the class mascot. If you downloaded this picture from the CreationGuide Web site at the beginning of this chapter, you should be good to go. To insert the picture, follow these steps:

1 Display the Ms. Koury Web site home page in Publisher, and then position a horizontal ruler guide at 140 px. (It should align along the top of the **Home** box.)

2 Click **Picture** on the **Insert** menu, click **From File**, navigate to the **C:\koury** folder, and then double-click **p_koury.jpg** to insert the image into your Publisher publication.

3 Drag the image so that the top of the image aligns with the 140 px horizontal ruler guide and the left edge aligns with the 8 px vertical ruler guide you created earlier in this project. Your page should look similar to the page shown in Figure 9-18.

You'll now want to add the picture to pages 2 and 3. You can do this by repeating the preceding steps for each page, or you can copy and paste the image. By default, Publisher pastes objects using the same pixel location measurements. This is a nice time-saver and helps to keep pages consistent.

**Figure 9-18**  *Inserting and aligning a picture*

4 With the image selected, press CTRL+C to copy the image and its position, use the **Page Sorter** to display page 2, and then press CTRL+V to paste the image.

5 Display page 3, press CTRL+V to paste the image again, and then save your changes.

## Inserting Clip Art

You might have noticed that the Bubbles template includes a piece of clip art on the home page that looks like a briefcase on some sort of pink surface. In our opinion, showing a briefcase on a Web site for a fifth-grade class seems a bit odd (unless it's career day of course). Therefore, we'll show you how to add clip art by replacing the briefcase with a clip art element that is more closely related to the class's "discovery" theme. As we mentioned earlier, adding clip art in Publisher follows the same series of steps as adding clip art in other Office applications:

1 Use the **Page Sorter** to show the home page (page 1), scroll right if necessary, right-click the briefcase clip art, click **Change Picture**, and then click **Clip Art**. Publisher displays the **Clip Art** task pane.

2   In the **Clip Art** task pane, type **science** in the **Search For** box, and then click **Go**.

3   Double-click a science-related clip art item that you think conveys the feeling of discovery. We found the picture used in this example about two-thirds down in the **Clip Art** task pane's search results window.

4   Place ruler guides at 576 px vertical and 236 px horizontal, and then align the clip art element with the ruler guides, as shown in Figure 9-19.

**Figure 9-19** *Inserting and aligning clip art*

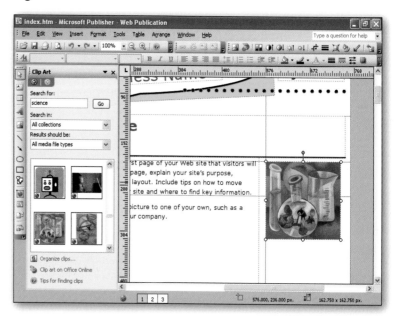

5   Place a horizontal ruler guide at 408 px, and drag the text box containing the words *Caption describing picture or graphic* to align with the 576 px vertical and 408 px horizontal ruler guides.

6   Replace the placeholder text with your own caption. In this example, we entered the text **Discovery happens every time you look at the world in a new way.**

7   Save your changes.

# Modifying AutoShapes

While you're in the mode of working with pictures and clip art, you
might as well turn your attention to the header area of the Web site
to work with the AutoShapes and other graphical elements. Publisher
templates tend to include a few graphical elements in the header area.
You have the option of keeping them, revising them, recoloring them,
reordering them (that is, changing any layering), or deleting them.
In this section, you'll delete, reorder, and modify template elements.
You'll start by deleting elements Ms. Koury doesn't need on the class
Web site:

1 On the home page, ensure that the top left corner of the page is
   visible, right-click the black box with the orange bull's-eye in it
   that appears above Ms. Koury's picture, and then click **Cut**.

2 Scroll right, right-click the organization logo placeholder
   element, and then click **Cut**. The header area should now start
   to look a little cleaner.

   Notice that the dotted line appears to be on top of the speaker
   bubble AutoShape. We think the dots should come from beneath the AutoShape, which means you need to change the
   layer order by sending the dotted line element back one layer.

3 Click the dotted line element to select it, click **Order** on the
   **Arrange** menu, and then click **Send Backward**, as shown in
   Figure 9-20.

   Next you'll customize the text in the text boxes in the header
   area.

4 Triple-click in the text box at the top-left corner of the page to
   select the text *Your business tag line here*, and type **Welcome!**

5 Triple-click the text *Business Name* to select it, click the **Font
   Size** drop-down arrow on the **Formatting** toolbar and select **16**,
   click the **Font Color** drop-down arrow and click the black color
   square, and then type **Koury's Kids are awesome!**

   Now you'll add a gradient to the solid AutoShape behind the
   speaker bubble, which will make that element carry out the
   gradient look you applied to the navigation buttons earlier in
   this project.

**Figure 9-20** *Changing the layering order of an object*

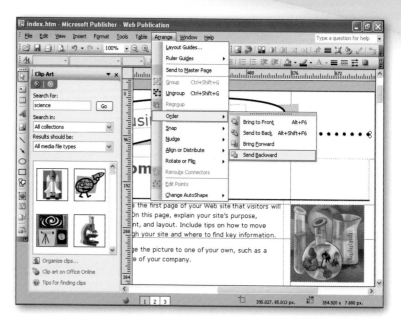

6 Right-click the yellow rectangular AutoShape in the header area, click **Format AutoShape**, click the **Color** box in the **Fill** area, and then click **Fill Effects**.

7 On the **Gradient** tab in the **Fill Effects** dialog box, click **Two Colors**.

8 In the **Shading Styles** area, click the **From Center** option, and in the **Variants** area, click the option on the right, as shown in Figure 9-21.

9 Click **OK** twice to close the open dialog boxes and to apply the new color settings, and then save your changes.

Now that you've made all these changes to the home page, you must repeat this process for pages 2 and 3. Here's a quick recap of the changes you made so you can quickly modify the other two pages in the Web site:

- Delete the orange bull's-eye.
- Delete the organization logo placeholder element.
- Send the dotted line element back one layer.

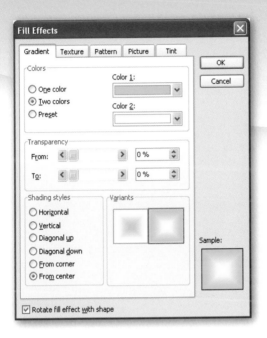

**Figure 9-21** *Adding a gradient to an existing AutoShape*

- Change the *Your business tag line here* text to **Welcome!**
- Change the *Business Name* text to 16-point, black text that states **Koury's Kids are awesome!**
- Add a gradient effect to the rectangular AutoShape.

Remember to save your Web publication after you make your changes. In the next section, you'll preview the site, so you can see how your project is coming along.

> **tip** If you don't want to repeat formatting steps for the header area on each page in your Web site, you can delete header elements on subpages and then copy and paste the formatted elements from the home page onto the subpages. Further, if an element's alignment gets shifted inadvertently at any time during development, you can delete the element on the subpages and then copy and paste the element from the home page onto subpages throughout your site to restore consistency. For example, if the *Welcome!* text at the top of the Web site looks like it moves around when you click from page to page, delete the element from all subpages, copy the element on the home page, and paste it onto each subpage.

# Previewing During Development

In addition to saving frequently while you develop your Web site, you should also preview your site frequently. As mentioned earlier, you can preview your Publisher site in two ways: you can use the Print Preview button for a quick look, or you can preview your site in a Web browser by using the Web Page Preview option. We suggest that you use both preview methods frequently. Figure 9-22 shows the Ms. Koury Web site in Web Page Preview mode. Your project should look similar.

**Figure 9-22**  *Previewing a Web publication in a browser*

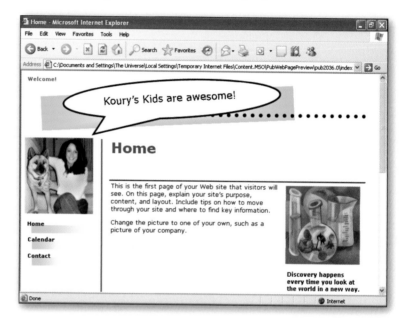

# Working with Text Boxes

You've created the site framework, added and customized a navigation bar, inserted an image and clip art, modified AutoShapes, and replaced text in a few small text boxes. The time has come to pay attention to the main content area of the Web site. In other words, it's time to add body text to those big text boxes. But before you start typing away, you should customize the templates' body area to suit your needs. Often Publisher's templates include objects that you don't need (as you saw when you configured the header area) or objects that you would like to resize. In this section you'll delete unnecessary template objects, resize text boxes, and add content by importing existing text.

## Deleting Objects

Publisher templates come chock-full of placeholder objects, many of which are unnecessary in some sites. Therefore, before you add content, you should delete any unnecessary objects, including text boxes. The detailed steps regarding deleting items from Ms. Koury's class site can be found at www.creationguide.com/ch09/extras. Figure 9-23 shows Ms. Koury's pages after the ruler guides are cleared and the unnecessary template objects are deleted from the content areas.

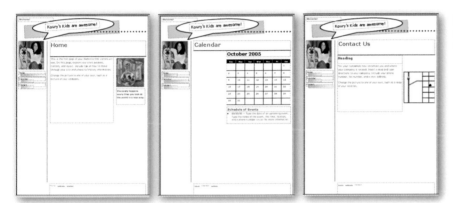

**Figure 9-23** *Deleting template objects on the home page and subpages*

## Adding and Importing Text

After deleting objects and extraneous text boxes, you're ready to add text. You can add text to a text box by typing, pasting, or importing text. We've provided online steps to help you master the following text-box-related tasks by practicing on Ms. Koury's Web site:

- Importing text from a Word document. (You can use the welcome.doc Word document that you downloaded from the CreationGuide Web site at the beginning of this walkthrough.)

- Resizing a text box.

- Creating and positioning a new text box using ruler guides.

- Inserting copyright information.

Visit www.creationguide.com/ch09/extras to view the online steps or print them for easy access.

**tip** To select multiple objects at one time for deleting, press CTRL while you click the objects to be deleted. When you execute the cut or delete process, all selected objects will be removed.

# Using Wizards to Format Objects

Publisher provides a number of custom wizards associated with specific objects. Each wizard helps you to control and format a particular object. For example, the calendar object included on the Calendar template page has a wizard you can use to format the calendar. The steps provided at www.creationguide.com/ch09/extras show you how to modify Ms. Koury's calendar page so that it looks like the calendar shown in Figure 9-24.

**Figure 9-24**   *Formatting an object by using a wizard*

# Formatting Page Headings by Using WordArt

Microsoft Office applications help you to create graphical text with a feature named WordArt. WordArt can help jazz up title text or call attention to special text, but we recommend that you use WordArt in moderation. You know that old saying about having "too much of a good thing." We show you how to use WordArt at www.creationguide. com/ch09/extras so that you'll know how to create stylized text when you need it. An especially nice aspect of WordArt is that you can use any of Word's drawing tools to format the text, including adding shadows and 3-D effects. In this walkthrough, you'll replace the three page headings with WordArt, as shown in Figure 9-25.

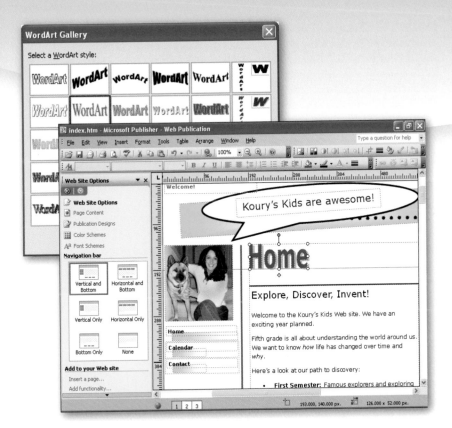

**Figure 9-25** *Selecting a WordArt style and positioning a WordArt object*

# Working with Hyperlinks

Last but not least, you need to know how to add hyperlinks to your Web publication. The navigation bar takes care of linking your Web pages together in a Web site, but you still need to provide hyperlinks within your content. For instance, you might want to link to pages in your Web site as well as link to online resources on other Web sites. You can even provide a hyperlink that opens a new e-mail message window if you want visitors to be able to send a message to you. In the bonus online steps located at www.creationguide.com/ch09/extras, you'll walk through the process of adding a sidebar element on your home page that includes links to the following resources:

- Calendar page within the same site
- Outside resource (the school newsletter, in this example)
- New e-mail message

**note** To change your Web publication's hyperlink colors, refer to the sidebar "Customizing Color Schemes," earlier in this chapter.

While publishing newsletters isn't the focus of this walkthrough, we're all for helping out whenever we can, so we are pleased to be able to provide you with a top 10+1 list from a design professional regarding how you can create great newsletters. You'll find the tips useful whether you're creating an online or print newsletter.

# Top 10+1 List for Creating Great Newsletters

Also available online, at www.creationguide.com/lists/newsletters.html.

*Sujata Soni* is a talented graphic designer who specializes in print design and publishing. Throughout the past several years, Sujata has worked in a variety of arenas, including magazine publishing houses, graphic art studios, and marketing departments. Currently, she contributes her eclectic experience to local organizations in the Portland, Oregon, area that range from education entities to wellness centers. Following are some tips Sujata recommends that you follow whenever you create a newsletter for any type of organization:

- **Ask yourself questions.** What is the purpose of the newsletter? Who is sending the newsletter? Who is the audience? What is the newsletter's intended style (informal, formal, classic, contemporary, and so forth)?

- **Include the parts that make up the whole.**
  - Nameplate. Banner or logo that identifies the publication.
  - Table of Contents. List of articles and page numbers for quick reference.
  - Masthead. Important data about the publication, such as the publisher, editors, and staff contributors.
  - Headers/Subheads. Text that identifies articles and important parts of articles.
  - Columns. Structural layout of newsletters.

- **Emphasize readability and flow.** Function takes precedence over form, so use legible fonts at appropriate sizes (no smaller than 9-point type for copy). Keep in mind that graphics and typographic elements imply a hierarchy, which enables readers to easily navigate the newsletter.

- **Err on the side of simplicity.**   Too many graphical elements and typographic treatments result in a cluttered, ineffective design. Avoid underlining copy and avoid overusing boldface or different-colored type—too much formatting decreases its effectiveness.

- **Add white space.**   If you think you have enough white space on a page, create more. White space makes pages look elegant and readable as well as makes headlines stand out.

- **Be consistent.**   Uniformity of design and style is a cardinal rule. Consistent margins and typefaces give the finished pages a neat and clean appearance.

- **Keep your balance.**   Use balance when designing the inside spread of a folded or four-or-more-page newsletter. If you place a photo on the left page of a spread, try balancing it with artwork or a pull quote on the right page.

- **Emphasize information visually.**   Selectively chosen illustrations, artwork, pull quotes, photos, charts, and graphs can emphasize information while conserving space.

- **Control your color.**   At a minimum for print or online newsletters, you have three important color-related topics to address: color of your paper or background, color of your text, and color of at least one *spot color,* which can be used in elements such as headlines, frames of photographs, charts and graphs, or pull quotes. (In printed publications, *spot color* refers to each color used in a publication in addition to the text color. For example, a newsletter might use black text with a green spot color to highlight the logo, headings, icons, notable quotations boxes, or other key elements.)

- **Proofread throughout the process.**   As the designer, you are often the last person to review the newsletter before it goes off to print or online. Use spelling and grammar checkers; make sure headings, subheadings, and text sizes are consistent; ensure captions are below the proper images; and make sure at least one other person has proofread the document.

- **Plus 1: Recognize that you have a very important job.**   With so much information, newsletters are often so packed they become quite boring. As a designer, you have the power to sift through the masses of information and turn the best parts into an enjoyable, informative, and aesthetically pleasing experience. Meet the challenge!

# Checking Your Publisher Site

At this point, if you've followed along and completed the bonus online steps, you probably think you've completed the Publisher project...Well, almost, but not quite. The final step in any Web creation endeavor is to check your work. Therefore, preview your Web site in Web Page Preview mode. Click every link, and check the alignment of all objects. Review content for typographical errors, and fix any anomalies you find. When you're satisfied that your Web site checks out and your pages look similar to those shown in Figure 9-26, *then* you've finished. Congratulations!

**Figure 9-26** *Reviewing the final project pages*

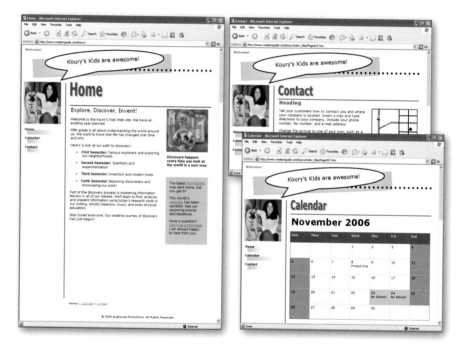

## Extra Credit

If you'd like to earn some extra credit, try your hand at adding content below the calendar object that describes and links to upcoming events, or complete the Contact page with a map and an e-mail link, or develop your own online newsletter using a Publisher newsletter template and the Top 10+1 list as guides. You now have the skills and knowledge to use Publisher to complete any of these tasks successfully and with flair.

## check it!

- You can create Web publications in Publisher by saving a print document as a Web publication, importing a text file, creating a blank Web publication, using the Easy Web Site Builder, or using a Web site template.

- Setting up a Web publication in Publisher entails choosing a design, specifying a navigation bar orientation, selecting a color scheme, and applying a font scheme.

- You can insert a new page and a navigation bar link for the page at the same time.

- Rulers and ruler guides help you to precisely align objects on each page and throughout your Web site.

- All text and images in Publisher Web publications must be inserted into text boxes or picture frames.

- Publisher provides special wizards for particular objects, such as calendars and navigation bars.

- To create a link that opens a page in a new window, you must use an HTML code fragment.

- Publisher offers numerous Web design options—experiment, mix and match, and create!

# swimming deeper into
## web waters with word and xml

# 10

Most of us are creatures of habit—we like to eat at favorite restaurants, hang with customary friends, shop at familiar stores, drive particular routes, and so on. Sometimes, life is more enjoyable (and easier) when we're surrounded by the familiar. Thus, you might feel most comfortable creating Web sites in an "old standby" application like Microsoft Office Word. Most people have used Word or a similar application to create standard documents and possibly e-mail messages. Therefore, we think Word serves as a widely recognized comfort-zone interface. Very likely, you'll find that creating Web pages in Word is quite similar to creating standard documents, with a few differences here and there. In this chapter, you'll put your Word and word processing skills to work as well as pick up a few new tricks. In addition, you'll learn how add a little spice to an old friendship by integrating a newer technology into your Word-based Web pages—Extensible Markup Language, or XML.

# Gathering Project Supplies

To create the Web pages described in this chapter, you'll need the following "supplies":

- Microsoft Office Word 2003 or later.

- A browser and an Internet connection. (An Internet connection is necessary only to download the walkthrough files from the CreationGuide Web site.)

- The following text files downloaded from www.creationguide. com/ch10. To obtain the files, create a folder named scuba on your computer's hard drive. For convenience, we'll refer to your hard drive as the C drive throughout this chapter. Connect to the Internet, open your, browser, display www.creationguide.com/ ch10, right-click the file name, click Save Target, and then save a copy of the file to the C:\scuba folder on your computer. Repeat this process for each file, or download the zip_files10.zip ZIP file, which contains all the files and images necessary for the walkthrough. The text files you need are:

| | | |
|---|---|---|
| home_text.doc | feature_text.doc | contact_text.doc |
| gallery.xml | gallery.xsl | |

- The following image files downloaded from www.creationguide. com/ch10/images and stored in C:\scuba\images on your computer:

| | | |
|---|---|---|
| arminacean.jpg | bg.gif | blue_anemone.jpg |
| clownfish.jpg | coral.jpg | dendronotid.jpg |
| diver.jpg | dorid.jpg | flag.gif |
| green_anemone.jpg | nudibranch.jpg | octopus.jpg |
| scubatank.jpg | titlebar.jpg | tube_sponges.jpg |

Figure 10-1 shows the files used in this chapter's walkthrough.

**tip**   If you prefer, you can download just the zip_files10. zip file and extract the necessary files and images folder locally. Your final file setup for this chapter's walkthrough should include the 5 text files in C:\scuba and 15 image files in C:\scuba\images.

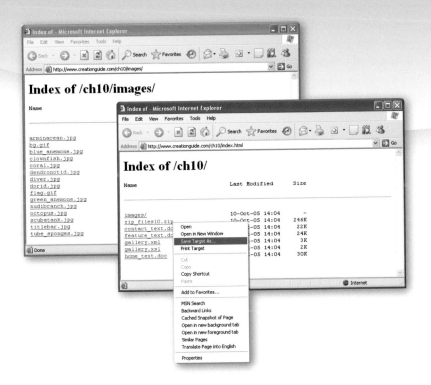

**Figure 10-1** *Download-ing the walkthrough files from the Internet*

# Word on the Web

In Chapter 7, "Posting a Web Site Within an Hour (or So)," the walkthrough shows how to create blogs using preconfigured settings. In Chapter 8, "Demystifying Basic CSS and XHTML," the walkthrough describes how to hand-code Web sites by using a text editor. Chapter 9, "Diving into Design with Publisher Templates," addresses designing Web sites in Publisher without worrying too much about source code. In this chapter, you get to combine your hand-coding and page design skills by creating a Web site in Microsoft Word 2003. In this walk-through, you'll hand-code a little bit of Extensible Markup Language (XML), instead of XHTML and cascading style sheets, in a very simple manner so that you can add another notch to your introductory hand-coding experience. You'll like this walkthrough—there's plenty of material included here for your experimentation pleasure, a few pictures you might like, and a chance to build a Web site in Word's familiar interface.

**tip**   To close the e-mail header pane without sending an e-mail message, simply click the E-Mail button on the Standard toolbar.

Speaking of Word, we've been watching for the past few years as the application has evolved by incorporating increasing levels of Internet and networking functionality in each new version. Word 2003 continues this networking-integration trend by building on existing Web capabilities and adding new features. Some of the main ways Word integrates with the Internet include the following:

- **View Web pages.**   You can click View, click Toolbars, and then click Web to display the Web toolbar. The Web toolbar provides basic Web navigation buttons and an Address bar.

- **E-mail messages.**   To create an e-mail interface within Word, you can click the E-Mail button on Word's Standard toolbar or click E-Mail Message in the New Document task pane. Clicking the E-Mail button on the Standard toolbar toggles the e-mail header pane within the current document view.

- **Create Web sites.**   You can use the Save As feature or Save As Web Page feature, click the Web Page link in the New Document task pane, or download templates from Microsoft Office Online to convert any Word document to a Web page or create Web pages from scratch. When you create a Web page in Word, Word automatically generates the source code and image directory necessary to display your document as a Web page or Web site. In essence, Word acts as a midrange Web editor.

**see also**   If you're interested in learning more about the e-mail features and Web browsing capabilities of Word 2003, pick up a copy of *Microsoft Office Word 2003 Inside Out* (Microsoft Press, 2003), by Mary Millhollon and Katherine Murray. The book was written by two seasoned Office experts and serves as a comprehensive resource for all topics related to Word.

Overall, Word offers quite a few basic Web development capabilities, and you can expand on those capabilities by shoring up your store of Web site development knowledge. For some people, learning to create Web sites in Word can fulfill their Web publishing needs, and they don't have to look further for a Web editor (but of course you'll be moving on to Microsoft Office FrontPage in Chapter 11, "Going All Out with FrontPage," because you're on a mission).

## Creating Web Pages

In Word 2003, you have two main options when it comes to creating a Web page—starting the creation process with a new, blank Web page or saving an existing document as a Web page. To start the process with a new, blank Web page, follow these steps:

**1** Click **New** on the **File** menu.

2 Click **Web Page** in the **New Document** task pane, as shown in Figure 10-2.

New Web Page icon

Web Page link

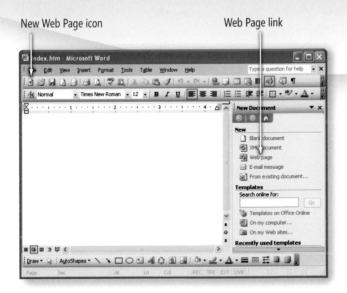

**Figure 10-2** *Creating a blank Web page in Word*

Like Microsoft Publisher, Word prohibits you from using application features that are not supported in online documents when you're working in Web mode. By default, Word provides only features that can be supported by Internet Explorer 4 (although the most current version is 6). You can tell if you are working on a Web page in Word because the New Document icon on the Standard toolbar displays a Web icon (as in Figure 10-2).

Another way to create a Web page is to use Word's Save As command. As you might know, you can save Word documents in various file formats and with various Save As Type file extensions, such as .txt, .doc, .rtf, and so forth. Among the file type options, Word includes the following collection of Web page options:

● **Single File Web Page (\*.mht; \*.mhtml)**   Saves all the elements of a Web page–including text, graphics, links, applets, and so forth–in a single file, called an *MHTML* document. Internet Explorer versions 4 and later support this format, but you can't count on other browsers to do so. For example, as of September 2005, Mozilla Firefox does not support MHTML Web pages. On the other hand, MHTML offers a convenient file format for those

**lingo**  *MHTML* stands for MIME (Multipurpose Internet Mail Extensions) encapsulation of aggregate HTML, which is a file type that contains all the text, graphics, links, applets, and other elements of a Web page in a single file.

times when you want to send an entire Web page, such as an online newsletter, in an e-mail message.

- **Web Page (*.htm; *.html)**   Saves a document as a Web page or Web site but retains Office-specific coding in the source code. You should use this Web page format for Web documents that serve as your working files or that you're sure will be viewed in Internet Explorer (such as on a company intranet). This ensures that you can take advantage of all of Word's built-in Web tools.

- **Web Page, Filtered (*.htm; *.html)**   Saves a document as a Web page without Office-specific coding in the source code. In theory, after you save a file using the Web Page, Filtered option, your text and the general appearance of the document will be preserved when you open the document in Office programs and online, but some features will work differently. For example, you will no longer be able to edit drawings you created on a drawing canvas. All in all, Web Page, Filtered files are smaller and have a higher propensity to be rendered properly in most browsers, but this format should be used only after you test your site in various browsers.

You can use the Save As dialog box to save any Word document as a Single File Web Page, a Web Page, or a Web Page, Filtered file. When you save a Word document as a Web page, Word generates the Web page's source code and image folder automatically.

## Previewing Web Pages

Regardless of the tool you use to create a Web site, you should preview your Web site frequently throughout the development process. This holds true for Word-created Web sites as well. To preview a document as a Web page in Word, open any Word document (such as the C:\scuba\home_text.doc file, if you downloaded it for this chapter's walkthrough), and then use any of the following methods:

- Click **View** on the menu bar, and then click **Web Layout**.

> **tip**   When you build a Web site in Word, save your documents using the Web Page option so that you can always make changes to your Web pages in Word. Before you post your Web site online, save a separate version of your Web site using the Web Page–Filtered option, without replacing your working files. That way, you can post smaller, filtered Web documents online for viewers without losing access to built-in Word Web editing features in the local versions of your files.

- Click the **Web Layout View** button, located in the lower-left corner of the document window.

- Click **File**, and then click **Web Page Preview**. When you click the **Web Page Preview** command, Word displays the current document in your browser (instead of within Word), as shown in Figure 10-3.

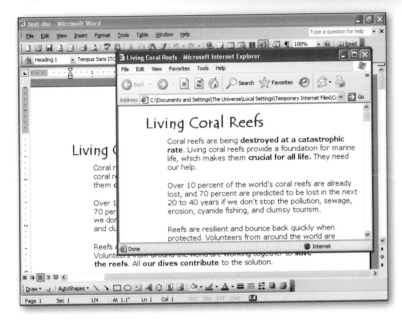

**Figure 10-3**   *Previewing a Word document in a browser*

You can use any of the preceding methods to preview your Web pages while you work in Word, as long as you preview the pages! Not to be overly bossy, but *don't wait until you think you've completed your Web site before previewing your pages.* Finding out that all your hard work just isn't going to fly online can be somewhat demoralizing, at least in the short term. And nobody wants that!

## Viewing Source Code

After you save a Word document as a Web page, you can view the Web page's source code in Word. In addition, you can edit most parts of a document's source code using WordPad or another text editor. Keep in mind, however, that the autogenerated code in Word is much more complex than the basic XHTML and cascading style sheet commands you worked with in Chapter 9, because Word includes XML, embedded cascading style sheets, and Office-specific coding used to display Web pages in Office documents. To view a Web document's source code in Word, click View, and then choose HTML Source. The Microsoft Script Editor window opens and displays the page's source code, as shown in Figure 10-4.

**Figure 10-4**  *An .htm page's source code in the Microsoft Script Editor window*

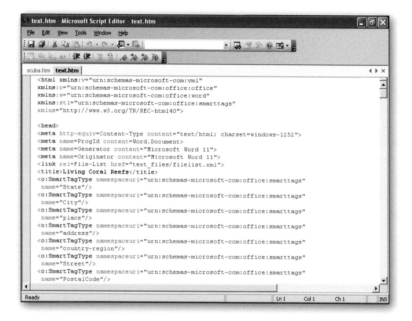

**note**    To open an .htm or .html file, you'll need to start Word, click File, and then click Open to open the file; or you'll need to drag the .htm document from a folder view into Word; or you'll need to right-click the file and then click Open With. If you double-click an .htm or .html file name in a folder, you'll open the document in your browser window. If you do double-click the file name of a Word document saved as a Web page and the page opens in Internet Explorer, all is not lost. You can still open the document in Word by using the Edit button on the Standard Buttons toolbar in Internet Explorer. To do so, click the Edit button's drop-down arrow and then click the Edit With Microsoft Office Word option.

## try this!

When you view a file's source code in Word, you might notice familiar tags, such as <head> and <title>. If you completed the Chapter 8 walkthrough, the <title></title> tags should look familiar to you, and you can work with the tag contents just as you would in a text editor. To try this, modify the Web page's title text directly in the source code within the Microsoft Script Editor by using standard editing techniques (deleting, inserting text, and so forth), as described here:

1 Start Word. You'll use a blank document to complete this procedure.

2 Click **File**, click **Save As**, and then click the **Desktop** button in the **Save In** pane (so that you can easily find and delete this file later).

3 In the **Save As Type** list, click **Web Page (*.htm; *.html)**, type **source_test** in the **File Name** box, click the **Change Title** button, type some title text, such as **This Is My Amazing Title Text**, and then click **OK**.

4 Click **Save**, click **HTML Source** on the **View** menu, and then find the title text between the <title></title> tags, as shown here:

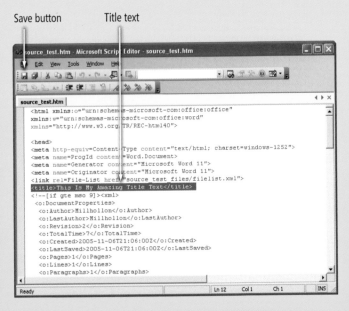

5 Change **This Is My Amazing Title Text** to any text you want, and then click **Save** in the Windows Script Editor window.

6 Scroll through the code in the Microsoft Script Editor window. See if you can recognize some cascading style sheet commands (shown in pink by default) and XHTML tags (shown in blue and red by default) amidst all the other commands that might not look so familiar just yet.

# Beware of the Drawing Canvas and
# AutoShapes
Generally, if we don't have something nice to say, we don't say anything at all. But in this case, we need to warn you about the temptations of Word's *drawing canvas* and AutoShapes when you build Web sites in Word. Naturally, when you create a Web site in Word, you'll be drawn toward Word's AutoShapes and the drawing canvas. They are easy to use and seem like a natural fit for creating attractive Web page elements. In fact, we initially created a perfectly wonderful Web site using Word's drawing features for you to build in this walkthrough. Unfortunately, after spending many hours on the site and congratulating ourselves for building such a pretty site, we realized there was no way the overlapping AutoShapes, transparent images, and toolbars we created in Word were going to be displayed properly in browsers other than Internet Explorer. We tried all kinds of workarounds, but to no avail.

With that said, the drawing canvas and AutoShapes *can* be used to design graphics. In this case, the most prudent way to proceed is to create the drawing in Word, copy it into a graphics program (such as Paint Shop Pro), modify and size the graphic in the graphics program, and then insert the graphic into your Word-based Web page as a picture. In fact, for this walkthrough, the site's banner was created by using the Rounded Rectangle AutoShape formatted as a text box, pasted into a graphics program, sized, and inserted into the Web site as a picture. We created the banner in that manner so that you could see how an AutoShape can be put to use (and so that you won't have an excuse for not building your own custom banners!). By saving Word drawings as graphics, you follow the most reliable path to cross-platform success.

Oh, and never fear. We came up with another great design for the walkthrough that bypasses the online trials and tribulations associated with AutoShapes and drawing canvas woes.

> **lingo**   The *drawing canvas* is an area where you can draw shapes. You can draw multiple shapes on a drawing canvas, add text and property settings to shapes, and modify the canvas properties. Further, the drawing canvas allows you to group, move, and resize the shapes included on the drawing canvas. By default, a drawing canvas is formatted without any background or outline color settings.

## Understanding Table Settings
When we say *table settings*, we're not talking forks and spoons here—we're talking about using tables to manage page elements. Many designers are beginning to shun using tables to lay out Web pages

and instead adhere to emerging Web standards that call for the use of cascading style sheets for page layout. That's all well and good, but the fact of the matter is that tables are used to lay out many, many Web pages. Table-based sites blanket the Web, and thousands of designers continue to rely on tables. Of course, we're studiously weaning ourselves from using tables and concentrating on maximizing the potential of cascading style sheets, but when you work with some Web design tools, Word and FrontPage included, tables can truly still save the day. As an added bonus, all browsers support tables, so you don't have to worry about ostracizing browsers with a table or two in the same way you might worry about cascading style sheet coding being properly interpreted. Therefore, while we encourage you to design without tables as much as possible, we also concede that there are times when only a table will do, at least for now. Ask us again in the next edition!

In this walkthrough, you'll use a table to hold the heading components in place. We found this was the best way to get Word to cooperate with us across platforms (including browsers and computers). That means you'll learn a bit about using tables in this walkthrough as well as in the Chapter 11 walkthrough, since FrontPage also relies on tables in some ways.

## XML, MSXML, XSLT—Oh My!

By far, HTML and XHTML are the most popular markup languages used on the Web today. With that said, XML is loudly making a case for itself as the most promising markup language on the horizon. Already, Office applications and Internet Explorer can process XML by using a software module called *Microsoft XML Core Services (MSXML)*. MSXML is installed automatically when you install Office applications and Internet Explorer. MSXML allows you to view XML data in various Office applications. For example, Figure 10-5 shows the gallery.xml data included with this chapter's walkthrough files in Microsoft Office Excel 2003 and Word 2003. Same data, different applications, different presentations.

Because XML is an emerging force on the Web, we thought you should know a little bit (and we really do mean "a little bit" here)

**note** Creating tables with HTML is much easier than you might imagine. If you'd like to learn how to hand-code an HTML table, visit www.creationguide.com/oldschool.

**lingo** The *Microsoft XML Core Services (MSXML)* software module (formerly known as the Microsoft XML Parser) is included in Office applications and Internet Explorer to provide support for XML. MSXML 5 shipped with Office 2003 applications. For Web content, one of the key benefits of MSXML 5 is that it supports the transformation of XML into HTML through Extensible Stylesheet Language Transformations (XSLT).

**Figure 10-5** *The gallery. xml document opened in WordPad, Excel, and Word*

about it and its associated technologies, such as MSXML, XSLT, and the XPath language. By learning some basic concepts and terms as well as seeing XML in action, you'll be one step ahead of many Web developers and ready to learn more XML in the future if you so desire. If you're not interested in XML, you'll still learn how to create Web pages in Word that don't use XML—no worries.

**tip** While XSLT can help you to control the XML data you want to show, you can (and most likely will) simultaneously use cascading style sheets to apply formatting to your Web site's contents. In Word, a cascading style sheet is generated automatically and embedded in your files, so you won't have to work directly with cascading style sheets in this walkthrough.

# Peeking In on XML

Fundamentally, XML is a markup language that allows you to create your own elements (tags), attributes, and document structures to describe your information. In XML, instead of using standard HTML or XHTML tags, you get to create your own tags. For example, if your data includes scientific information about plants and animals, you might include the following XML tags in your data (among others, of course):

-
-
-
-
-
-
-

Looking at the preceding collection, you might imagine how convenient the tags would be when you want to label, format, and organize data. Further, by storing data in an XML format, you can easily update your data as well as update any other documents that access the data. Those are two of the main ideas behind using XML. A third benefit of using XML is that it allows you to easily filter and format data when you also use *Extensible Stylesheet Language Transformations (XSLT)*.

# Meeting XSLT and XPath

As mentioned, XML documents can be used effectively to label, organize, and update information. Because XML data is highly structured, you can use XSLT (sometimes simply referred to as a *transformation* or a *transform*) to instruct browsers to find, extract, sort, filter, and manipulate XML data in specific ways. When you associate an XSLT document with an XML document, you can control what information is pulled from your XML data and how the selected data appears on your Web page. You'll learn how to perform this action in this chapter's walkthrough.

Returning to the plant and animal classification elements shown earlier, you could use an *XPath* command in XSLT to tell browsers to show

**lingo** *Extensible Stylesheet Language Transformations (XSLT)* is an XML-based language that allows you to create new XML documents based on content in an existing XML document without changing the original document. In other words, XSLT lets you pick and choose the data you want to use from the data stored in an XML document. XSLT then lets you apply custom formatting to the selected information. All this without altering a single pixel of the original data. In a way, XSLT is to XML as cascading style sheets are to XHTML. XSLT can define what and how data appears (although cascading style sheets can also be used in conjunction with XSLT to format a Web site, but no need to worry about that at this point).

**lingo**   *XPath* is a special notation system used to navigate through the hierarchical structure of XML documents. XPath expressions are used in XSLT to describe how to access parts of an XML document.

only the data in an XML document that is associated with a specific element. For example, you could add an XPath command in an XSLT document that tells a browser to show only the data  associated with the Anura order (<order>Anura</order>). If you did that, your page would display only information about frogs, toads, and tree toads.

We think that's just about enough X-alphabet soup for now. We invite you to reread this section later after you complete this chapter's walk-through. We bet you'll be surprised to see how much more clearly this explanation comes across after you've had some hands-on XML practice.

# Planning Your Word 2003 Web Site

In this chapter's walkthrough, you'll learn how to create an informational site for a group of coral reef divers. As you probably know, informational sites account for many online Web sites. There-fore, we thought this walkthrough could provide a handy template. In this walkthrough, a group of coral reef divers is committed to volun-teering its services toward the global effort of restoring, saving, and protecting coral reefs around the world. The main goal of the site is to inform members and potential members by presenting the following:

- Information about coral reefs and the organization's mission
- Images from diving expeditions
- Regularly updated feature articles submitted by members throughout the year
- Information about upcoming diving opportunities
- Contact information

With the basic information pinned down, we turned to design considerations. The organization indicated that its target audience consists of divers, researchers, and activists who tend to be well connected online. Therefore, we felt comfortable including images (optimized for the Web, of course), and we assumed that visitors ac-cess the Web with fairly updated Internet browsers and computers. As far as overall design, we knew we wanted to keep the site looking clean and uncluttered to reflect the divers' goal of cleaning up coral reef sites around the world. On a more detailed level, we also considered color schemes, page layout, and content management. Here's a quick rundown of what we came up with:

- **Color scheme**   As you might imagine, our first thoughts turned to the red-and-white flag used by divers around the world. There-fore, red quickly became a palette color. The next obvious choice was a deep blue to reflect the ocean waters. We chose Dark Teal on Word's default color palette. Then we added a splash of yellow as a complimentary color that's commonly found in coral reefs and that is a natural complement to blue and red. We also took advantage of using black and white throughout the site. Black edges seem indicative of diving masks and hoses, while the white background creates a very clean feel (although a light blue back-ground—the color of clean water—also would work nicely, if you prefer to use a color background in place of white).

- **Basic layout**   Because the main goals of the site are to convey information and present photo galleries to entice visitors to par-ticipate in dives, we decided on a simple design that could easily adapt to both page types. We also liked the idea of having a top navigation bar because visitors' eyes "dive down" the page to find information and then "resurface" at the top of the page to catch their breath, click a navigation bar link, and move to another page. We know that sounds a bit corny, but it did come to mind!

- **Content management**   Last but not least, we considered the types of content the site would present. The home page and contact page present fairly static information, while the feature article page and galleries present changing information. To create a consistent look for the site, the home and content pages have the same basic layout. The feature page is very similar to the other informational pages, with a simple content area that can be easily updated with new information. Because the coral reef divers hope to continually update their galleries, we had to think of a way to keep the information dynamic. We did this by creating one XML document that contains all the photo gallery information. The divers could then use the XML document to update and modify their online galleries while storing all of their data in one file.

After reaching the preceding conclusions, we created the site's framework and sketched storyboards for the basic page layout and gallery pages. Figure 10-6 shows the framework of the coral reef divers' site, which we refer to as the scuba site. Notice that the feature article shows a custom gallery page. Figure 10-7 shows the storyboard sketches.

**Figure 10-6**  *The scuba site's framework*

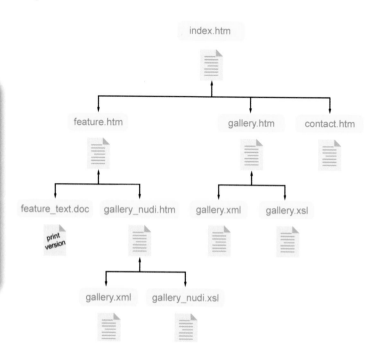

> **note**  Notice in the framework chart that we indicated to include a print version link on the feature article page. As you'll see, the feature article is designed to be read both online and in print because it's strictly an informative piece for site visitors.

**Figure 10-7**  *The scuba site's storyboard sketches*

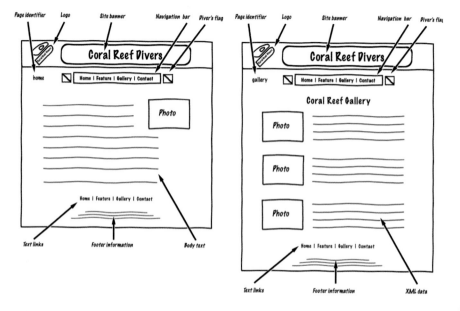

# Creating Your Main Template

The first order of business in creating a Web site is to set the standard. In other words, you should place all the standard elements first, such as the background, Web site title, navigation bar, logo or home icon, and footer text. In this section, you'll create the standard elements found throughout the scuba site. That way, this page can serve as a template for the subpages, before you add content.

## Creating and Saving a Blank Web Page

All creative projects start with a blank slate—a Web site in Word is no different. To set up a blank Web page, follow these steps:

1 Start Word, which automatically opens a new blank document by default, and then click **Save As** on the **File** menu.

2 In the **Save As** dialog box, display the contents of **C:\scuba**, click **Web Page (\*.htm; \*.html)** in the **Save As Type** list, and type **in-dex** in the **File Name** box, as shown in Figure 10-8. Notice that the **Save As** dialog box now includes a **Change Title** button.

**Figure 10-8** *Configuring the Save As dialog box to create an .htm file*

> **tip** The left pane in the Save As dialog box includes a My Network Places button. By clicking the My Network Places button, you can save Web documents directly to your server if it supports Network Places. See Chapter 12, "Sending Web Pages into the Real World," for details about creating and using Web Folders to upload and manage Web pages.

3 Click the **Change Title** button, and then type **Coral Reef Divers** in the **Set Page Title** dialog box, as shown in Figure 10-9. Click **OK**, and then click **Save**.

**Figure 10-9** *Adding title bar text for a Web page*

**tip**   To check your Web document's title bar text, click Web Page Preview on the File menu. Your browser should open the blank document, and the text *Coral Reef Divers* should appear in the title bar.

After you save the document, you can see in Word's title bar that the current file is index.htm. You can now edit and upload the Web document just as you would any Web file you created using a text editor or another Web editing program.

## Inserting a Background Image

For this project, you'll insert a 1-pixel-wide graphic that will repeat, or tile, across your Web page. Web developers use this type of small tiling background graphic extensively on the Web because the graphic is small and automatically fills the browser window. To insert a background image that creates a dark teal, black-edged bar across the top of a Web page regardless of window resizing, follow these steps:

**1** With C:\scuba\index.htm open in Word, click **Background** on the **Format** menu, and then click **Fill Effects**.

**2** In the **Fill Effects** dialog box, click the **Picture** tab, and then click the **Select Picture** button.

**3** In the **Select Picture** dialog box, display the contents of the **C:\scuba\images** folder, and then double-click the **bg.gif** file.

**4** The **Fill Effects** dialog box displays the 1-pixel-wide image, which is dark teal on top, 3 pixels of black below the dark teal, and white on the bottom, as shown in Figure 10-10. Click **OK**. The image tiles across the page to fill the window (as shown in the image on the left in Figure 10-10).

**5** Save your work.

**try this!**
You can customize the 1-pixel-wide background image to create a custom tiling background by starting with the bg.gif file provided in the scuba site walkthrough. To do this, open the bg.gif graphic in your editing program, recolor the 1-pixel-wide graphic using the colors you want, and then save the file with a new name. You can then view your background by inserting the graphic into a blank Web page in Word.

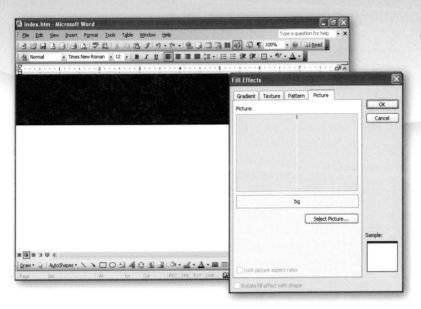

**Figure 10-10**   *Adding a background image*

## Building a Table and Inserting Pictures

For this site, the title banner, the home page graphic, and the navigation bar are held in place on each page by the judicious use of a table. You'll start by creating a three-row, two-column table:

1 On the **Standard** toolbar, click the **Insert Table** button, and then drag to create a 3 × 2 table, as shown in Figure 10-11.

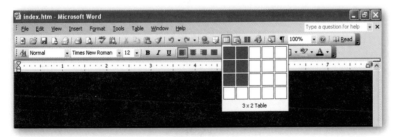

**Figure 10-11**   *Inserting a table*

2 By default, the insertion point is positioned in the first cell. Click **Insert**, click **Picture**, and then click **From File**.

3 In the **Insert Picture** dialog box, navigate to the **C:\scuba\ images** folder, and then double-click the **scubatank.jpg** image.

4 Click in the second cell in the first row, click **Insert**, click **Picture**, and then click **From File**.

5 Double-click **titlebar.jpg** in the **Insert Picture** dialog box.

6 Double-click the **titlebar.jpg** image to open the **Format Picture** dialog box.

7 Click the **Size** tab, locate the **Height** box in the **Size And Rotate** section, change the **Height** setting to **.71**, click **OK**, and then click **Save**. Your page should look similar to the page shown in Figure 10-12.

**Figure 10-12** *Inserting graphics into a table*

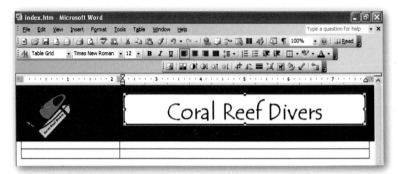

Next you'll format the table and align the graphics in the table.

8 Click anywhere in the table other than on a graphic, and then click **Table Properties** on the **Table** menu to open the **Table Properties** dialog box.

9 On the **Table** tab, click the **Borders And Shading** button.

10 In the **Borders and Shading** dialog box, on the **Borders** tab, click the **None** icon in the **Setting** area, and then click **OK** to return to the **Table Properties** dialog box.

11 On the **Table** tab, in the **Size** area, select the **Preferred Width** check box, and then type **100** in the text box. The value in the **Measure In** list automatically changes to **Percent**.

12 On the **Row** tab, verify that the **Specify Height** check box is *not* selected.

13 On the **Column** tab, clear the **Preferred Width** check box so that it is *not* selected for **Column 1**.

14 Click the **Next Column** button, and then clear the **Preferred Width** check box so that it is *not* selected for **Column 2**.

15 On the **Cell** tab, clear the **Preferred Width** check box, click **OK** to apply your table settings, and then click **Save** to save your work.

Your Web page should look similar to the page shown in Figure 10-13. Notice that the table borders appear light gray so that you can see the table cells while you work, even though the borders won't be shown when a browser displays the page.

**Figure 10-13** *Viewing a table with elements aligned*

## Building the Navigation Bar

Your next order of business is to build the navigation bar. The navigation bar is created by nesting a table within the table you've already created. In addition to the navigation text links, the navigation bar includes two graphics, one on each end. To build the navigation bar, follow these steps:

1 Click in the third row, second column cell of the table you created in the preceding section, click the **Insert Table** button on the **Standard** toolbar, and then create a 1 × 3 table (one row, three columns).

2 By default, the insertion point is positioned in the first column of the nested table. Click **Insert**, click **Picture**, click **From File**, double-click the **flag.gif** image in the **Insert Picture** dialog box, and then click **Align Right** on the **Formatting** toolbar with the **flag.gif** image still selected.

3 Click in the third column cell in the nested table, click **Insert**, click **Picture**, click **From File**, and then double-click the **flag.gif** image in the **Insert Picture** dialog box.

4 Right-click the center cell of the nested table, click **Borders And Shading**, click the **None** setting on the **Borders** tab, click the **Red** color square in the **Fill** area on the **Shading** tab, click **Cell** in the **Apply to** area, and then click **OK**.

5 On the **Table** menu, click **Table Properties**.

6 In the **Table Properties** dialog box, on the **Column** tab, clear the **Preferred Width** check box for all three columns (remember to use the **Next Column** button), and then on the **Cell** tab, clear the **Preferred Width** check box and click **OK**.

Now you will add text to the center cell in the navigation bar; this text will later be formatted as hyperlinks. Make sure that your insertion point is still positioned in the center cell of the nested table.

7 On the **Formatting** toolbar, click **Tempus Sans** (or **TmpsS**, or another font family if necessary) in the **Font** drop-down list, click **14** in the **Size** list, click the **Bold** button, click the **Center** button, and then click **White** on the **Font Color** drop-down color palette.

8 Type **Home**, press SPACEBAR three times, type a pipe character (|), press SPACEBAR three times, type **Feature**, press SPACEBAR three times, type |, press SPACEBAR three times, type **Gallery**, press SPACEBAR three times, type |, press SPACEBAR three times, and then type **Contact**.

9 Right-click in the center cell of the nested table, click **Cell Alignment**, and then click the **Center** option, which centers content both horizontally and vertically. The Center option looks like this:

**caution**   The Tempus Sans font is included in Office 2003 as well as in some earlier versions of Microsoft Windows and Office applications. But Tempus Sans, while generally accessible, is *not* one of the sure-fire cross-platform fonts defined in Part One of this book. Therefore, all systems might not support this font. Use Tempus Sans and other nonstandard fonts at your own risk (or convert them to graphical text). Generally, you should use nonstandard fonts only when you're familiar with the systems your visitors will be using (such as a company intranet). In this walkthrough, the coral reef divers thought most visitors would have up-to-date systems, and because this chapter is written for Word 2003, using the Tempus Sans font seemed acceptable.

**10** Select the pipe character between **Home** and **Feature**, click **Black** on the **Font Color** drop-down color palette, and then color the other two pipe characters black.

**11** Finally, carefully drag the nested table to the right slightly so that it appears centered below the page banner graphic, and then save your work.

Your navigation bar should now look similar to the one shown in Figure 10-14. You will link the navigation bar to the subpages after you create the subpages. Unfortunately, Word won't let you add hyperlinks to yet-to-be-made files.

**Figure 10-14**  *Creating the navigation bar*

## Adding Page Identifiers

For this Web site, you'll identify the current page in two ways. You'll show the page's name in gray text in the top-of-the-page table, and you'll color the current page's name on the navigation bar. To set up the home page, follow these steps:

**1** Select the word **Home** on the navigation bar (or double-click the word **Home**), and then click **Black** on the **Font Color** drop-down palette.

**2** Click in the first cell of the top-of-the-page table (not the navigation bar table).

**3** On the **Formatting** toolbar, click **Verdana** in the **Font** list, click **10** in the **Size** list, click the **Bold** button, click **Gray-25%** in the **Font Color** drop-down palette, and then type **home**.

**4** Right-click in the cell, click **Cell Alignment**, and then click the bottom, left-aligned option.

5 Save your work. Your page should look similar to the page
shown in Figure 10-15.

**Figure 10-15** *Adding page identifiers to the home page*

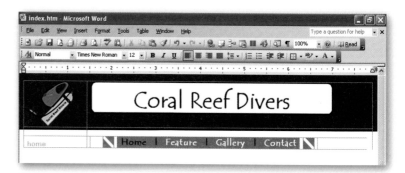

## Adding Footer Information

Now that you have the top of the page well on its way, you're ready to add the footer information. Footer information comes in many forms. For this site, we'll keep it basic. You'll include text-based navigation links, a last-updated date, and copyright information. As with the navigation bar, Word won't let you link the footer links to the sub-pages yet because you haven't created them. You'll have to add the hyperlink information later, after you build the site framework. To add footer information, follow these steps:

1 Double-click near the bottom of the window, click the **Center** alignment button on the **Formatting** toolbar, click **Verdana** in the **Font** list, click **11** in the **Size** list, and then click **Black** on the **Font Color** drop-down palette, if necessary.

2 Type the following, adding a space before and after each pipe character:

Home | Feature | Gallery | Contact

3 Press ENTER three times, click **8** in the **Size** drop-down list on the **Formatting** toolbar, type **Last updated** *current month and year*, press ENTER, type **(c)**, and then press SPACEBAR. By default, Word inserts a copyright symbol when you type the **(c)** combination.

4 Type your name or company name followed by the phrase **All Rights Reserved.**, press ENTER two or three times to add a bit of space below your footer information, and then save your work.

Your footer should look similar to the footer shown in Figure 10-16. You now have the standard page format setup for your entire Web site.

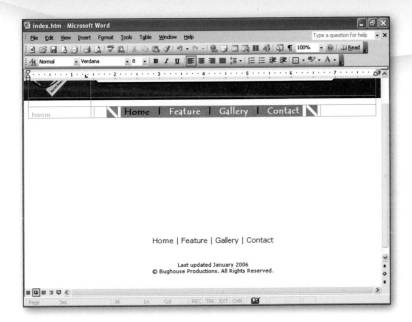

**Figure 10-16**  *Inserting footer information*

# Building the Site Framework

Before you start adding content, you need to set up your site. In Word, this is especially important, because you can't link to your pages until they actually exist. Apparently, Word has a "see it to believe it" mentality when it comes to subpage development. Therefore, instead of trying to convince Word to have a little faith, we'll show you how to quickly create subpages, and then we'll get the navigation bars linked and ready to go.

## Putting the Save As Command to Work

By default, Word organizes supporting files in a folder for you. Because this is the default setting, you'll retain that setting for this walkthrough. Working with Word means you'll probably end up with more folders than you would normally have for a Web site, but it saves you quite a bit of hassle when you're developing in Word to just go with the application's default on this one. Therefore, the best approach here is to simply use the Save As command from within index.htm, as described here:

1  Click **Save As** on the **File** menu, type **feature** in the **File Name** box, and then click **Save**.

2  Click **Save As** on the **File** menu, type **gallery** in the **File Name** box, and then click **Save**.

3  Click **Save As** on the **File** menu, type **contact** in the **File Name** box, and then click **Save**.

4  Click **Save As** on the **File** menu, type **gallery_nudi** (trust us on this one) in the **File Name** box, and then click **Save**.

5  Close Word, and then open the **C:\scuba** folder. Your folder should contain the files shown in Figure 10-17.

> **note**   You'll add page titles later in this chapter, in the section "Replacing Subpages with the Updated Template."

**Figure 10-17**  *Viewing the Web site's documents and folders*

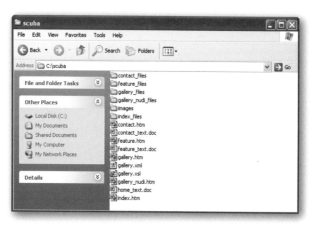

## Linking the Navigation Links

As we're sure you're aware, a navigation bar has to actually link to the pages in your site. Because you have now created a framework, Word will let you link the navigation bar links to your subpages. You might think this means that you'll have to repeat this process for every subpage. Luckily, we have a little workaround for you. To add links to your navigation bars (top and bottom), follow these steps:

1  In the **C:\scuba** folder, right-click **index.htm**, click **Open With**, and then click **Microsoft Office Word**.

2  In the top navigation bar, select the word **Home**, and then click
   **Hyperlink** on the **Insert** menu. The **Insert Hyperlink** dialog box
   opens.

3  Click the **ScreenTip** button, type **Home** in the **Set Hyperlink
   ScreenTip** dialog box, click **OK**, type **index.htm** in the **Address**
   box, and then click **OK**. The link changes to blue, underlined
   text—you'll fix that in a moment.

> **lingo**  A Screen-
> Tip is descriptive
> text that pops up
> when the mouse
> pointer hovers over
> a hyperlink.

4  Select the word **Feature**, click **Hyperlink** on the **Insert** menu,
   click the **ScreenTip** button, type **Feature**, click **OK**, type **feature.
   htm** in the **Address** box, and then click **OK**.

5  Select the word **Gallery**, click **Hyperlink** on the **Insert** menu,
   click the **ScreenTip** button, type **Gallery**, click **OK**, type **gallery.
   htm** in the **Address** box, and then click **OK**.

6  Scroll down to the bottom navigation bar, and then repeat steps
   2 through 5 to link the text-based navigation bar links.

7  While you're in creating-hyperlink mode, you might as well link
   the logo to the home page, so right-click the **scubatank** logo in
   the upper-left corner, click **Hyperlink**, click the **ScreenTip** button, type **Coral Reef Divers Home**, click **OK**, type **index.htm** in
   the **Address** box, and then click **OK**.

8  Now, to reformat the links in your top navigation bar, select the
   **Home** link, click the **Underline** button on the **Formatting** toolbar to remove the underline, click **Font** on the **Format** menu,
   click **White** on the **Font Color** drop-down palette, click **(none)**
   in the **Underline Style** list, and then click **OK**.

9  With the word **Home** still selected, double-click the **Format
   Painter** button on the **Standard** toolbar to copy the **Home**
   button's formatting, and then drag your mouse pointer across
   the word **Feature** to reformat it. Next drag across the word
   **Gallery**, and then drag across the word **Contact**. Click the
   **Format Painter** button to turn off the formatting tool.

10 Last but not least, select the **Home** text once more, and then
   click **Black** on the **Font Color** drop-down palette. One way to
   quickly indicate the current page to visitors is to format the
   link to the current page differently than other links on the
   navigation bar.

**11** Save your work. Hover the mouse pointer over various links to check the ScreenTip text. Your linked index.htm page should look similar to the page shown in Figure 10-18.

**Figure 10-18** *Linking the navigation bars*

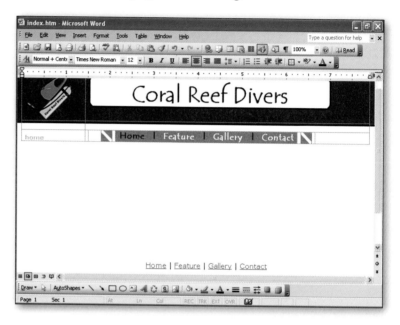

## Replacing Subpages with the Updated Template

At this point, you have a fully linked index.htm page, but none of the subpages are formatted with links. You could go in and add hyperlinks to both navigation bars all over again on each page, or you could replace each page with the new index.htm page, as follows:

**1** With the **index.htm** file still open in Word, click **Save As** on the **File** menu, click the **Change Title** button, type **Feature** in the **Set Page Title** box, and then click **OK**.

**2** Click the **feature.htm** file in the **Save As** dialog box, and then click **Save**. You'll see a dialog box asking whether you want to replace the existing file (the option selected by default); click **OK**.

**3** Double-click (or drag to select) the light gray **home** text in the first cell in the third row of the top-of-the-page table, and then type **feature**. This indicates to viewers that they are on the Feature page.

4 Double-click the **Home** text in the red navigation bar, and use the **Font Color** drop-down palette to change the font color to **white**.

5 Select the **Feature** text in the red navigation bar, and change the font color to **black**.

6 Click **Save**. Make *sure* that you save the changes to feature.htm before moving on to formatting the Gallery page in step 7.

7 Repeat steps 1 through 6 to set up the Gallery page, adding the title bar text, changing the gray text to **gallery**, and modifying the navigation bar link colors as appropriate. Click the **Save** button before you move on to format the next page.

8 Repeat steps 1 through 6 to set up the Contact page, adding the title bar text, changing the gray text to **contact**, and modifying the navigation bar link colors as appropriate. Click the **Save** button before you move on to the next page.

9 Click **Save As** on the File menu, click the **Change Title** button, type **Nudibranch Gallery**, click **OK**, click the **gallery_nudi.htm** file name in the **Save As** dialog box, click **Save**, and then click **OK**.

> **tip** If you're not sure which document you're working in, look at the title bar in Word to see the current document's file name.

10 Replace the gray **contact** text with **feature : gallery** (all lowercase, with a space on each side of the colon, and resized to **Font Size 8**), color the **Feature** link in the red navigation bar **black**, color the **Contact** link in the red navigation bar **white**, save your changes, and close Word.

11 In the **C:\scuba** folder, double-click the **index.htm** file to open your Web site in your browser. Click each link to make sure that the gray text, the link color in the red navigation bar, and the title text change each time you click a link. Hover the mouse pointer over links to check your ScreenTip text. Figure 10-19 shows the Gallery page in a Web browser. Notice that the Gallery link color, ScreenTip text, gray text, and title bar text are all in order. If you see any errors on your pages, open the corresponding file in Word and make changes before moving on.

12 Close your browser window after you've checked all your pages.

**Figure 10-19** *Previewing the site framework and checking navigation links in a browser window*

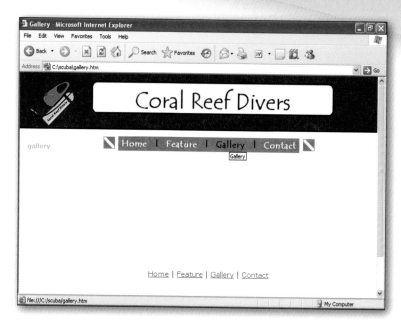

**note**  Because the gallery_nudi. htm page isn't linked to any pages yet, you need to either type the C:\ scuba\gallery_nudi. htm address in your browser's Address bar or you need to double-click the file name in the folder to view and check the page's setup.

## Adding Basic Content

You've been pretty busy formatting hyperlinks and text up to now, so we've decided to cut you a break here. We assume you've used Word before, so there's no dire need to rehash the wonders of typing and formatting text. With that thought in mind, we developed all the content for the Web site, and you presumably downloaded the text documents at the beginning of this chapter. Therefore, adding content will just be a matter of importing text. After you import text, you'll add a couple images and then create print, mailto, and standard links before moving on to the XML portion of the walkthrough.

Because you're already familiar with the steps for adding content and formatting hyperlinks, we've opted to include the steps for filling and linking the Home, Feature, and Contact pages on the companion Web site at www.creationguide.com/ch10/extras. Figure 10-20 shows the finished home page after you've followed the online steps.

## Working with XML Data

As discussed earlier, importing XML data stores all your related data in a single file. For the scuba site, the XML file stores data and related image file names for creatures photographed on various dives. The

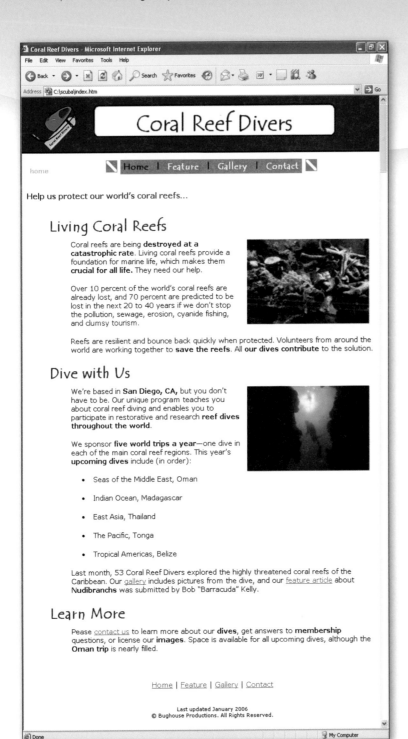

**Figure 10-20**   *Previewing the finished home page*

Web site includes two galleries—one showing all the XML data, and another one that filters the data and shows only the nudibranchs. To keep this project manageable, we've included only eight creatures. You might want to experiment with the files later to add additional entries.

As we mentioned, XML data is highly structured, much like XHTML. XML uses tag pairs that must be nested properly. (The Chapter 8 walkthrough describes *nesting*.) Uppercase and lowercase letters much match exactly; we tend to use all lowercase as much as possible. Figure 10-22 shows the gallery.xml file opened in WordPad.

**Figure 10-22**  *Viewing simple XML data in WordPad*

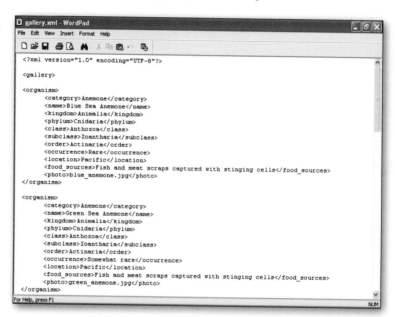

Although some versions of Word 2003 support editing XML, not all versions do, so you'll complete the XML editing portions of this walkthrough using WordPad. To open the gallery.xml file in WordPad, right-click gallery.xml, click Open With, and click WordPad. The main structure of the data is as follows:

```
xml statement
start gallery
start organism entry
        organism detail
        organism detail
                etc.
end organism entry
more organism entries
end gallery
```

To get a little practice entering XML data, scroll down in the gallery. xml file, and then add the following organism entry between the final </organism> and </gallery> tags:

```
<organism>
        <category>Nudibranch</category>
        <name>Dendronotid</name>
        <kingdom>Animalia</kingdom>
        <phylum>Mollusca</phylum>
        <class>Gastropoda</class>
        <subclass>Opisthobranchia</subclass>
        <order>Nudibranchia</order>
        <occurrence>Less common</occurrence>
        <location>Warm Pacific</location>
        <food_sources>Sponges, corals, anemones, jellyfish (varies by
                species)</food_sources>
        <photo>dendronotid.jpg</photo>
</organism>
```

Your document should look like the one shown in Figure 10-23. Save and close the gallery.xml document. You'll import the data from within Word.

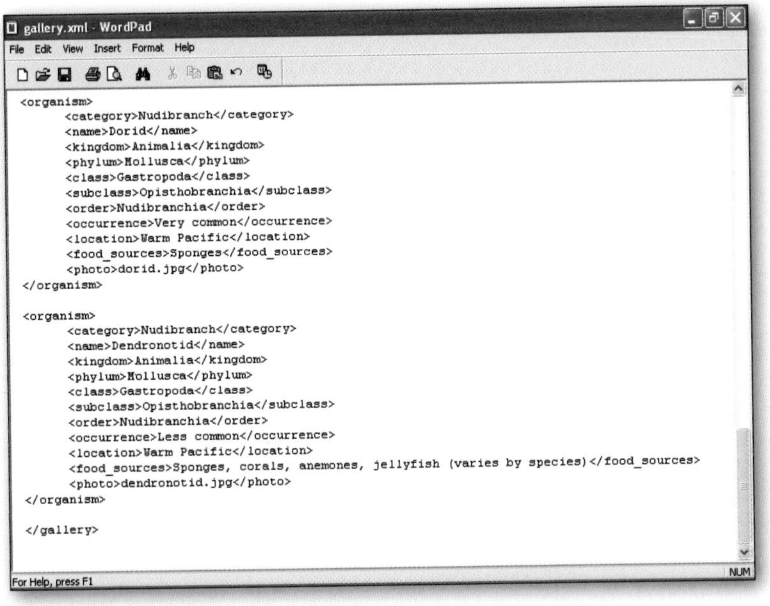

**tip** To help speed the process of adding a new organism entry to the gallery. xml file, you can copy and paste an existing entry and then modify the content information that appears between each tag pair.

**Figure 10-23** *Adding data to an XML file*

## Viewing and Modifying XSL Transformations

Now that you've seen the type of data you're working with, you should take a look at the XSL transformations (XSLT) that you'll apply to the data. We've created the XSL transformation for importing all the gallery.xml data without any filters. This document is named gallery. xsl, and the code stored in the gallery.xsl document is shown here:

```
<?xml version="1.0" encoding="UTF-8"?>
<xsl:transform version="1.0" xmlns:xsl="http://www.w3.org/1999/XSL/
Transform">
<xsl:output method='html' version='1.0' encoding='UTF-8' />
<xsl:template match="/">
<html>
<body>
<table align="center" border="0" cellpadding="10" cellspacing="0">
<xsl:for-each select="gallery/organism">
<xsl:sort select="name" />
<tr>
  <td align="center" width="250">
    <img>
    <xsl:attribute name="src">
      <xsl:value-of select="photo" />
    </xsl:attribute>
    </img>
  </td>
  <td>
    <p>
    <span style="font-family: verdana;">
    <strong>Category: </strong> <xsl:value-of select="category" /><br />
    <strong>Name: </strong> <xsl:value-of select="name" /><br />
    <strong>Kingdom: </strong> <xsl:value-of select="kingdom" /><br />
    <strong>Phylum: </strong> <xsl:value-of select="phylum" /><br />
    <strong>Class: </strong> <xsl:value-of select="class" /><br />
    <strong>Subclass: </strong><xsl:value-of select="subclass" /><br />
    <strong>Order: </strong> <xsl:value-of select="order" /><br />
    <strong>Occurrence: </strong> <xsl:value-of
        select="occurrence" /><br />
    <strong>Location: </strong> <xsl:value-of select="location" /><br />
    <strong>Food source: </strong> <xsl:value-of
        select="food_sources" />
    </span>
    </p>
  </td>
  </tr>
</xsl:for-each>
</table>
</body>
</html>
</xsl:template>
</xsl:transform>
```

You don't really need to understand every bit of the code, although if you're familiar with HTML, you might recognize the basic table <table>, table row <tr>, table data <td>, and strong emphasis (boldface) <strong> tag pairs, among others. To illustrate the effect of using a transformation, Figure 10-24 shows XML imported into a Word document with and without an XSL transformation.

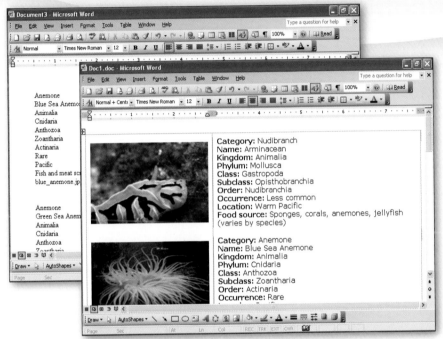

**Figure 10-24** *Comparing XML data without and with an XSL Transformation applied*

For this walkthrough, you'll add a one-line XPath command that filters the gallery.xml data to include only nudibranchs, and then you'll give the XSL transformation file a new name so that you'll have two XSL files to work with when you're importing XML data to the two remaining pages in the scuba site. To create the second XSL transformation, follow these steps:

1 In the **C:\scuba** folder, right-click **gallery.xsl**, click **Open With**, and then click **WordPad**.

2 Before any unwanted data changes take place, you should save the file with a new name. In WordPad, click **Save As** on the **File** menu, change the file name to **gallery_nudi.xsl** in the **Save As** dialog box, and then click **Save**. You should see the new file name in WordPad's title bar.

3 **To add the XPath filter command that selects, formats, and displays only nudibranch data, find the following line of code in the gallery_nudi.xsl file:**

```
<xsl:for-each select="gallery/organism">
```

and change it to:

```
<xsl:for-each select="gallery/organism[category='Nudibranch']">
```

4 **Save the file, and then close WordPad.**

## Including XML Data in a Web Site

Now that you've updated the XML file by adding data for an organism and added an XPath filter to an XSL transformation, you're ready to insert the data into your Web site. At this point, we should mention that we've discovered that Word has a hard time finding images referenced in an XML file. Word tends to point and hard-code image references to a temp directory, which means the images referenced in the walk-through's gallery.xml file are not found and you can't change the image references in Word. You can either edit the Web page's Word-generated source code in WordPad or insert pictures manually. Since placeholders are included next to the imported XML data, we opted to show you how to insert the images manually instead of editing Word's source code, because that's a tricky business. We hope future versions of Word are more friendly about following image references in XML files, but for now, the workaround is easy enough. If we discover a way to force Word to access the proper paths to image references in the XML file, we'll post our findings on the CreationGuide Web site.

### Inserting Data

Inserting data in a Word document entails inserting a field. To insert XML data, you insert the IncludeText field and reference the related XML file and XSL transformation. Here are the steps:

1 **Open gallery.htm in Word, and then click below the gray gallery page identifier text so that you can add the page's heading text.**

2   On the **Formatting** toolbar, click **Tempus Sans (or TmpsS** or
    another font) in the **Font** list, click **26** in the **Size** list, click the
    **Center** alignment button, click **Dark Teal** on the **Font Color**
    drop-down palette, press ENTER, type **Coral Reef Gallery**, and
    then press ENTER twice.

3   On the **Insert** menu, click **Field**.

4   In the **Field** dialog box, click **IncludeText** in the **Field Names**
    list, type **gallery.xml** in the **Filename Or URL** box, and then type
    **gallery.xsl** in the **XSL Transformation** box (which will be se-
    lected automatically after you type a path in the text box). The
    **Field** dialog box should look similar to the dialog box shown in
    Figure 10-25.

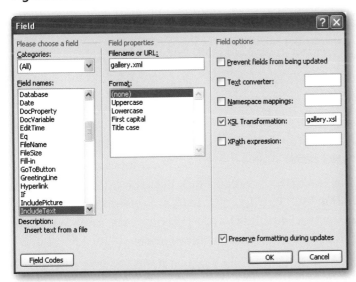

**Figure 10-25**  *Importing an XML file and an XSL
Transformation*

5   Click **OK**. The data is imported without the images.

6   Click in the table, click **Table Properties** on the **Table** menu,
    select the **Preferred Width** check box on the **Table** tab, change
    the width to **80 percent**, and then click **OK**. Your Gallery page
    should appear similar to the page shown in Figure 10-26.

**Figure 10-26** *Viewing XML data in Word*

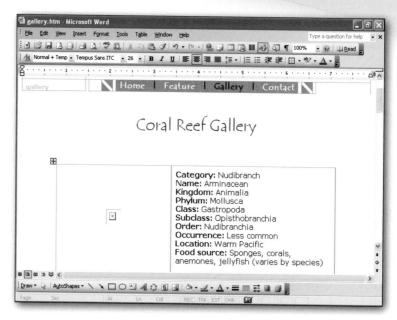

Next you'll add text to the Nudibranch Gallery, and then you'll insert images into both galleries.

7 Click the **Open** button on the **Standard** toolbar, open the **gallery_nudi.htm** file, and then click below the gray **feature : gallery** page identifier text.

8 On the **Formatting** toolbar, click **Verdana** in the **Font** list, click **11** in the **Font Size** list, click the **Center** alignment button, click **black** on the **Font Color** drop-down palette, press ENTER, and then type **Return to the Feature Article**.

9 Format the **Return to the Feature Article** text as a hyperlink that links to **feature.htm**, and then press ENTER.

10 On the **Formatting** toolbar, click **Tempus Sans** (or **TmpsS,** or another font) in the Font list, click **26** in the **Size** list, click **Dark Teal** in the **Font Color** palette, press ENTER, type **Nudibranch Gallery**, and then press ENTER twice.

11 Click **Field** on the **Insert** menu, click **IncludeText** in the **Field Names** list, type **gallery.xml** in the **Filename Or URL** box, type **gallery_nudi.xsl** in the **XSL Transformation** box, and then click **OK**.

**12** Click the table, click **Table Properties** on the **Table** menu, set the **Preferred Width** to **80 Percent** on the **Table** tab, click **OK**, and then save your work.

## Adding Images to the XML data

Even though it would be nice if Word would properly insert the referenced images, this step is fairly easy for this project. We'll walk you through inserting the images for the Nudibranch Gallery, and then you can work your way through the Coral Reef Gallery on your own. To insert images into the XML data table, follow these steps:

> **tip**   All images have the same name as the organism's common name, shown in the Name field.

1 Click the image placeholder icon next to the first entry, and note the entry's name.

2 Click **Picture** on the **Insert** menu, click **From File**, double-click the **arminacean.jpg** file, click **Table Properties** on the **Table** menu, click the **Cell** tab, click the **Top** option in the **Vertical alignment** area, and then click **OK**.

3 In the **gallery_nudi.htm** file, click the second image placeholder icon, insert the **dendronotid.jpg** file, click the third and final image placeholder icon, and then insert the **dorid.jpg** file.

4 Delete the extra space between the XML table and the footer information, and then click **Save**. Figure 10-27 shows the Nudibranch Gallery in a browser window.

5 Add images to the XML table inserted into the gallery.htm file. Remember to apply **Top** vertical alignment after inserting the first image, and then save your work after you've added the eight images.

## Previewing the Completed Web Site

Congratulations! You've completed the scuba site and plowed through an introduction to XML. As a reward, the final task of the walkthrough is an easy one. Simply preview your Web site in a browser. You've checked your pages a few times during the process, so you shouldn't receive any major surprises at this point. Hopefully, by now, you can casually click through your site and enjoy the fruits of your work.

> **note**   To view the final project online saved with Word's Web Page, Filtered option, visit www.creationguide.com/scuba.

**Figure 10-27** *Viewing the Nudibranch Gallery in a browser window*

# check it!

- You can use Word 2003 to create Web pages by using the Save As feature or by starting with a blank Web page document.
- After you save a document as a Web page in Word, you can view the document's source code, which is automatically generated by Word.
- Many Web page creation tasks in Word are similar to standard Word processing tasks.
- You can create Web page objects using AutoShapes, but you should save the AutoShape creation in a graphics program and then reinsert the AutoShape as a typical graphic.
- The Insert Hyperlink dialog box enables you to create standard and mailto hyperlinks.
- Being consistent, saving frequently, and previewing your work often are key tasks in creating effective Web sites.
- Word can import XML and XSL transformations and include XML data in Web sites.

# going all out
## with frontpage

# CHAPTER

# 11

When you watch the news on TV, the only "equipment" you need is the TV and a place to sit. But what about when you rent a DVD or order a pay-per-view movie that's filled with outrageous special effects and has an awesome soundtrack? Instead of turning to grandma's 13-inch hand-me-down TV, you'd probably prefer the ultimate in home entertainment systems. You know, the rare setup that can be easily controlled by a *single* remote control and includes a huge plasma TV, digital cable, and surround sound components artfully blending into the shadows—all strategically placed for optimal viewing and listening pleasure from the comfort of an oversized, overstuffed down sofa or body-forming recliner. Granted, these "extras" aren't strictly necessary, but they sure can make a big difference sometimes. The same can be said of Web editors. Notepad (a basic text editor) can be likened to the TV-and-chair way of creating Web pages, whereas Microsoft Office FrontPage provides the luxury home entertainment system approach to Web site development. In this chapter, you're going for the extras.

# Gathering Project Supplies

To create the Web site described in this chapter, you'll need the following "supplies":

- Microsoft FrontPage 2003 or later.

- An Internet connection. (An Internet connection is necessary to download the sample project's graphics and text files from the CreationGuide Web site.)

**tip**   If you prefer, you can download the zip_files11. zip file and extract the necessary files and images folder locally. Your final file setup for this chapter's walkthrough should include the 3 text files in C:\notebooks and 14 image files in C:\ notebook\images.

- The home_text.doc, notebooks_text.doc, and events_text.doc text documents, downloaded from www.creationguide.com/ch11. To download these files, create a folder named notebooks on your hard drive. For convenience, we'll refer to your hard drive as the C drive throughout this chapter. Then connect to www.creationguide.com/ch11, right-click home_text.doc, and save the file to the C:\notebooks folder on your computer. Repeat the process to save notebooks_text.doc and events_text. doc to your C:\notebooks folder.

- The following figures, downloaded from www.creationguide.com/ ch11/images (or zip_files11.zip):

| | |
|---|---|
| b_add.gif | imagemap.jpg |
| logo.gif | p_nb01.jpg |
| p_nb02.jpg | p_nb03.jpg |
| p_nb04.jpg | p_nb05.jpg |
| p_nb06.jpg | p_nb07.jpg |
| p_nb08.jpg | p_nb09.jpg |
| p_nb10.jpg | p_nb11.jpg |

To obtain these figures, download the ZIP file and extract the files to C:\notebooks, or create an images folder in C:\notebooks, right-click an image file on the www.creationguide.com/ch11/images page, and save a copy of the file to the C:\notebooks\images folder on your computer. Repeat the process for each image. Figure 11-1 shows the files used in this chapter's walkthrough.

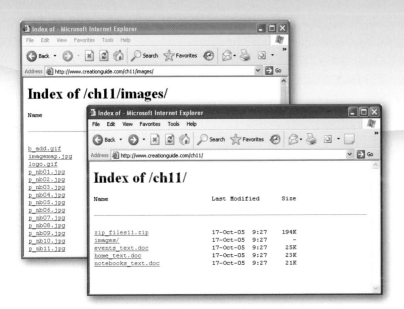

**Figure 11-1** *Organizing the Chapter 11 walkthrough files*

# Introducing FrontPage: A Full-Featured Web Editor

For this book's final walkthrough, we show you how to use Microsoft Office FrontPage to create a simple online store. FrontPage is a full-featured Web editor that you can purchase as a stand-alone application. As you'll see in this chapter, using a true Web editor such as FrontPage opens numerous doors to Web page design for beginning designers. Full-scale Web editors also provide handy shortcuts for seasoned designers. Our goal is to give you firsthand experience in creating a Web site that uses a number of FrontPage features. That way, you can see how an advanced Web editor can actually simplify and speed up the Web design process. But before you start building, let's give the FrontPage interface a quick once-over to preview where you're headed.

> **tip** If you're familiar with older versions of Front-Page, you can see a nice table illustrating the upgrades and additions included in FrontPage 2003 by visiting www.microsoft.com/office/front-page/prodinfo/compare.mspx.

## Strolling Past the FrontPage Window

Much of the FrontPage interface is similar to that of other Office applications. In other words, when you first open FrontPage, you'll probably feel that it looks quite familiar if you're used to working in Office. In fact, at first glance, you'll see the menu bar across the top along with the Standard and Formatting toolbars, a workspace area below, and a status bar along the bottom. But in addition to the standard fare, FrontPage offers a couple key interface options to assist you in creating Web sites. Namely, the FrontPage interface includes Web page tabs, a tag selector bar, and view tabs—such as Design, Split, Code, and Preview (although other view tabs are available, depending on the current view)—as shown in Figure 11-2. These elements will help you keep track of the multiple files and folders of your Web site, preview Web pages during development, edit source code, manage hyperlinks, select and format page elements, and more. Figure 11-3 shows a Web page in Split view, which enables you to view source code and design layout simultaneously.

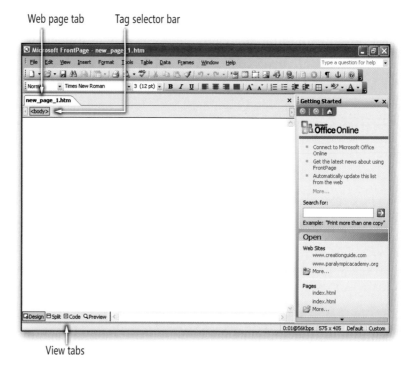

**Figure 11-2**   *Looking over the FrontPage 2003 window*

As you'll soon see, taking advantage of many FrontPage features generally requires you to select menu options, click toolbar buttons, and complete dialog boxes—familiar activities for most computer users. Therefore, although FrontPage is considered a high-end Web editor with advanced Web development capabilities, you should feel comfortable working within its interface by the time you finish this walkthrough—even if you've never composed so much as a single text-based Web page in a Web editor.

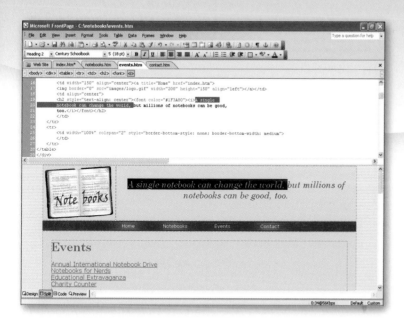

**Figure 11-3** *Viewing a Web page in Split views*

> **note** As you can imagine, you'll need more than a walk-through to learn the ins and outs of FrontPage 2003. This chapter shows you how to create a nice-looking site in FrontPage, but to really learn Front-Page, you should pick up a compre-hensive resource, such as *Microsoft Office FrontPage 2003 Inside Out* (Microsoft Press, 2004), by Jim Buyens. Further, we hope to write our own FrontPage book soon—when we do, we'd be happy to meet up with you again to walk you through the many features of FrontPage.

## FrontPage Server Extensions

The final issue we need to touch on before we get going on the walkthrough is a technology called *FrontPage Server Extensions*, which is a technology specific to FrontPage. Before the onset of advanced Web editors, developers had to write, buy, or copy code to enable cer-tain Web page features, such as forms, counters, rollovers, JavaScript, and so forth. Nowadays, FrontPage provides the code for many of these features. This enables designers to easily include functionality that requires some coding—without having to manually insert code or acquire the code in some other way. The catch is that your server (or your hosting service) needs to support FrontPage Server Exten-sions. So before you go crazy using the advanced design features of FrontPage, check with your Web hosting service to verify that it supports FrontPage Server Extensions.

You can control whether a Web site you're making includes components that require FrontPage Server Extensions. To turn off the availability of features requiring FrontPage Server Extensions, do the following:

1 On the **Tools** menu in FrontPage, click **Page Options**.

2 On the **Authoring** tab, clear the **Browse-time Web Components** check box, and then click **OK**.

> **lingo** *FrontPage Server Extensions* are installed on servers to enable additional function-ality in Web sites created or imported in FrontPage. FrontPage Server Extensions 2002 work with Front-Page 2003.

After you complete the preceding steps, all features that require extensions appear as dimmed options in menus and dialog boxes, and any components already installed on the page are disabled and the related source code appears as gray text. This chapter's walk-through assumes that FrontPage Server Extensions are installed on your server even though you won't be publishing the walkthrough site online. Therefore, the Web site is built with the Browse-Time Web Components option selected and all features available.

At this point, you know enough to get started on the walkthrough. The time has come for you to explore the final frontier of this book's Part 2—FrontPage!

> **note**   Most hosting services support FrontPage Server Extensions, although you'll definitely find some exceptions, including hosting services that support some but not all of the FrontPage Server Extensions. If you're shopping for a hosting service and think you'll be using FrontPage Extensions (such as for a FrontPage page rollover buttons or hit counters), you'll want to ensure that your hosting service supports FrontPage Server Extensions before you plunk down any cash and commit to the hosting service's plan.

## Editing Existing FrontPage Sites   One of the most

convenient features of FrontPage is its online editing capabilities. When you install FrontPage, the Edit With Microsoft Office FrontPage command is automatically added to the Edit drop-down menu on the Microsoft Internet Explorer Standard Buttons toolbar, as shown here:

You can quickly edit your online Web pages by displaying your Web page in Internet Explorer and clicking the Edit button to display the drop-down menu. After you select Edit With Microsoft Office FrontPage, FrontPage opens, asks for your user name and password if required by your server, and then displays the page for editing. When you're satisfied with your changes, you can click Save in FrontPage to automatically save the changes to your online Web site. See Chapter 13, "Updating, Archiving, Moving On," for more information about saving and archiving Web information.

# Planning Your FrontPage Web Site

Many readers from past editions of this book have asked us questions about online stores. Frequently, people want to build a site that offers or advertises items for sale. For example, people often want to build online stores to showcase items they offer for sale on eBay. Building a simple store site is similar to building many other types of Web sites. For instance, a store site might include a background, page banners, navigation bars, footer text, images, and so forth. A store Web site makes a fine walkthrough project, so in this chapter, you build a Web site for a notebooks store—as in the paper type, not computer laptops!

Our fictional notebooks store sells new, used, and collectible notebooks; collects notebooks from around the world; and often holds special charity events. At this time, the store owners merely want a simple Web presence that grants them the ability to sell a few notebooks online, provides a venue to advertise upcoming events, and enables people to contact them. With that information, you can see that a basic four-page Web site—Home, Notebooks, Events, and Contacts—could serve as a suitable solution.

Design-wise, the notebooks store has an international clientele. With a worldwide audience, the Web site should be fairly conservative and professional looking. FrontPage provides a number of Web site templates and design themes that you can combine to create professional Web sites. For this site, you'll use a Web site template and customize a theme by adding old leather colors (such as dark blue, dark green, and burgundy). Figure 11-4 shows the framework for the notebooks store, and Figure 11-5 shows storyboards for the Home page and the Notebooks page. The Notebooks page is the page that displays some of the notebooks that are for sale.

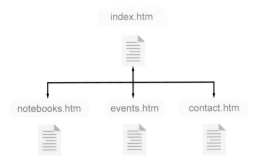

**Figure 11-4** *Creating a framework for the Notebooks Web site*

**Figure 11-5** *Story-boarding the Home and Notebooks pages*

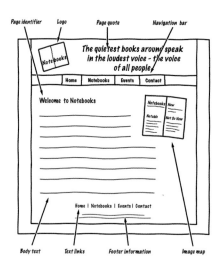

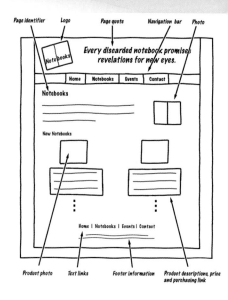

# Building the Site Structure

Whenever you build a Web site, the first step almost always involves setting up the site's structure. FrontPage can help out enormously with this task when you create a Web site using one of the Web site templates, as you'll see in just a moment.

## Customizing a New Web Site Template

FrontPage offers both Web page and Web site templates. When you set up a Web site using a Web site template, FrontPage generates all the files and folders necessary for your basic site. While the Web site template might not provide the exact setup you're looking for, using a template is a good way to start, because you can delete and modify pages and folders FrontPage creates to customize the template to suit your needs. To create a site structure for the Notebooks Web site, follow these steps:

**tip** Make sure you click the More Web Sites Templates link in the New task pane, *not* the More Page Templates link.

1  In FrontPage, click **New** on the **File** menu, and then click **More Web Site Templates** in the **New** task pane. The Web Site Templates dialog box opens.

2  In the **Web Site Templates** dialog box, click **Personal Web Site**, click the **Specify the location of the new Web site** box, type

C:\notebooks (or use the **Browse** button to locate **C:\note-books**), and then click **OK**. FrontPage generates the files and folders necessary to create a personal Web site and adds them to the documents and images folder in your C:\notebooks folder, as shown in Figure 11-6.

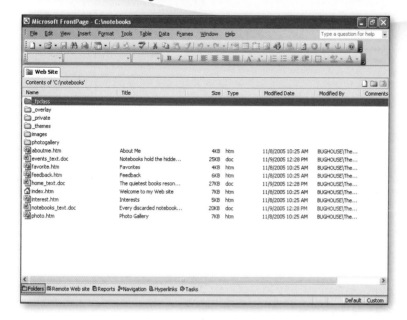

**Figure 11-6** *Viewing the files generated by FrontPage before modification*

3  Right-click **aboutme.htm**, click **Rename**, type **events.htm**, and then press ENTER. A message box indicates that **aboutme.htm** is being renamed **events.htm**.

4  Right-click **events.htm**, click **Properties**, type **Events** in the **Title** box on the **General** tab, and then click **OK**. This sets the Web page's title bar text.

5  Right-click **favorite.htm**, click **Rename**, type **notebooks.htm**, press ENTER, and then click **Yes** in the **Rename** message box.

6  Right-click **notebooks.htm**, click **Properties**, type **Notebooks** in the **Title** box on the **General** tab, and then click **OK**.

7  Right-click **feedback.htm**, click **Rename**, type **contact.htm**, press ENTER, right-click **contact.htm**, click **Properties**, type **Contact** in the **Title** box on the **General** tab, and then click **OK**.

8  Right-click **interest.htm**, click **Delete**, and then click **Yes** to delete a template page you don't need.

**note** The Properties dialog box for the contact. htm file shows a message on the Error tab that a FrontPage Save Results component will not function properly until the Web site is published. This message refers to the form included on the contact.htm page. Basically, the form won't work until you publish the site. In this walkthrough, you learn how to format the form's interface.

**Figure 11-7**  *Viewing the C:\notebooks files and folders (with hidden folders shown)*

**9** Delete **photo.htm**, and then delete the **photogallery** folder. Your FrontPage Web site Folders view should now match to the Folders view in Figure 11-7.

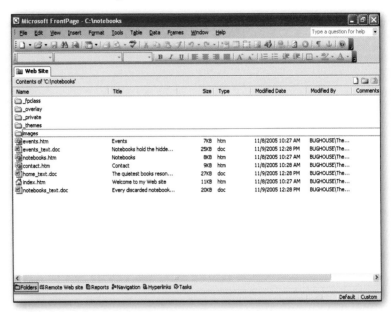

**10** Double-click the **images** folder, and then delete **mount.gif**, **mycat.jpg**, and **parrot1.jpg**. FrontPage adds these files to your images folder by default.

## Adjusting the Navigation Links

FrontPage offers a view that looks just like a Web site framework– Navigation view. Navigation view allows you to see your site's organization as well as rename and rearrange the navigation elements in your site, as described here:

**1** Click the **Navigation** view button (located at the bottom of the window) or click **Navigation** on the **View** menu, right-click the **Welcome to my Web site** page and rename it **Home**, rename **About Me** to **Events**, rename **Favorites** to **Notebooks**, and rename **Feedback** to **Contact**. The names you enter in this view are used on your navigation bar, meaning that your navigation bar will show Home, Events, Notebooks, and Contact buttons or links.

2 Click and drag **Notebooks** to the left of **Events** to specify the order of the navigation bar buttons. Your Web site's navigation bar should appear as shown in Figure 11-8.

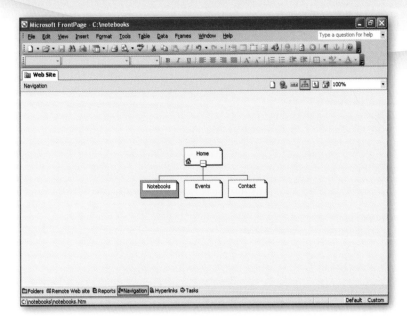

**Figure 11-8**   *Configuring a Web site's navigation settings*

## Creating and Adding a Custom Theme

Themes have been a Microsoft Office staple for a while now, slowly improving and becoming more flexible over time. In FrontPage, you can now customize themes and apply them to Web sites:

1 In **Navigation** view, double-click the **Home** page icon to open the Home page document in Design view, and then click **Theme** on the **Format** menu. The **Theme** task pane opens.

2 In the **Theme** task pane, scroll through the available themes, point to the **Bars** theme, click the drop-down arrow, and then click **Customize**, as shown in Figure 11-9. The **Customize Theme** dialog box opens, as shown in Figure 11-10.

**note**   When you customize a theme in FrontPage, the custom theme is also available in Microsoft Word.

**Figure 11-9**   *Choosing to customize a theme*

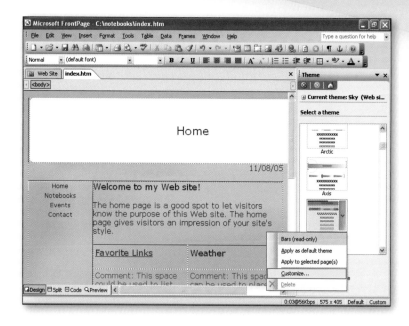

**Figure 11-10**   *Viewing the Customize Theme dialog box*

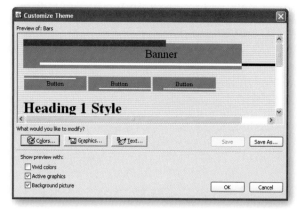

3 In the **Customize Theme** dialog box, click the **Colors** button, and then click the **Custom** tab.

4 To set the default hyperlink colors, click **Hyperlinks** in the **Item** list, click **Blue** in the **Color** list, click **Hyperlink (Followed)**, click **Purple**, click **Hyperlink (Active)**, and then click **Teal**. A *followed* hyperlink is a link that has been clicked, and an *active* hyperlink is a link that is being pointed to with the mouse pointer.

5 To modify heading styles, click **Heading 1** in the **Item** list, click **Teal** in the **Color** list, click **Heading 2**, click **Teal**, and click **OK**.

6 Click the **Graphics** button so that you can modify the bullet styles.

7 In the **Item** list, click **Bullet List**, and then change the file names in the **List Bullet 1** and **List Bullet 2** boxes to **barbul3e.gif**. All three bullet levels should now appear in the preview window as triangle bullets. If you want to include a custom bullet, click **Browse**, and navigate to the custom bullet image.

8 Click **OK**, and then click the **Text** button so that you can modify the default font styles. Notice that the **Body** style appears in the **Item** list by default.

9 In the **Font** list, scroll down and click **Verdana** for the **Body** style, click **Heading 1** in the **Item** list, click **Century Schoolbook** in the **Font** list, change the font for Headings 2 through 6 to **Century Schoolbook**, and then click **OK**.

10 Click **Save**, type **Bars_Notebooks** in the **Save Theme** dialog box, click **OK**, and then click **OK** to close the **Customize Theme** dialog box.

11 Point to the **Bars_Notebooks** theme on the **Theme** task bar, click the drop-down arrow, select **Apply As Default Theme**, click **Yes**, and then close the task pane.

## Building the Logo Area

After you open the Home page and customize the theme, the insertion point is located in the top-left corner of the page by default. This seems like a good time to insert the logo and format the logo area:

1 Click in the table cell to the left of the template-generated **Home** banner, click **Insert**, click **Picture**, click **From File**, and then double-click **logo.gif** in the **C:\notebooks\images** folder to insert the image.

2 To link the logo image to the home page, right-click the logo image, click **Hyperlink**, click the **ScreenTip** button in the **Insert Hyperlink** dialog box, type **Home**, click **OK**, and then double-click **index.htm (open)** in the list of files.

3 To set the logo image's picture properties, click the **logo** image, and then double-click the **<img>** tag on the tag selector bar to open the **Picture Properties** dialog box.

4 On the **Appearance** tab, click **Left** in the **Wrapping Style** area, and then click **OK**.

5 To replace the template-generated **Home** banner with custom text, click the banner to select it, and then type **The quietest books resonate with the clearest tones of notes written in time.** The image is replaced with the text.

6 To format the new text, select the text you typed in step 5, click **Heading 2** in the **Style** drop-down list on the **Formatting** toolbar, click the **Italic** button, and then click the **Center** alignment button. With the text still selected, click the **Font Color** drop-down arrow on the Formatting toolbar, click **More Colors**, click the **Custom** button, type **31** in the **Red** box, type **58** in the **Green** box, type **128** in the **Blue** box, click **Add to Custom Colors**, and then click **OK** twice.

7 To position and resize the logo and banner area table, right-click anywhere in the row containing the logo image and text you just added, click **Table Properties**, click **Center** in the **Alignment** list, and type **90** in the **Specify Width** box (but don't click OK just yet!).

8 To recolor the table, click the **Color** drop-down arrow in the **Background** area, click **More Colors**, and then click the **Select** button. To specify the darker tan color found on the thin horizontal stripes in the Web site's background, move your mouse pointer over the background pattern in the Web site until the darker tan color appears in the **New** box in the **More Colors** dialog box, click to select the dark tan, click **OK** to close both open dialog boxes, and then save your work. The logo and banner area of your home page should look similar to the banner area shown in Figure 11-11.

**Figure 11-11**   *Viewing the logo and banner area in Design view*

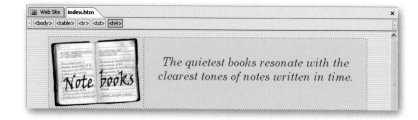

## Adding the Logo and Banner Area to Subpages

Now that your home page is shaping up, you're ready to start paying attention to the subpages. Using the tag selector bar, you can easily select the banner table. Then you can copy and paste the banner table into the subpages, as described here:

1 Click in the logo and banner area table, click **<table>** on the tag selector bar to select the table, and then click **Copy** on the **Standard** toolbar or press CTRL+C.

2 To configure the Notebooks page, click the **Web Site** tab (near the top-left corner of the design area), make sure the **Navigation** view button is selected, double-click the **Notebooks** page icon, click in the **Notebooks** page's banner area, click **<table>** on the tag selector bar to select the existing table, click **Paste** on the **Standard** toolbar to replace the old table with the new table, select the blue text, and then type **Every discarded notebook promises fresh revelations for new eyes.**

3 To set up the Events page, click the **Web Site** tab, double-click the **Events** page icon, click in the **Events** banner area, click **<table>** on the tag selector bar, click **Paste**, select the blue text, and then type **A single notebook can change the world, but millions of notebooks can be good, too.**

4 To set up the Contact page, click the **Web Site** tab, double-click **Contact**, click in the **Contact** banner area, click **<table>** on the tag selector bar, click **Paste**, select the blue text, and then type **Notebooks speak volumes!**

5 To save the changes made to all pages, click **File**, and then click **Save All**. FrontPage should now display tabs for all the pages in your Web site without asterisks, as shown in Figure 11-12.

**Figure 11-12** *Working with multiple Web pages in FrontPage*

## Formatting the Navigation Bar

By default, the Web site template creates a vertical navigation bar, but the Notebooks Web site design calls for a horizontal navigation bar below the logo and banner area. In this section, you change the orientation of the navigation bar as well as the style to fit the site's storyboard design:

1 Click the **index.htm** tab, click to the right of the date, and press BACKSPACE to delete the date.

2 To access the table's properties, point to **<table>** on the tag selector bar, click the **<table>** drop-down arrow, and click **Tag Properties**. The **Table Properties** dialog box opens.

3 To format the table, change the **Alignment** setting to **Center**, type **90** in the **Specify Width** box, click the **Color** box in the **Background** section, click the blue **RGB(1F,3A,80)** color square in the **Document Colors** area, and then click **OK**.

4 To move and format the navigation bar, drag the navigation bar into the blue box you just formatted, right-click it, and then click **Link Bar Properties**. On the **Style** tab, click the **Deep Blue** style in the **Choose a style** area, click **Horizontal** in the **Orientation and appearance area**, select **Use Vivid Colors**, and select **Use Active Graphics**, as shown Figure 11-13. Then click **OK**.

**Figure 11-13** *Restyling the navigation links*

5 The blue area is wider than you'd like because an **<h4>** tag is formatting the area. To delete the tag, point to **<h4>** on the tag selector bar, click the drop-down arrow, and then click **Remove Tag**.

6 To center the navigation bar in the blue area, click any area outside of the selected table to deselect the table, click the navigation bar, click **Center** on the **Formatting** toolbar, and then save your work.

**7** Repeat steps 1 through 6 for the notebooks.htm, events.htm, and contact.htm pages to restyle the navigation bar for each page. (Unfortunately, you can't copy and paste the navigation bar because FrontPage won't be able to properly publish the code later.) Figure 11-14 shows the logo and navigation bar areas on the home page in Design view.

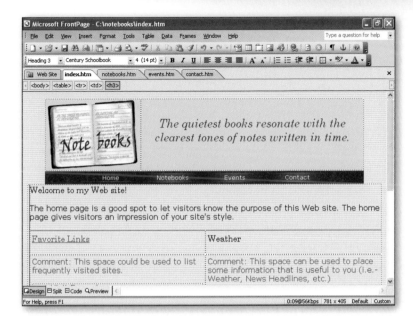

**Figure 11-14**   *Customizing the navigation bar in Design view*

## Preparing the Main Area for Content

The final part of the site structure you need to configure is the main content area. FrontPage's Web site templates come packed with placeholder text. You don't need any of it! To remove all the sample text and insert an empty table cell surrounded by 25 pixels of padding (or space), follow these steps:

**1** To cut the placeholder text, click the **index.htm** tag (if necessary), click anywhere in the table below the navigation bar, point to **<table>** on the tag selector bar, click the drop-down arrow, click **Select Tag Contents**, and then click **Cut** on the **Edit** menu.

**2** To align, size, and color the content area table, point to the **<table>** tag, click the drop-down arrow, click **Tag Properties**, click **Center** in the **Alignment** drop-down list, type **90** in the **Specify Width** box, type **25** in the **Cell Spacing** box, click the

**Color** box in the **Background** section, choose the **tan** color square in the **Document Colors** section, and then click **OK.**

3  To display the empty table cell, click toward the right-side of the small table box, making sure **<table>** is selected on the tag selector bar, and press SPACEBAR once to add content (which is just a space at this point) and expand the table.

4  To remove excess space at the top of the page, right-click on the page, click **Page Properties**, click the **Advanced** tab, type **0** in the **Top Margin** box, and then click **OK.**

5  To copy and paste the new empty content area to the Notebooks page, click in the main body area on the index.htm page again, click the **<table>** tag to select the table, click **Copy**, click the **notebooks.htm** tab, click in the main body table, and click the **<table>** tag to select it. Click **Paste**, right-click on the page, click **Page Properties**, click the **Advanced** tab, type **0** in the **Top Margin** box, and then click **OK.**

6  To format the Events page, click **events.htm** tab, click in the main body table, click the **<table>** tag, and click **Paste**. Right-click on the page, click **Page Properties**, click the **Advanced** tab, type **0** in the **Top Margin** box, and then click **OK.**

7  To format the Contact page, click the **contact.htm** tab, right-click on the page, click **Page Properties**, click the **Advanced** tab, type **0** in the **Top Margin**, and then click **OK.** You don't want to replace the Contact page's form with the empty content area; instead, you will customize the autogenerated form later.

8  To format the footer text, click the **index.htm** tab, click within the **This site was last updated** text, click **Center** on the **Formatting** toolbar, click at the end of the line of text, and then press ENTER.

9  Click **Insert**, click **Symbol**, click the **copyright** symbol, click **Insert**, and then click **Close** to add the copyright symbol. Type the year, your name, and **All Rights Reserved.**

10  Repeat steps 8 and 9 for the notebooks.htm, events.htm, and contact.htm pages, and then click **Save All** on the **File** menu. Your pages should resemble the events.htm page shown in Figure 11-15.

**tip**  You can copy and paste the last-updated and copyright information from page to page to save time.

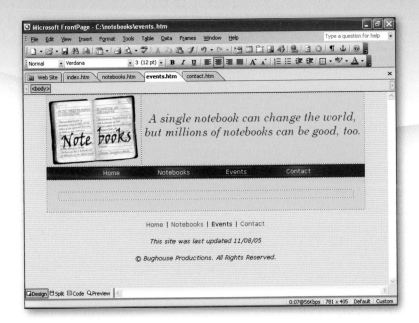

**Figure 11-15** *Preparing the content area*

# Adding Content

With the site's structure taken care of, you are now ready to add content. In FrontPage, you can add content in all the typical ways. We're confident that you know how to type and paste text, so we've provided content for you to insert. This way, we'll all be spared from step after step of "Type this..." instructions. Never fear, though—we saved plenty of other tasks for you to complete, as you'll soon see.

## Inserting Text

Often, inserting text from a Microsoft Office Word document or text file proves to be wise because you can use the text in a variety of ways and in a variety of applications. For example, you might want to include text from a Word document in both a brochure created in Publisher and a Web site created in FrontPage. In this walkthrough, you insert text from Word documents into your FrontPage Web site:

1 In FrontPage, to insert and left-align text on the home page, click the **index.htm** tab, click the center of the content table, click **Align Left** on the **Formatting** toolbar (the insertion point jumps to the left within the table cell), click **Insert**, and click **File**.

**tip**  If you insert a Word document into a FrontPage Web page and the document contains unexpected formatting marks (such as dashed underlines or empty picture placeholders), open the Word document in WordPad, delete any extraneous marks you find, and then save the document as a Rich Text Format (RTF) file. You can then import the RTF file into FrontPage.

2  In the **Select File** dialog box, navigate to the **C:\notebooks** folder, click **All Files (*.*)** in the **Files of Type** list, and then double-click the **home_text.doc** file.

3  To add and align on the Notebooks page, click the **notebooks.htm** tab, click in the center of the content table, click **Align Left**, click **Insert**, click **File**, and double-click **notebooks_text.doc**.

4  To add and align text on the Events page, click the **events.htm** tab, click in the center of the content table, click **Align Left**, click **Insert**, click **File**, double-click **events_text.doc**, and then click **Save All**.

## Formatting Text

Now that you've added text, you can format it using your custom theme settings:

1  Click the **index.htm** tab, select the **Welcome to Notebooks** text, click the **Style** drop-down arrow on the **Formatting** toolbar, and then click **Heading 1**.

2  Select the three consecutive paragraphs that start with **New…**, **Not-So-New…**, and **Notable…**, and then click the **Bullets** button on the **Formatting** toolbar. The text on your index.htm page should look similar to the text shown in Figure 11-16.

**Figure 11-16**  *Formatting text using a theme*

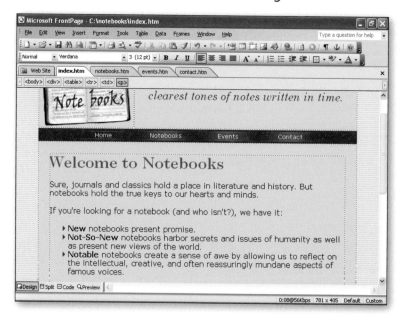

3 Click the **notebooks.htm** tab; format the **Notebooks** heading using the **Heading 1** style; select the **New...**, **Not-So-New...**, and **Notable...** paragraphs; click the **Bullets** button; select the **New Notebooks**, **Not-So-New Notebooks**, and **Notable Notebooks** headings; and click **Heading 2** in the **Style** list.

4 Click the **events.htm** tab, format the **Events** heading text using the **Heading 1** style, and format the remaining headings as follows:

| | |
|---|---|
| Annual International Notebook Drive | Heading 2 |
| Summer | Heading 3 |
| Notebooks for Nerds | Heading 2 |
| January | Heading 3 |
| Educational Extravaganza | Heading 2 |
| January, March, August, November | Heading 3 |
| Charity Counter | Heading 2 |

5 Click **Save All** on the **File** menu.

## Placing Bookmarks

You can add hidden markers, called *bookmarks*, to Web pages that allow you to link to specific areas on Web pages. After you add bookmarks to your Web site, you can link to a bookmark on the same page, or you can link to a bookmark on another page. But before you can link to a bookmark, the bookmark must exist. Here are the steps for adding bookmarks to the notebooks.htm page:

1 Click the **notebooks.htm** tab, position the insertion point before the heading **New Notebooks**, click **Insert**, click **Bookmark**, type **new notebooks** in the **Bookmark name** box to name the bookmark, and then click **OK**.

2 Position the insertion point before the heading **Not-So-New Notebooks**, click **Insert**, click **Bookmark**, type **not-so-new notebooks** in the **Bookmark name** box, and then click **OK**.

3 Position the insertion point before the heading **Notable Notebooks**, click **Insert**, click **Bookmark**, type **notable notebooks** in the **Bookmark name** box (see Figure 11-17), click **OK**, and then save your work.

**lingo** *Bookmarks* in Web sites are hidden markers that allow you to name and link to specific locations on Web pages. When you create a bookmark, you basically provide a name for a specific location on a page—such as a heading, table, or list. Then when you use the bookmark in a hyperlink, the location's name is added to the hyperlink's reference so that when users click the hyperlink, the specified location on the target page is shown in the browser window.

**Figure 11-17** *Viewing bookmark names in the Bookmark dialog box and bookmark markers in the text*

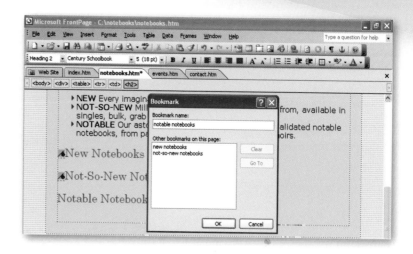

## Linking to Bookmarks on the Same Page

As mentioned, after you add a bookmark, you can create a hyperlink that takes readers to the bookmark's location. In these steps, you format links at the top of the page that jump to bookmarks lower on the page (a technique often used on product pages as well as other long pages):

1 In **notebooks.htm**, scroll up to view the bulleted list, double-click **NEW** to select it, click **Hyperlink** on the **Insert** menu, click the **Bookmark** button, click **new notebooks** in the **Select Place in Document** dialog box to specify the bookmark you want to link to, click **OK**, click the **ScreenTip** button, type **Go to New Notebooks**, and then click **OK** twice.

2 Select **NOT-SO-NEW**, press CTRL+K, click the **Bookmark** button, click **not-so-new notebooks**, click **OK**, click the **ScreenTip** button, type **Go to Not-So-New Notebooks**, and then click **OK** twice.

3 Select **NOTABLE**, press CTRL+K, click the **Bookmark** button, click **notable notebooks**, click **OK**, click the **ScreenTip** button, type **Go to Notable Notebooks**, click **OK** twice, and then save your work.

## Inserting Images

All Office applications share the same steps for inserting images. If you're comfortable inserting images in Microsoft Word or Excel, you'll find that inserting images into your FrontPage Web site is a familiar task. Because this is a basic task, we've included the steps to insert images online. If you'd like to insert pictures on the notebooks.htm and events.htm pages, visit the online steps at www.creationguide.com/ch11/extras.

## Creating an Image Map

Image maps allow you to link parts of one image to different Web resources. To create an image map in FrontPage, you insert the picture, draw a shape called a *hotspot* on the picture, and then format the hotspot as a hyperlink. Pretty simple (especially in FrontPage), and yet an effective way to add a professional touch to a Web site. To create an image map on the home page:

1 Click the **index.htm** tab, click before the heading **Welcome to Notebooks**, and insert the **imagemap.jpg** picture.

2 To set the image properties, double-click the image to open the **Picture Properties** dialog box, click **Right**, type **25** in the **Horizontal spacing** box, and then type **15** in the **Vertical spacing** box. On the **General** tab, type **notebooks.htm** in the **Location** box (by adding a default hyperlink, you assist older browsers that don't support image maps), and then click **OK**.

3 To draw and link a hotspot, click **Toolbars** on the **View** menu, click **Pictures**, click the **Rectangular Hotspot** button on the **Pictures** toolbar, draw a rectangle around the **New notebooks present promise.** text in the image, click **notebooks.htm** in the **Insert Hyperlink** dialog box, click **Bookmarks** to link to a book-marked location, click the **new notebooks** bookmark, and then click **OK** twice.

4 Repeat step 3 for the **Notable** and **Not-So-New** sections in the image to link to the proper bookmarks on the notebooks.htm page, and then save your changes. Figure 11-19 shows the completed image map in Design view.

**lingo** In an image map, a *hotspot* is a specified area of an image that is formatted to link to a particular Web resource. Hotspots are generally not visually distinct until a user positions the mouse pointer over the area. When the mouse pointer hovers over the hotspot area, the cursor changes shape to indicate a hyperlink.

**Figure 11-19** *Building an image map*

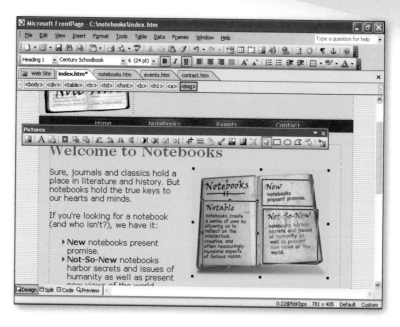

## Customizing the Contact Form

**note**  Check out the online bonus content at www. creationguide. com/ch11/extras to learn how to create product tables for the notebooks.htm page.

At this point, the Notebooks site is almost complete, but you might have noticed that the walkthrough has been neglecting the Contact page for the most part. That's because you don't have much to do on this page. FrontPage has already done a nice job of creating a contact form for you. All you need to do is to customize the form elements here and there and tell FrontPage to send the form information to you when people complete it. To do this, follow the steps provided on www.creationguide.com/ch11/extras. Figure 11-20 shows how the form will look after you follow the online steps.

## Publishing Your Site

**see also**
Chapter 12, "Sending Web Pages into the Real World," provides some Web publishing tips.

FrontPage offers a publishing feature that uses an interface somewhat similar to many FTP applications. In FrontPage, you'll see your local Web site files in the left pane and your online files on your server space in the right pane. When you upload a FrontPage site, you need to use FrontPage's Publishing tool to *publish* it (not just save your pages or copy them to an online space), at least the first time, to ensure that your site functions properly. You can publish your Web site to a server or a location on your computer or local network. To start the publishing process, simply click Publish Site on the File menu.

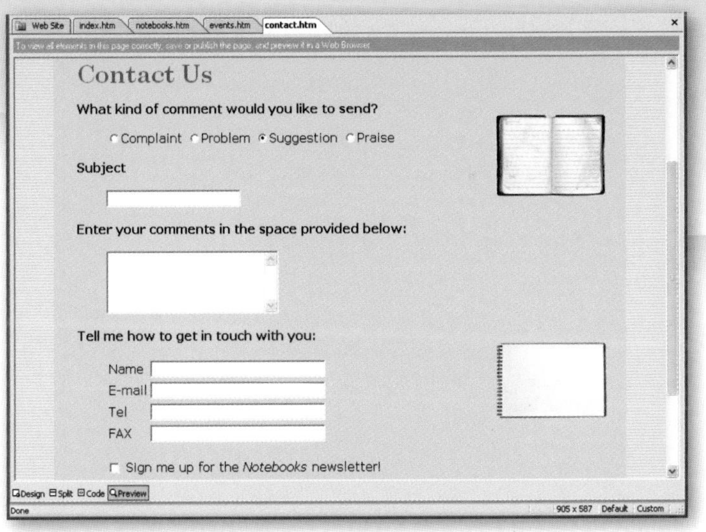

**Figure 11-20** *Customizing the default form*

Keep in mind that there are a few nuances to publishing Web sites. You should consult a FrontPage resource, the FrontPage Help files, Microsoft's FrontPage Web site, Microsoft's Knowledge Base (support.microsoft.com), or your ISP for instructions if you run into problems.

# check it!

- You can use FrontPage to easily create advanced Web page features, such as button rollover effects, image maps, forms, and so forth.

- The FrontPage interface enables you to display your Web pages in a number of views, including Design, Split, Code, Preview, and Navigation.

- Learning to use FrontPage opens doors to using other full-service Web editors because FrontPage exemplifies the types of capabilities Web editors can provide.

- Before you create your Web pages using FrontPage, you should ensure that your Web hosting service supports FrontPage Server Extensions.

- FrontPage provides a number of Web site and Web page templates, and you can define custom themes and apply them to your Web sites.

- For best results, upload FrontPage files using the Publishing feature, at least the first time you upload the site to your server.

the rest—
**going live**

# PART

# 3

A few years ago, a couple friends of ours hatched a plan to build a cabin in the White Mountains. It all started one day when they were chatting over coffee. Their conversation turned to vacations and getaways, and soon they were half-jokingly sketching their "dream" mountain cabin. Not long after their initial conversation, they found themselves talking to an architect. In a few weeks, the blueprints were solidified, and they were gathering supplies and laying the cabin's foundation. Within the year, the cabin was built. But they didn't stop there. Ever since, they've been improving their cabin. They regularly take on "big" jobs (such as installing cabinetry and building a stone fireplace) as well as undertake "not-so-big" jobs (such as planting a garden and hand-stitching drapes). As a result of our friends' hard work, attention to detail, and dedication, even the most casual passerby can see that their cabin is a unique and well-loved mountain escape.

You might be wondering how in the world this little story relates to Web site development. Simple—it serves as a foundation for Part Three. Specifically, after you post your Web site (as described in Chapter 12, "Sending Web Pages into the Real World"), you should count on providing continuing attention to your Web pages (as discussed in Chapter 13, "Updating, Archiving, Moving On"). Sure, you could slap any old Web site onto the Web and leave it unattended, but you'd hardly be the proud owner of a successful site. To achieve success on the Web, you need to tend your Web pages regularly. In the chapters in this part, we show you how to get your site online and keep it alive and well.

# send web pages

## pages

into the real world

# 12

The troupe is well rehearsed, and the set is a work of art. The time has come to put the show's name up in lights, meet for a last-minute dress rehearsal, hand out flyers, and let the show begin.

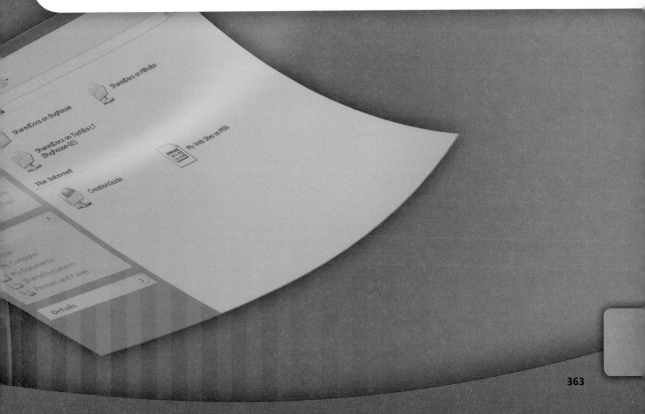

# Now That Your Pages Have Taken Shape

After you create a Web site, you'll probably be all set to get it online. That's what this chapter is all about—moving your pages off the "for your eyes only" desktop and onto the "for everyone to see" Internet. Most likely, you've built a Web site so that you can create a Web presence—not just as an intellectual exercise—so we'll go with that assumption.

The key to going "live" and getting your site onto the Web is to copy your Web site's files onto a server. Chapter 5, "Considering Tools and Stockpiling the Goods," covers server space, domain names, and Internet service providers (ISPs) in detail, so no need to rehash those subjects here. If you need an in-depth refresher on those topics, refer to Chapter 5. If you feel comfortable with just a summarization of requirements, here's a short list of items you'll need to gather before your Web site can go live:

- Source code (.html), style sheets (.css), possibly data files (.doc, .xml, and so forth), and image files (.gif, .jpg, .png), properly named and organized.

- Server space. You can pay a monthly fee to a hosting service for server space, you can use free server space, or you can use server space provided by your ISP as part of your Internet connection account.

- A software application that enables you to transfer files from your computer to a server. We discuss this requirement later in this chapter.

- A Web address. You need to purchase a domain name and register it with a hosting service, or you need to set up a Web address on a free server, or you need to obtain your Web address from your ISP—free server space Web addresses are usually based on the ISP's domain name followed by your user name.

At this point in the book, the preceding list shouldn't sound too daunting. Further, we describe in just a bit exactly which file transfer applications you can use and how you can copy files onto a server. So even if you have a few questions about the preceding requirements, hang on—this chapter addresses each requirement shortly.

In addition to transferring your files to a server, you have a couple other tasks to attend to. Namely, you'll need to check your Web site after you transfer your files to a server, and you'll need to let others know that your site is available for viewing.

These three postproduction tasks—transferring files, checking live Web pages, and getting the word out—are the main points we touch on in this chapter. If you have all your files, an Internet connection, and some server space on hand, your site can be available online by the end of this chapter.

## Transferring Your Files to the Internet

Having HTML and image files as well as some server space and an Internet connection means that you're ready to post your Web site. You can transfer files across the Internet in several ways. Here are some of the methods you can use to transfer files:

- File Transfer Protocol (FTP) programs
- My Network Places and Web folders
- Web publishing wizards
- ISP interfaces and Web editors
- Browsers

There's really no way around it—you're going to have to use some method to post your site. After all, one of the most common transactions a Web designer has with a server is to *upload* Web documents, including .html, .css, image, data, and media files. Therefore, read on. Uploading is fairly straightforward as long as you keep in mind the process's main goal, which is moving files from your computer to a server in an organized manner.

Whenever you upload files from your desktop to the Internet, you use FTP. The trick to transferring files using FTP is to use an application or interface that's designed specifically to serve as an FTP agent. Although that "trick" doesn't seem too profound, stating the obvious is well worth the space necessary to clarify what it means to use FTP. We've seen people's eyes glaze over as soon as we've uttered those three mysterious letters—*F-T-P*. Fortunately, as with many other

> **lingo** *Uploading* refers to the process of copying files from your computer to a server. *Downloading* refers to copying files from a server to your computer (such as when you downloaded graphics from the CreationGuide Web site to complete the projects in Part Two of this book).

> **lingo** *File Transfer Protocol (FTP)* is a client/server protocol that enables you to use a computer to transfer files between computers over the Internet.

Web site creation technologies, using FTP to transfer files isn't rocket science. You just need to learn a few basics.

## FTP Applications

We think FTP applications provide one of the easiest, most widely supported, and most straightforward methods of uploading files to the Internet. Apparently we're not alone in this thinking because lots of FTP applications are available as freeware, shareware, and commercial software. For the most part, we use a program named CuteFTP for Microsoft Windows–based PCs and a program named Fetch for Macintosh computers. But you can find numerous other FTP applications online (free for download as well as available for purchase) and at computer software retailers.

Figure 12-1 shows the CuteFTP interface, which is a fairly typical FTP application interface.

**Figure 12-1**   *The CuteFTP Professional interface*

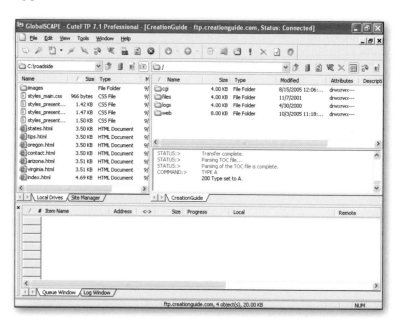

**tip**   You should be able to buy a good FTP program for a very reasonable price. Generally, purchasing an FTP application means you'll have added functionality compared to most bare-bones freeware and shareware utilities. Keep in mind that you probably received an FTP application from your ISP with your startup package. If so, contact your provider or leaf through your ISP documentation for application-specific instructions.

The beauty of most FTP applications is that you can drag and drop the files you want to upload from one window into another. For example, in CuteFTP, you can display a local folder in the left pane and display your server space in the right pane. Figure 12-1 shows the C:\roadside folder created in the Chapter 8 walkthrough project. To upload your Web documents, you simply click and drag the files or folders from the left pane into the right pane.

We've heard from a number of users that the most intimidating part of using an FTP application is configuring the initial connection. Fortunately, after you initially configure a connection, most FTP applications keep the connection data "on file" for future use.

Even though every FTP application has a custom interface for gathering account information, you'll need to provide the following few basic types of information to establish an FTP connection to a server, no matter which application you use:

- **FTP site label**   A name you provide for the FTP account you're creating. The sole purpose of the site label is to help you remember which FTP account goes with which server. So be sure to name your connections logically.

- **FTP host address**   The address of your server space. For example, the CreationGuide site's host address is ftp://ftp.creationguide.com.

- **FTP site user name**   The user name you use to access your server space. An FTP site user name is generally the same as your e-mail address, such as admin@creationguide.com. Some providers allow you to enter your user name without the @*domain.com* portion, in which case only *admin* would be necessary in the preceding example.

- **FTP site password**   A password associated with your user name that enables you to access your server space.

**Try This!**
Visit www.tucows.com or www.shareware.com to find listings of available FTP programs. Download and install an FTP program of your choice, and then put the application through its paces. You can always uninstall the FTP program you downloaded and try some others if the one you chose doesn't suit your working style. If you do find a shareware program that you like, be sure to register it.

Figure 12-2 shows an example of a completed FTP connection form. On many forms, you'll also be asked whether you want to transfer information in ASCII or binary format, or use autodetect to have the program determine the correct format. The default is usually autodetect (or some variation of that terminology), and we recommend that you retain the default setting.

**Figure 12-2**  *Configuring an FTP connection*

To create an FTP connection, you insert the proper information into the respective fields (in CuteFTP, you use the Site Properties dialog box) and finalize the configuration by clicking OK, Finish, or Connect (depending on your application). After you configure an FTP connection to your server space, you can connect to the Internet, activate the FTP connection, and upload your pages. Contact your ISP or visit your ISP's help pages if you have trouble connecting.

At this point, we want to mention a couple uploading rules you need to follow religiously when you copy your Web site's files to a server. You can't copy files and folders willy-nilly—you have to keep

**tip**   Your .html and .css files should be transferred in ASCII, text, or MS-DOS text mode. Multimedia files, including images, sounds, and videos, must be transferred in binary mode. Ensuring that the Auto, Autodetect, All Files, or Raw Data option is selected in your FTP application's options generally means that the application can differentiate between the common file types, so you won't have to worry about distinguishing between multimedia and text files. By default, CuteFTP (as well as most other FTP applications) is configured to autodetect common file types. In CuteFTP, you can find the Transfer Type setting on the Type tab in the Site Properties dialog box.

the process orderly; otherwise, you'll risk creating broken links and erroneously overwriting files that have the same name. For example, most subfolders contain a file named index.html—if you upload your files into the wrong folders, you might inadvertently replace one index.html file with another, unrelated index.html file. Here's the key point to remember when you're uploading your Web site:

*Retain the file and folder structure of your Web site.*

In other words, if a Web site consists of one index.html document and a folder named images, make sure that you upload the index.html file and the images folder along with all its contents to your server space. Nowadays, FTP programs usually let you copy a folder and all its contents to your server by dragging the folder to the server area in the FTP window. As mentioned, retaining your site's structure is crucial to avoiding broken links on your pages.

Here's another extremely important point:

*Name your online folders with exactly the same names as your local folders.*

Don't rename any folders or files when you're uploading—especially don't rename any folders that contain images. (By the way, accidentally creating a folder named *image* when it should be *images* constitutes renaming a folder; further, altering capitalization within file and folder names also qualifies as an unacceptable renaming practice.) The reason for retaining your existing naming structure is simple—your Web documents probably contain commands that tell browsers where to look for graphics. Image instructions (contained within the <img /> tag, if you worked through the XHTML project in Chapter 8) specifically point to images stored in a particular location. If you change a folder's name without changing your source code, browsers won't be able to find your graphics and the graphics won't be displayed on your Web pages. To reiterate, uploading is *not* the time to rename your Web site's folders and files. In fact, the opposite is true and is well worth repeating one last time:

*Uploading is the time to replicate your local Web page file setup onto a server in as exact a manner as possible.*

**tip**    ISPs generally tell you where you should store your Web files within your server space. On our server space for the CreationGuide Web site, we copy all our information into the folder named Web. Check with your ISP to see whether you must work within any parameters. Some ISPs simply provide you with the top-level folder that you can use to store your Web files.

After you've successfully copied your Web site's files onto a server, terminate your FTP connection, open your browser, and enter your Web site's URL in your browser's Address bar. Your Web site's URL is the same as the FTP host address we mentioned earlier except that *www* appears in place of *ftp*. For example, the FTP address for the Bughouse Productions site is ftp.bughousepro.com, and the Web address is www.bughousepro.com. If you've uploaded an index.htm or index.html document, you should be able to access your new home page by entering your URL in your browser's Address bar without having to type a file name. For example, you can simply type **www. bughousepro.com** instead of **www.bughousepro.com/index.html** to view the Bughouse Productions home page.

As you can see, most FTP applications serve the sole purpose of providing a means to transfer and manipulate (rename, delete, move, and so forth) files across a network. If you're looking for other file transfer options or a more automated approach, you'll find that more than a few applications have built-in FTP capabilities, as discussed in the next section.

## My Network Places and Web Folders

Microsoft provides another method of uploading and managing a Web site's files and folders—using My Network Places to create and manage network places that contain Web folders and files. My Network Places was introduced in Microsoft Office 2000 and is a staple in every version of Office since. (Prior to Office 2000, the feature was known strictly as Web Folders, and it was a tad more cumbersome than My Network Places to manage.) Using My Network Places, you'll be able to use the familiar interface in Windows to conduct the file and folder management tasks necessary for you to create and maintain your Web site.

**caution**    Before you can set up a link to your Web space in My Network Places, you must ensure that your Web server supports network places. The My Network Places feature requires the Web Extender Client (WEC) protocol and Microsoft FrontPage Extensions, or the Web-Based Distributed Authoring and Versioning (WebDAV) protocol and Internet Information Services (IIS). Call your hosting service or check the service's online FAQ pages to see if your Web space qualifies to take advantage of network places technology.

**tip** You might have to activate FrontPage Extensions on your hosting service before you can create a network place that leads to your Web space. Although this task might sound a bit daunting, most likely, it's a matter of a few mouse clicks. To find out how to turn on FrontPage Server Extensions on your hosting service, perform a quick search on your hosting service's support pages or contact the support department.

Basically, when you use the My Network Places feature, you can create shortcuts to network locations that contain folders stored on your Web space. After you create a link to a network place, you can manipulate the contents of Web folders stored in your Web space (typically, your Web space is the space you purchase on your hosting service's server) in the same manner you manipulate local files and folders. The difference is that changes made to files in a Web folder are made to the online files when you save your changes. In short, a network place serves as a shortcut to the Web folders (and the folders' contents) on your server space.

**lingo** *My Network Places* enables you to create shortcuts on your computer to files and folders located on an Internet or intranet server.

To access network places and Web folders, click My Network Places on the Start menu. The My Network Places window is displayed (see Figure 12-3), which enables you to create new network places as well as open existing links. Notice that the My Network Places window includes a link named Add A Network Place in the Network Tasks section along the left side of the window. You can probably guess the purpose of that small gem!

When you open a My Network Places folder and view its contents, you'll see a list of online folders and files, along with their associated Web addresses (URLs), as shown in Figure 12-4. Within the Web folder, you can move, copy, rename, and delete folders and files as well as view folder and file properties. You can also drag files between Web sites (if you have multiple Web sites), between Web servers, and between a Web server and your hard disk or other storage device (such as a CD or flash drive). In other words, Web folders make Web site file management as straightforward as local file management.

**note** In views other than My Network Places, Windows also provides the options Publish This Folder To The Web or Publish This File To The Web (depending on the type of item that's currently selected), as described later in this chapter. When you select a folder or file and click either of the preceding options, Windows enables you to copy the folder or file to a Web storage space, such as MSN or Xdrive Plus. This feature caters to people who want to share, transfer, and store non-HTML documents on the Web in addition to Web files.

**Figure 12-3**  *Accessing My Network Places*

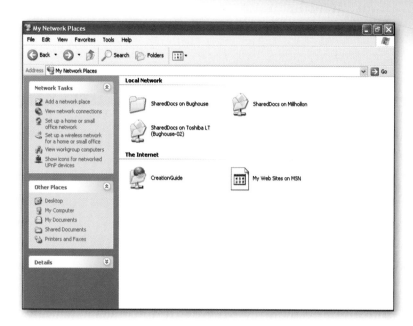

**Figure 12-4**  *Viewing the contents of a Web folder*

Now let's take a quick look at how you can create network places on your system.

### Creating a network place

Before you set up a network place, you need to have the following information on hand:

- Domain information, which is your Web site's Internet address (such as www.creationguide.com)
- The password to access your server space

Once you have the preceding two pieces of information, you're good to go. To create a network place by using My Network Places, follow these steps:

1 Click **My Network Places** on the **Start** menu, and click the **Add A Network Place** link in the **Network Tasks** section to start the Add Network Place Wizard, as shown in Figure 12-5.

**Figure 12-5**  *Accessing the Add Network Place Wizard*

2 Click **Next**. The Add Network Place Wizard provides an option to set up a network place on MSN or another network location. In most instances, you'll be setting up a network place in a location other than on MSN.

3 Select the **Choose Another Network Location** option, and then click **Next**.

4 On the next page of the wizard, in the **Internet Or Network Address** box, type the Internet address of your network location. (This example uses **http://www.bughousepro.com**.)

5 Click **Next**. If your Web space requires you to enter a user name and password, you'll see a dialog box requesting this information, as shown in Figure 12-6.

6 Enter your user name and password, and then click **OK**.

**Figure 12-6**  *Providing a user name and password to a network place*

**tip**  After you create a network place, you can save any Office document to the network place from within the application. For example, if you want to save a Word document on your server space, click Save As on the File menu, click the My Network Places button in the Save As dialog box, double-click your network place, type your user name and password if necessary, and save the document to your server space in the same way you would save it to any folder on your desktop.

**7** Type a name for the network place item in the **Type A Name For This Network Place** box (for example, **Bughouse Productions**). The name you type here is displayed in your my Network Places window, so be nice to yourself and choose a name that will make sense to you down the road.

**8** Click **Next**, and then click **Finish** to complete the process.

You should now see a network place link in your My Network Places folder. You can double-click the network place icon to access the network place's Web space. If you have trouble setting up your connection, ensure that your Web server has the proper configuration to handle network places (as mentioned earlier in this chapter).

Now that you've created your Web folder, you can transfer files to your Web site by dragging them into your Web folder in your newly created network place or by saving files directly to your Web folder from any Microsoft Office 2000 or later program. You'll find that you can use network places to modify and maintain your Web site in a number of ways. For instance, you'll be able to open a network place and right-click file names and folders to rename them, select and delete files and folders, replace files and folders with updated information, and otherwise modify your Web documents and directories.

**tip**  When you set up a network place, we recommend that you *don't* instruct Windows to remember your password. Your Web folders contain the files you display online, so you'll want to protect them. If someone logs on to your computer, you probably don't want them to be able to easily access the online version of your Web site. By requiring your password to be typed each time you go online, you'll protect your files from others. Furthermore, when you have to type a password to access your online files, you'll always clearly indicate to yourself when you're working with online files instead of local versions.

# Other FTP Options

If you don't want to install an FTP program on your computer or if you don't want to configure My Network Places and Web folders, all hope is not lost. You can copy files to a Web server in other ways as well. Namely, you can use the FTP functions built into any of the following types of applications:

- Web publishing wizards, such as the Web Publishing Wizard that comes with Microsoft Windows
- ISP online services and Web editors, such as Microsoft Publisher and Microsoft FrontPage
- Browsers, such as Microsoft Internet Explorer

### Web Publishing Wizard

The Web Publishing Wizard offered in Microsoft Windows XP mainly serves to provide file storage and file sharing capabilities. Therefore, this tool isn't the ideal tool to publish your Web site, other than to update your MSN group site. But you can easily upload and store Web documents and other files (including images) by using the Web Publishing Wizard in Windows. You might want to use this feature while you're creating documents as a backup storage medium or as a means to share your working documents with others.

> **note** The Web Publishing Wizard is available in most versions of Windows. It was first added to Windows in the OSR2.5 release of Windows 95.

The Web Publishing Wizard works in the same way as other wizards—it provides a series of dialog boxes that you can complete to upload a folder or file to an online service provider, such as MSN or Xdrive. If you become a "serious" Web designer and you have your own Web space, you'll quickly crave the greater flexibility (and simplicity) that FTP applications and My Network Places offer.

The best way to understand how the Web Publishing Wizard works is to walk through the process. Because the process comes in wizard form, there's no reason for us to show you the pages you can see on your computer. To access the wizard, complete the following steps:

1 On the **Start** menu, click **My Computer**, and then click the file or folder that you want to publish to the Web.

2 In the **File And Folder Tasks** section, click either **Publish This Folder To The Web** (if you've selected a folder) or **Publish This File To The Web** (if you've selected a file).

To kick off the wizard, click the Next button. Then work your way through each page, providing the proper information—if you don't have Web space, Windows helps you to set up an MSN space. When you select the option to publish a folder, the wizard displays a dialog box in which you can select the files you want to publish by selecting or clearing check boxes. When you complete all the wizard pages, you'll need to click Finish to upload your files. If you have the correct information on hand, the process should flow smoothly without incident, and your newly added information will be displayed in your browser by default.

## ISP interfaces and Web editor features

Other resources for transferring files include ISP interfaces and software applications that provide Web document creation features. Basically, these tools are variations or hybrids of FTP applications, My Network Places, and the Web Publishing Wizard. The main benefits of ISP interfaces and Web editor features are that the tools are often easily accessible. For example, some ISPs offer online tools that you can use to upload files from your computer to the server. Personally, we've found online uploading tools to be cumbersome, so we never use them to manage a site's files. If you're shopping for a hosting service, look into the file management services the hosting service offers. If the hosting service provides a number of quality features—such as detailed logging statistics (including tracking the number of page hits and visitor traffic), fast Internet connectivity, very few interruptions in service, lots of space, and round-the-clock support—you might want to overlook a weak file manager feature, because you can whip a few pages across an FTP application interface pretty quickly. In our opinion, if you're planning to use an ISP file transfer interface, make sure that the online tool is at least as intuitive as an FTP application or My Network Places.

Similar to an ISP's online FTP forms, a number of Web editors, including Publisher and FrontPage, offer automatic file uploading or "publishing" features (as discussed in Chapter 11, "Going All Out with FrontPage"). Using a Web editor to upload files can be extremely convenient. The main concern is that you should be keenly aware of which files are being uploaded and where they're going. Further, know when you're replacing existing online files ("knowing" is always good, no matter how you're uploading files); otherwise, you might not be able to backtrack to a previous version of a page if you decide you don't want to keep your most recent modifications. To illustrate, if you're using Internet Explorer and you have FrontPage installed, you can visit your Web site and then click the Edit button on the Internet Explorer toolbar to open a local version of your Web page in Front-Page. You can then make modifications to the page and click Save to save and upload the modified page directly to the server. When you do this, if you don't rename the newly modified page, the existing page is replaced with the updated page. As you'll see in Chapter 13, you should archive your unused Web pages in case you need to revert to older pages or borrow elements from past publications. When you modify and save a page using the online access feature in FrontPage, you overwrite your existing document. That's definitely something to keep in mind.

To learn how to use ISP forms or a Web editor's uploading features, refer to the application's help files or published documentation. Too many variations exist among systems to adequately provide procedural descriptions in this chapter.

> **tip** Using the FrontPage Publish Web command to initially upload Web pages you've created in FrontPage ensures that FrontPage features that rely on FrontPage Server Extensions are properly implemented. Even if you haven't added advanced capability to your FrontPage Web site, we highly recommend that you use the Publish Web command to upload your Web site—at least the first time you upload your site.

## Reviewing Your Work

After you upload your Web site, immediately surf to your site and check it. As recommended in Part Two, you should preview your Web documents throughout the creation process—and we consider upload-ing part of the creation process. So check your live site. If you've been careful, you shouldn't find too many surprises after your site goes live. Nevertheless, before you start calling all your friends and directing people to your Web site (unless you're asking them to help you review

> **tip** This chapter introduces a number of tools that you can use to transfer your local Web site's files to a server. Try a few of the options, and see which works best for you. We recommend that you start with My Network Places because it's the easiest method and then move on to FTP applications if your hosting service doesn't support My Network Places. FTP applications have the most universal support and are also easy to use. If you're uncomfortable with one process, try another approach. As long as you have the appropriate connection information, you'll be able to get your site online.

your Web site), you should review your site thoroughly. After you display the home page, check for the following details:

- Ensure that all images are displayed properly. You don't want any broken image markers on your site.

- Click your links to ensure that they work, including the buttons on your navigation bar, linked logo graphics, text links, and image maps, if those appear on your site.

- Verify whether the site and its elements fit within the standard browser window. Remember—users report that having to scroll left and right to view Web content is highly annoying.

- Complete and submit a test form to yourself, if your site uses forms.

- Read each page title in the title bar for accuracy.

- Verify that text and text links are easy to read against the Web site's backgrounds.

Basically, take the time to scrutinize your site. Click everywhere, test each interactive element, and employ your critical eye. Better to take a little extra time after uploading to check your work than to have a viewer send you an e-mail message to tell you that your Web site is lame because it isn't displayed properly or doesn't respond as expected.

The last postproduction task we cover in this chapter is getting the word out that your Web site exists. The most common way to begin publicizing your site is to ensure that your Web site is readily recognizable by search engines and search directories.

## Registering with Search Engines and Directories

After you upload your site and it passes your rigorous error-checking analysis, you're ready to start publicizing your Web site's existence. The most popular way to start the process is to register your site with search engines and directories. You've probably used search engines, such as MSN Search, Lycos, Yahoo!, Google, and AltaVista, to find Web pages in the past. Now you need to approach search services from the opposite angle—instead of searching for other people's sites, you want to enable others to find your site. But first, a little background information.

The term *search engine* has come to encompass true search engines, such as MSN Search, as well as search directories, such as Yahoo! Distinct differences exist between the two major types of information retrieval systems (although after the following brief explanation, we'll go with the crowd on this one and continue to refer to both of the following setups as search engines):

- **Search engines**   Search engines create listings automatically or with a little assistance (such as a URL submission) and via *spiders* that crawl the Web. Whenever you post or change Web pages, search engines will eventually find your pages. Page titles, headings, body copy, and other page elements can affect how your Web site is categorized. Generally, you don't need to supply any specific information to a search engine, although sometimes you might be required to submit your URL.

- **Directories**   Directories rely on human input. To be listed in a directory, you must submit a short description of your site. Directory editors also write brief descriptions of the sites they review. When users run a directory search, the process looks for matches in the descriptions (not for matches within the Web site's titles, body text, or other elements).

Popular search engines that don't require any input from you—which means they'll find your site automatically—include the following:

- All The Web (www.alltheweb.com)
- AltaVista (www.altavista.com)
- Dogpile (www.dogpile.com)
- Go.com (www.go.com)
- Google (www.google.com)
- HotBot (www.hotbot.com)
- iWon (www.iwon.com)
- Lycos (www.lycos.com)
- WebCrawler (www.webcrawler.com)

**lingo**   *Spiders* are automated programs that search (or *crawl*) the Internet for new Web documents. The spiders then index all the addresses they find along with content-related information in a database that search engines can use.

**caution**   If you pay a fee to have your Web site submitted to a search engine, be sure that you note which services are included with your fee. Many fees cover registering your site with a number of services, and you don't want to inadvertently pay for registering with the same search engine twice.

**tip**    Some search engines query other search engines to get results from multiple sources (sometimes referred to as *metasearch engines*). Prime examples are the DogPile and Web-Crawler sites.

Some search engines that require you to provide additional information or that pick and choose which sites get listed in their directories include the following:

- AOL Anywhere (search.aol.com)
- Ask Jeeves (www.askjeeves.com)
- LookSmart (www.looksmart.com)
- MSN Search (search.msn.com)
- Netscape (search.netscape.com)
- Yahoo! (www.yahoo.com)

Some sites, such as AltaVista, will list your site within a day or two after submission, but others, such as Yahoo!, can take months to list your site, if they choose to list your site at all.

In addition to registering your sites with search engines and directories, you can use code within your Web documents to help search engines properly classify your Web pages or ignore your Web pages altogether. The key to assisting search engines is to add <meta /> tags within your Web document's header section.

## Adding <meta /> Tags

To some extent, you can control how search engines "see" the contents of a Web page. To do this, you can add <meta /> tags to your .html documents that specify keywords and descriptions that should be associated with your pages. Adding <meta /> tags is especially helpful if you want to classify a page that contains little textual content, such as a photomontage page.

To use <meta /> tags, you nest them within the <head></head> tag pair in your Web document's source code. (See Chapter 8, "Demystifying Basic CSS and XHTML," for an explanation of source code and the <head></head> tag pair.) You can use **keyword** or **description** meta tag attributes, or both. You'll also see **generator** and **author** attributes in meta tags, which specify the program used to create the Web page and the Web designer's name. For instance, a simple example using all four types of meta tags would look like similar to the following:

```
<head>
<meta name="author" content="bughouse productions and extracheese" />
<meta name="description" content="lunchtime!" />
<meta name="generator" content="Microsoft FrontPage 6.0" />
<meta name="keywords" content="salad, pesto ravioli, garlic bread"/>
</head>
```

And for comparison purposes, here's a more in-depth use of just the keywords and description meta tags:

```
<head>
<meta name="keywords" content="bughouse productions, extracheese,
    content specialists, web design, writing, editing, multimedia,
    mary millhollon, jeff castrina, animation, web site, microsoft,
    macromedia, graphic design, illustration, portland, oregon" />
<meta name="description" content="bughouse productions and extracheese
    are multimedia, publishing, and design firms specializing in
    content, education, web development, and interactive media. we
    create educational materials, original content, web sites,
    interactive media, animations, illustrations, and other high
    quality content."/>
</head>
```

> **tip** Limit your meta *keyword* tags to 10 to 25 keywords, with the most important keywords listed first. Some search engines will catalog only the first dozen or so words in meta *description* tags, so keep your descriptions short as well, and place the most important information up front.

You can also instruct search engines not to catalog your site to prevent sensitive, personal, or incomplete information from being indexed. In other words, you can display a virtual "Do Not Enter" sign for search engines by including the following tag within your Web document's <head></head> section:

```
<head>
<meta name="robots" content="noindex, nofollow" />
</head>
```

If you don't include meta tag information in your Web documents, search engines will catalog your site according to the text information on your home page, which can work for or against your site.

## Calling Attention to Your Site
Other ways you can attract attention to your site include participating in any of the following activities:

- Telling others about your site via word of mouth, e-mail messages, newsgroups, or list servers

- Participating in reciprocal programs in which you display links on your page to other sites and vice versa (if possible)

- Displaying banner ads for other Web sites on your Web pages as well as submitting banner ads for your site on other sites

- Getting your site publicly reviewed by a third party

- Putting your Web site address on your printed and marketing collateral, including business cards, stationery, brochures, and advertisements

After copying your Web files to a server, checking your online pages, and publicizing your site, you're ready to sit back and enjoy the fruits of your creative endeavor—at least for a little while. But don't get too comfortable. It won't be long before you're ready to update, archive, and modify your site. In Chapter 13, "Updating, Archiving, Moving On" (the final chapter in this book), we'll provide you with a few pointers that you can use to keep your site alive and dust-free.

# check it!

- You can use FTP applications to copy files from your computer to a server.
- You can transfer files and folders by using FTP applications, My Network Places and Web folders, the Web Publishing Wizard, ISP online forms, Web editors, and browsers such as Internet Explorer.
- If your server supports network places, you can use the My Network Places feature to easily upload and manipulate your Web site's files and folders in the same manner you manage local folders.
- When uploading Web files to a server, retain your Web site's file and folder structure, including using the exact naming and organizational parameters as the files and folders on your local computer.
- After you upload Web pages, always view them online and thoroughly check them for errors and broken links.
- To publicize your Web site, register with search engines.
- Consider adding meta tags to your .html documents to help define how search engines categorize your site.
- Finally, let others know that your site is live—via word of mouth and other typical communication channels—and start the exchange of online information.

# updating,
## archiving,
## moving on

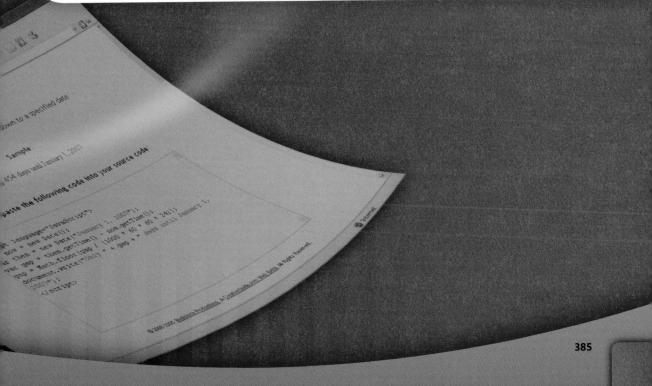

Most people would gladly accept the opportunity to drive around in a new Porsche. But even an expensive sports car loses its appeal if it's never tuned up or if it's allowed to gather dust, rust, and cobwebs. Similarly, Web sites can quickly lose their glow if they're neglected and left to fend for themselves on the Internet.

# After the "Going Live" Dust Settles

By the time you've reached this point in the book, you've probably posted your Web site online and you're enjoying a little breather. Congratulations! Soon, though, you'll want to explore ways in which you can modify and improve your site's visual appeal and content. In this chapter, we give you some practical instructions for Web site postproduction tasks as well as provide you with a few pointers for additional Web site creation opportunities that will arise now that you've passed the "beginner" stage of Web development.

# Updating Your Web Site

**note**  Keep in mind that even though this is the final chapter of the book and you're no longer sitting in the neophyte section among Web developers, your Web site creation education is far from over. The Web site creation skills you've learned in this book can carry you a long way, but your skills have only just begun to blossom. In the words of Winston Churchill, "This is not the end. It is not even the beginning of the end. But it is, perhaps, the end of the beginning."

One of the beauties of Web sites is that they're never really "done." Just as most self-actualized people never stop learning, effective Web sites are evolving works-in-progress. So after a few days away from your Web site, you might want to think about ways you can update your site to make it more interesting and useful for visitors.

## Reasons to Update

Quite a few reasons bolster the argument for updating your Web site regularly. The following list includes some of the reasons we've run across. Pick and choose whichever reasons seem relevant for your needs, or concoct some custom reasons of your own. Generally, you should update your site because you want to:

- Supply new and updated information.
- Show viewers that you're just as interested in your Web site as you want them to be.
- Encourage people to return to your site (not bore them with the same old stuff).
- Provide additional features for visitors that you didn't address when you first created the site.
- Remove features that visitors find distracting or confusing.
- Promote special causes.
- Celebrate an upcoming holiday or event.

- Reflect changes in the site's parent entity (such as a company that might want to incorporate a new logo, slogan, or color scheme).

- Incorporate up-to-date technologies or update code to meet new Web standards.

Keep in mind that the overriding reason you update your site should be to *benefit your viewers*. You shouldn't update your site just to provide a forum for your experimentation with Web page gimmicks (unless that's the whole point of your Web site). Likewise, if you have a popular item on your Web site, resist the urge to remove it just because you're tired of it. If viewers find an item useful and they voice their opinions through your feedback page, guest book, or other avenues, keep the component or upgrade it to make visitors even happier. Just as you had a reason for adding each element when you first created your Web site, make sure you have reasons for adding and removing items when you modify your site. In other words, think before you act.

## Easily Updateable Elements

Certain Web elements lend themselves to being updated easily. For the most part, you'll probably want to preserve your Web site's overall structure, navigation bars, logos, and contact information. Occasionally, though, such as when a company revamps its image or embarks on a new marketing campaign, these elements are changed intentionally. While you shouldn't make arbitrary changes, here are the five Web site elements that change most often:

- **Complementary colors or themes.** Changed in moderation, of course, such as Google's seasonal themes; this change can be easily accomplished when you use style sheets.

- **Copyright or last-updated date.** We show you some JavaScript that can automate the copyright date later in this chapter, and you can find scripts to update the last-updated date online as well.

- **Graphics.** Readers always appreciate updated photographs.

- **Links.** Especially update and check links if you link to resources outside of your site.

- **Text.** One of the easiest ways to update your site.

The reason the preceding elements are easy to change and are changed more frequently than others is because they generally express a Web site's content or message. Most viewers can appreciate a well-styled Web site, but they return to and use sites that contain dynamic (as opposed to static) information.

## Updating Tip and Tricks

Now that we've briefly outlined why you might want to update your site in the future as well as the types of elements you might want to change, let's look at some guidelines you should follow when you're updating your Web pages. Most of these guidelines are based on common sense, but they're worth noting here anyway.

> **tip** If your site doesn't require an update or you just don't have time for revisions this month, at least take a moment to refresh the last-updated date on your home page to indicate to viewers that you've recently checked in.

Above all, avoid taking a perfectly good page and rendering it useless through unnecessarily complex design or coding modifications. We've seen clean, once-working sites "updated" with the latest and greatest Web features that were rendered unviewable by the majority of browsers. Here's a motto to keep in mind: *Aim for better not deader.*

And because change is inevitable, consider the next guideline as well: *Create a regular schedule for updates.*

A regular schedule forces you to clearly plan how you want to update your Web site as well as provides a target date for completing future changes. For example, let's say you decide that you'll update your site every third Monday of each month. Throughout the month, you can jot down update notes to yourself or create local versions of live pages. When the third Monday rolls around, commit yourself to implementing any planned changes and uploading modified pages. Then start taking notes for the next month's update. Of course, in some instances, a quick nonscheduled update might be in order—for example, you might want to quickly change a phone number, correct a typo, or fix a broken graphic link. But for more routine changes, you

> **tip** Before an updated Web page goes live, consider temporarily uploading the page with a "fake" name, such as index2.html. You can then enter the path to the "fake" page in your browser's Address bar and view the page online before granting users easy access to the page. After you're sure the page properly reflects your changes, rename your old file (using a name with a numeric date, such as index121505.index or index2005.html, for archiving), and rename the new file (to index.html, in this example) to update your Web page with the newly created file. Safely replacing your files is discussed in the next section.

should try to stick to some regular schedule. Randomly updating your site can lead to slovenly or chaotic practices, in which your Web site can either gather too much dust or change too frequently (which can cause regular visitors to miss some of the updates).

Here's the next rule of thumb: *Avoid updating a live site, especially during peak hours.*

Some HTML editors (Microsoft FrontPage included) enable you to edit live sites. This feature can be useful for performing emergency fixes, such as the slight informational errors, typos, and broken links mentioned a moment ago. In most cases, though, you should follow these steps when beginning your update:

1 **Download the most recent version of the page you want to update. This step is extremely important, because it ensures that you're working on the most up-to-date version of the page.**

2 **Redesign the page locally and preview it in a browser.**

3 **Upload the modified page only after you've ensured that it operates correctly and displays the layout properly.**

Updating a live site might result in users seeing half-completed changes as you work on the page. Further, you might be hard pressed to revert to an earlier version of your site if you need to recover from disastrous or undesirable changes. (Later in this chapter, we talk about archiving to avoid losing "old" data.) With that said, at times you'll find that it's okay to make some tweaks to live pages. We sometimes make quick text changes to live pages, but we try to limit those edits to times when we know few visitors will be visiting the site.

Finally, as part of your routine maintenance on your site, you should follow this practice: *Regularly check hyperlinks on your pages.*

As you know, the Web is extremely fluid; pages come and go. So check your links frequently, because nothing signals a neglected Web site as clearly as hyperlinks to nonexistent pages. Remember, you can use link checking software and online services to perform this task. Further, whenever you replace pages in your site, check your navigation links to make sure the new page is properly incorporated into your site.

**note** Keep in mind that if your online Web documents are saved in Microsoft Office in Web Page, Filtered format, you should edit your unfiltered pages that you've stored locally on your computer instead of downloading the filtered pages.

**tip** If you've uploaded an "in-progress" site while you're developing it and you haven't advertised it to anyone yet, by all means—update the live pages. Just ensure that you have backup files to revert to if you make changes you'd rather not keep.

# Archiving Web Elements

Updating your Web site goes hand in hand with saving past versions of your Web pages. This practice is referred to as *archiving*. The underlying concept of archiving is this: *When you update your site, don't throw away your old Web page elements!* At least not right away.

Best practices dictate that you let your has-been Web documents and graphics hang around for a while. You should keep old documents for at least six months in most cases and possibly a year, if you can foresee any chance that you'll need the "old" information or graphics, especially if you can't easily re-create the information. The most notable reason for archiving instead of deleting is that you never know when you might need old text, graphics, JavaScript, style sheets, and so forth. Many times, you can use old pages as templates or reuse old graphics in new ways. You'll find that creating an archive folder to store past page elements is much easier than re-creating graphics and data after you've obliterated them.

> **lingo**  *Archiving* refers to copying files onto tape or disk for long-term storage.

You can store archived information in several ways. The easiest way is to create a folder named archives and copy past Web elements into subfolders within that folder. You can store an archive folder and its subfolders in several places:

- Removable storage devices, such as CDs, USB flash drives, or other external hard drives
- Local computer or local networked computer
- Web site's hosting service, since you'll probably have more than enough server space for a while
- Online storage space, such as the document storage space available on the MSN Groups site, at groups.msn.com

> **tip**  When archiving Web documents, remember also to archive any associated graphics files and folders. Further, you should store graphics in a folder with the same name as the original graphics folder so that your archived page's links will work properly.

Another way to think of archiving is as a method to copy and store Web pages before you choose to stop displaying them for visitors. For example, let's say you created a new Web document that shows the racing times for the members in a local cross-country team. Your updating and archiving procedures might take the following form:

**1** You've given the name *times2.html* to the new page showing the runners' updated racing times, and you've uploaded it to the

Internet. The page checks out, so you're now ready to display the new page (times2.html) in place of the existing outdated page (times.html).

2  Before you rename times2.html to times.html and replace the existing times.html page, you create a subfolder named times inside the archives folder. Then you copy the existing times.html page into the times subfolder, and rename the document something like times2005.html. That way, the page will be available online, at www.domain.com/archives/times/times2005.html.

3  After copying the outdated times.html document to the archives folder, you delete the outdated times.html file in your Web site's main directory.

4  You then rename times2.html to times.html and place the new times.html file in your Web site's main directory.

In the preceding steps, the outdated times.html file is safely stowed away for future use and the new times.html page displays the updated information. Creating an organized archiving storage system and directory-naming scheme can make finding "old" information a snap.

After you master updating and archiving—it shouldn't take you long—and you've worked your way through this book, you can safely say that you've covered all the basics of Web site creation. The next logical progression is to forge beyond the basics and into the realm of intermediate and advanced Web site development.

# Moving Beyond Easy Web Design

As we wrap up this book, we hope you've found that you've gained a strong foundation for basic Web site development. Although we could go on for a few hundred more pages describing more advanced Web development techniques (and we really wouldn't mind doing that, either), we realize that we've had to pick and choose what's most helpful when it comes to "easy" Web design and development. We want to point out, though, that while we've covered quite a bit of information in this book, we haven't explained everything—many more advanced techniques for creating Web documents are available to you as well. At some point, you'll probably want to incorporate additional multimedia

**tip** Whenever you add JavaScript to a Web document, test the code in various popular browsers to verify that it works and appears properly for the greatest number of visitors.

elements, such as video, animation, and audio. Or maybe you'll want to add security features to your Web site by employing encryption algorithms or password protection schemes. At this point in the book, we're confident that your understanding of the Web should enable you to move on to more complex issues if you so desire.

Just for fun, we've provided the following four quick JavaScripts that you can experiment with and use on your Web sites:

| | |
|---|---|
| Copyright generator | Countdown element |
| Daily tip | Pop-up window |

To find these code snippets, working online samples, and directions on how to use the code, visit www.creationguide.com/javascript.

### Additional JavaScript on the Web

You can find all sorts of free JavaScript online—just search for *JavaScript*. When you find free JavaScript online, you can copy the code and paste it directly into your Web documents—no typing required! So keep those CTRL+C (copy) and CTRL+V (paste) keyboard commands in mind when you want to quickly and efficiently add JavaScript (or other freely offered Web code) to your Web documents.

## check it!

- Consider updating your Web site regularly to keep content fresh and visitors happy, and archive old Web documents and graphics (at least for a while) in case you need to reuse elements.

- Don't fear the unknown! Have fun—cautiously move beyond easy design and development techniques and try your hand at various advanced procedures. You might be surprised to find how much you've learned.

- Finally—our last key point in this book. We hope you've enjoyed learning about Web design and development as much as we've enjoyed creating this book and the companion site. Feel free to use all the resources incorporated into the companion site, and drop us a line (mm@creationguide.com and jc@creationguide.com) if you ever have a question or want to share your Web creation results. We'd certainly enjoy hearing from you, and we'll do our best to respond to your queries as quickly as possible. Best wishes for success on the Web!

# Index

## Symbols

# Author Bios

### Mary Millhollon, writer, editor, consultant, educator, Web designer

Mary founded Bughouse Production and has years of publishing, design, and computer experience, including hands-on experience in the book, magazine, newspaper, courseware, IT, Web publishing, and screenwriting industries. Mary works around the clock with technology on instructional and creative ventures. Her educational background is a blend of art, English, journalism, and computer science. Her most recent works include Microsoft Word Version 2003 Inside Out, the Paralympic Academy Web site (www.paralympicacademy.org), and scripts for DMiller Studios in Portland, OR. She's also written numerous publications covering topics such as HTML, Microsoft Office, interactive education, graphics, online communities, browsers, online auctions, science, sports, and other completely unrelated creative topics.

### Jeff Castrina, multimedia developer and Web designer

Jeff owns ExtraCheese (www.extracheese.com), a multimedia, Web design, and consulting firm based in Portland, OR. Jeff has created Web sites and interactive CD-ROMs for a number of established clients as well as coauthored the books Easy Web Page Creation and Faster Smarter Web Page Creation. Prior to founding ExtraCheese, Jeff worked as a Multimedia Services Manager and held graphic design and video production positions in Rochester, NY. Before that, he jump-started his multimedia career by graduating from the Rochester Institute of Technology where he studied film/video production and computer science.

## Leslie Lothamer, interactive media developer and Flash specialist

Leslie is trained and experienced in Web design and programming, and she is currently working as a developer with The New Group in Portland, OR. She's extremely masterful with Flash programming, Web scripting, and building interactive components that provide a dynamic element to online communication. Leslie's design sense is outstanding, and she's a treasure trove of ideas. She also kindly donated a childhood picture of herself for the Space Camp for Kids sample Web site shown in Part One of this book.

In addition, the following professionals contributed to the content for both the book and companion Web site (www.creationguide.com):

John Phillips, Black Star Photo Agency

Justin Garrity, PopArt Inc.

Katherine Murray, reVisions Plus, Inc.

Kevin Martonick, Cartoon Network

Natalie Koury, Teacher (yes, she's the Ms. Koury in the Chapter 9 walkthrough)

Sarah Spencer, 26 Letters

Sujata Soni, Marketing and Public Relations

# What do you think of this book? We want to hear from you!

Do you have a few minutes to participate in a brief online survey? Microsoft is interested in hearing your feedback about this publication so that we can continually improve our books and learning resources for you.

To participate in our survey, please visit:

**www.microsoft.com/learning/booksurvey**

And enter this book's ISBN, 0-7356-2252-3. As a thank-you to survey participants in the United States and Canada, each month we'll randomly select five respondents to win one of five $100 gift certificates from a leading online merchant.* At the conclusion of the survey, you can enter the drawing by providing your e-mail address, which will be used for prize notification *only*.

Thanks in advance for your input. Your opinion counts!

Sincerely,

Microsoft Learning

*Learn More. Go Further.*